SIXTH EDITION

MOSAIC 1

Reading

Brenda Wegmann

Miki Knezevic

Lawrence J. Zwier
Contributor, Focus on Testing

McGraw Hill

Mosaic 1 Reading, Sixth Edition

Published by McGraw-Hill ESL/ELT, a business unit of The McGraw-Hill Companies, Inc., 1221 Avenue of the Americas, New York, NY 10020. Copyright © 2014 by The McGraw-Hill Companies, Inc. All rights reserved. Printed in the United States of America. Previous editions © 2007, 2001, and 1995. No part of this publication may be reproduced or distributed in any form or by any means, or stored in a database or retrieval system, without the prior written consent of The McGraw-Hill Companies, Inc., including, but not limited to, in any network or other electronic storage or transmission, or broadcast for distance learning.

Some ancillaries, including electronic and print components, may not be available to customers outside the United States.

This book is printed on acid-free paper.

4 5 6 7 8 9 0 QVS/QVS 1 0 9 8 7 6 5 4

ISBN: 978-0-07-759511-1
MHID: 0-07-759511-4

Senior Vice President, Products & Markets: Kurt L. Strand
Vice President, General Manager, Products & Markets: Michael J. Ryan
Vice President, Content Production & Technology Services: Kimberly Meriwether David
Director of Development: Valerie Kelemen
Marketing Manager: Cambridge University Press
Lead Project Manager: Rick Hecker
Senior Buyer: Michael R. McCormick
Designer: Page2, LLC
Cover/Interior Designer: Page2, LLC
Senior Content Licensing Specialist: Keri Johnson
Manager, Digital Production: Janean A. Utley
Compositor: Page2, LLC
Printer: Quad/Graphics

Cover photo: Shutterstock.com

All credits appearing on page iv or at the end of the book are considered to be an extension of the copyright page.

The Internet addresses listed in the text were accurate at the time of publication. The inclusion of a website does not indicate an endorsement by the authors or McGraw-Hill, and McGraw-Hill does not guarantee the accuracy of the information presented at these sites.

www.mhhe.com

McGraw-Hill ELT

www.elt.mcgraw-hill.com

The **McGraw-Hill** Companies

A Special Thank You

The Interactions/Mosaic Sixth Edition team wishes to thank our extended team: teachers, students, administrators, and teacher trainers, all of whom contributed invaluably to the making of this edition.

Maiko Berger, **Ritsumeikan Asia Pacific University**, Oita, Japan • Aaron Martinson, **Sejong Cyber University**, Seoul, Korea • Aisha Osman, Egypt • Amy Stotts, **Chubu University**, Aichi, Japan • Charles Copeland, **Dankook University**, Yongin City, Korea • Christen Savage, **University of Houston**, Texas, USA • Daniel Fitzgerald, **Metropolitan Community College**, Kansas, USA • Deborah Bollinger, **Aoyama Gakuin University**, Tokyo, Japan • Duane Fitzhugh, **Northern Virginia Community College**, Virginia, USA • Gregory Strong, **Aoyama Gakuin University**, Tokyo, Japan • James Blackwell, **Ritsumeikan Asia Pacific University**, Oita, Japan • Janet Harclerode, **Santa Monica College**, California, USA • Jinyoung Hong, **Sogang University**, Seoul, Korea • Lakkana Chaisaklert, **Rajamangala University of Technology Krung Thep**, Bangkok, Thailand •Lee Wonhee, **Sogang University**, Seoul, Korea • Matthew Gross, **Konkuk University**, Seoul, Korea • Matthew Stivener, **Santa Monica College**, California, USA • Pawadee Srisang, **Burapha University**, Chantaburi, Thailand • Steven M. Rashba, **University of Bridgeport**, Connecticut, USA • Sudatip Prapunta, **Prince of Songkla University**, Trang, Thailand • Tony Carnerie, **University of California San Diego**, California, USA

Greetings and Acknowledgments from the Authors

Once again we are proud and pleased to be part of the McGraw-Hill team presenting a new edition of our *Mosaic* reading books in a vibrant, updated, and flexible form. We believe that the combination of provocative, authentic selections with a strategy-development program that enables students to internalize reading, vocabulary, and critical-thinking skills continues to be a winning formula for academic English success.

We wish, first of all, to honor the memory of Tina Carver, whose expert guidance, research, and responsiveness laid the foundation from which this new edition grew. In addition, we thank those who worked with her and with us in past editions and Pam Hartmann for her ongoing counsel and inspiration through all editions. We also owe a debt of gratitude to Arley Gray with his keen editorial eye, to Anita Raducanu for her superb direction and flexibility during production, to Anné Knezevic for effective suggestions and advice about materials, and to Dr. Jessica Wegmann-Sanchez for her creative ideas and cogent criticism of strategies and exercises. Above all, we wish to express our heartfelt gratitude to Valerie Keleman for her outstanding management, resourcefulness, and ingenuity in bringing this new edition of our reading books through many hurdles and into actualization.

Finally, we extend our appreciation to the dedicated ESL/EFL teachers who bring their boundless energy and imagination to the task of teaching English, and to their students who have the determination to learn this distinctive language of international discourse.

—Brenda Dominski Wegmann and Miki Prijic Knezevic

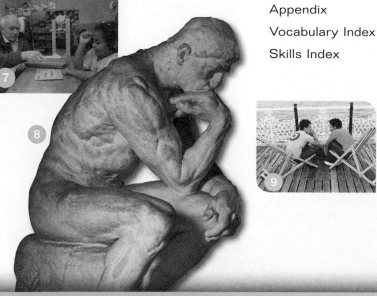

Table of Contents

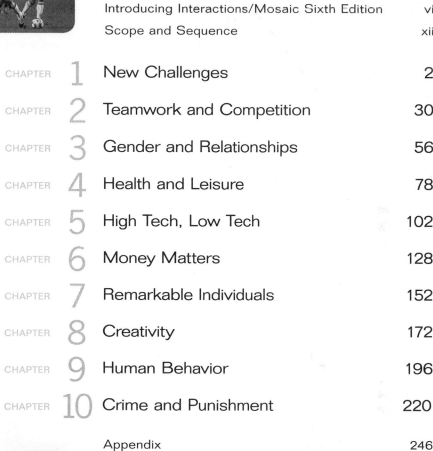

A 21st-Century Course for the Modern Student

Interactions/Mosaic prepares students for university classes by fully integrating every aspect of student life. Based on 28 years of classroom-tested best practices, the new and revised content, fresh modern look, and new online component make this the perfect series for contemporary classrooms.

Proven Instruction that Ensures Academic Success

Modern Content:

From social networking to gender issues and from academic honesty to discussions of Skype, *Interactions/Mosaic* keeps students connected to learning by selecting topics that are interesting and relevant to modern students.

Digital Component:

The fully integrated online course offers a rich environment that expands students' learning and supports teachers' teaching with automatically graded practice, assessment, classroom presentation tools, online community, and more.

- **3 Revised Chapters**, updated to reflect contemporary student life:
  Chapter 1: New Challenges
  Chapter 3: Gender and Relationships
  Chapter 8: Creativity
- **6 all-new readings** focusing on global topics and digital life
- **Over 80 new vocabulary words** that enhance conversational proficiency
- **New photos** that showcase a modern, multi-cultural university experience

Emphasis on Vocabulary:

Each chapter teaches vocabulary intensively and comprehensively. This focus on learning new words is informed by more than 28 years of classroom testing and provides students with the exact language they need to communicate confidently and fluently.

Practical Critical Thinking:

Students develop their ability to synthesize, analyze, and apply information from different sources in a variety of contexts: from comparing academic articles to negotiating informal conversations.

Highlights of *Mosaic 1 Reading* 6th Edition

Part 1: Reading Skills and Strategies
Each chapter begins with an engaging assignment, making learning more efficient and fun.

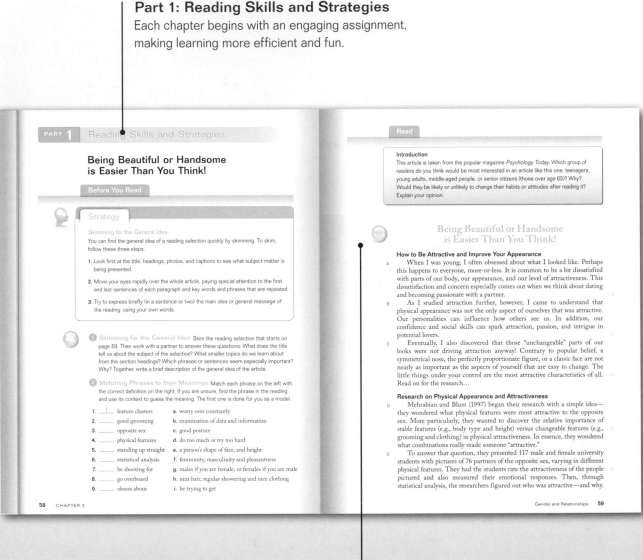

PART 1 Reading Skills and Strategies

Being Beautiful or Handsome is Easier Than You Think!

Before You Read

Strategy

Skimming for the General Idea
You can find the general idea of a reading selection quickly by skimming. To skim, follow these three steps.

1. Look first at the title, headings, photos, and captions to see what subject matter is being presented.
2. Move your eyes rapidly over the whole article, paying special attention to the first and last sentences of each paragraph and key words and phrases that are repeated.
3. Try to express briefly (in a sentence or two) the main idea or general message of the reading, using your own words.

1 Skimming for the General Idea Skim the reading selection that starts on page 59. Then work with a partner to answer these questions: What does the title tell us about the subject of the selection? What smaller topics do we learn about from the section headings? Which phrases or sentences seem especially important? Why? Together, write a brief description of the general idea of the article.

2 Matching Phrases to their Meanings Match each phrase on the left with the correct definition on the right. If you are unsure, find the phrase in the reading and use its context to guess the meaning. The first one is done for you as a model.

1. __i__ feature clusters — a. worry over constantly
2. ____ good grooming — b. examination of data and information
3. ____ opposite sex — c. good posture
4. ____ physical features — d. do too much or try too hard
5. ____ standing up straight — e. a person's shape of face, and height
6. ____ statistical analysis — f. femininity, masculinity and pleasantness
7. ____ be shooting for — g. males if you are female, or females if you are male
8. ____ go overboard — h. neat hair, regular showering and nice clothing
9. ____ obsess about — i. be trying to get

Read

Introduction
This article is taken from the popular magazine *Psychology Today*. Which group of readers do you think would be most interested in an article like this one: teenagers, young adults, middle-aged people, or senior citizens (those over age 65)? Why? Would they be likely or unlikely to change their habits or attitudes after reading it? Explain your opinion.

Being Beautiful or Handsome is Easier Than You Think!

How to Be Attractive and Improve Your Appearance

A   When I was young, I often obsessed about what I looked like. Perhaps this happens to everyone, more-or-less. It is common to be a bit dissatisfied with parts of our body, our appearance, and our level of attractiveness. This dissatisfaction and concern especially comes out when we think about dating and becoming passionate with a partner.

B   As I studied attraction further, however, I came to understand that physical appearance was not the only aspect of ourselves that was attractive. Our personalities can influence how others see us. In addition, our confidence and social skills can spark attraction, passion, and intrigue in potential lovers.

C   Eventually, I also discovered that those "unchangeable" parts of our looks were not driving attraction anyway! Contrary to popular belief, a symmetrical nose, the perfectly proportionate figure, or a classic face are not nearly as important as the aspects of yourself that are easy to change. The little things under your control are the most attractive characteristics of all. Read on for the research…

Research on Physical Appearance and Attractiveness

D   Mehrabian and Blum (1997) began their research with a simple idea—they wondered what physical features were most attractive to the opposite sex. More particularly, they wanted to discover the relative importance of stable features (e.g., body type and height) versus changeable features (e.g., grooming and clothing) in physical attractiveness. In essence, they wondered what combinations really made someone "attractive."

E   To answer that question, they presented 117 male and female university students with pictures of 76 partners of the opposite sex, varying in different physical features. They had the students rate the attractiveness of the people pictured and also measured their emotional responses. Then, through statistical analysis, the researchers figured out who was attractive—and why.

Topics for the Modern Student
Selected readings are pulled from current publications and relevant to students' lives.

Jane Eyre (Extract from the classic English novel)

Introduction to Jane Eyre

Jane Eyre is a famous British novel published in 1847. It has been immensely popular ever since and has served as the basis for ballets, musicals, radio adaptations, TV shows, and more than 15 movies (including one in 2011). The story is told in the first person (using "I") as if it were an autobiography, and in fact, some parts really do reflect the true experiences of the author, Charlotte Brontë.

▲ Charlotte Brontë

The main character is an orphan (a person whose parents die when he or she is a child) named Jane Eyre, who suffers great difficulties in her childhood from poverty to physical and emotional abuse by relatives and some teachers. Nevertheless, Jane manages to do well in school and gains employment at a wealthy estate called Thornfield Hall as a governess (private female teacher) for a young girl who is being raised by the eccentric owner, a widower named Edward Rochester. The owner does not abuse or look down upon Jane for being poor; instead, he spends time with her, conversing about interesting subjects and sharing ideas and opinions. Jane enjoys this and becomes strongly attracted to her employer. Then she finds out something that threatens to change everything!

One reason for the continuing appeal of this novel is the remarkable character of Jane. Jane Eyre burst onto the literary world of the 19th century as a new kind of heroine (female protagonist). Up to that point, female characters in novels were usually *damsels in distress*: lovely, weak, and helpless creatures in need of rescue by a hero (a tradition that persists today in many adventure movies). In contrast, Jane is strong and self-reliant and speaks her mind. Some critics suggest that Jane Eyre represents an early version of the feminist woman.

Before You Read

① Scanning for Words with a Specific Meaning Be a word detective and read the clues below about nine key words in the first section of the reading selection. Review the scanning strategy (Chapter 2, Part 2) if necessary and use it to find those words. Write each word in the blank beside its description. The words are asked for in the order of their appearance in the text.

1. a word that begins with *b* and means "a man who is going to be married soon"
   bridegroom

2. a word meaning "employee" that begins with *d* _____

Part 2: Main Ideas and Details
Each chapter teaches crucial skills such as reading for main ideas and scanning.

---

3. a word beginning with *h* that means "an obstacle or difficulty that is in the way"
   _____

4. a word beginning with *s* that means "crying in a loud or noisy way"
   _____

5. a descriptive word that starts with *a* and means "similar in thoughts and feelings" _____

6. a word beginning with *n* that is the name of "a European bird known for its beautiful song" _____

7. a word that begins with *o* and means "a vow or serious promise declared with God as a witness" _____

8. a word beginning with *a* that means "a robot or machine that acts like a person but has no emotions" _____

9. an action word that starts with *s* and means "express disdain or contempt (looking down on someone as worthless and inferior)" _____

Strategy

Making Inferences about a Relationship from Dialogue
By reading the exact words two people speak to each other, it is possible to make inferences (draw conclusions) about their relationship. Do they talk to each other as equals, or is one dominant (superior) and the other subordinate (inferior)? Are they both involved in the conversation, or is one person interested and the other indifferent? As you read, look for words that show what emotions each person feels. For example, do they express fondness, admiration, love, hatred, annoyance, or disdain (looking down on someone)?

② Making Inferences about a Relationship from Dialogue Read the following excerpts (parts) from the conversation between the young governess Jane Eyre and her middle-aged employer Mr. Rochester. Choose the correct options from the words in parentheses, and complete the statements that follow.

1. (Jane speaking) "It is a long way off, sir."
   "No matter—a girl of your sense will not object to the voyage or the distance."
   "Not the voyage, but the distance; and then the sea is a barrier—"
   "From what, Jane?"

   This shows that the two characters are (equal / not equal) socially because

   Jane Eyre calls Mr. Rochester "_____" and he calls her

   "_____." Therefore, in the society of that time Jane is

   (dominant / subordinate) and Mr. Rochester is (dominant / subordinate).

Practical Critical Thinking Key communication strategies are taught that support language learning and encourage independent thinking.

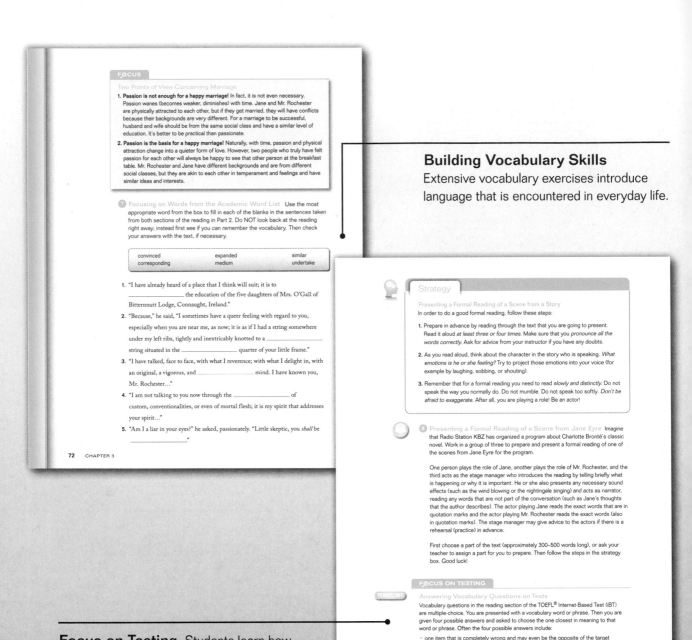

FOCUS

Two Points of View Concerning Marriage

1. **Passion is not enough for a happy marriage!** In fact, it is not even necessary. Passion wanes (becomes weaker, diminishes) with time. Jane and Mr. Rochester are physically attracted to each other, but if they get married, they will have conflicts because their backgrounds are very different. For a marriage to be successful, husband and wife should be from the same social class and have a similar level of education. It's better to be practical than passionate.

2. **Passion is the basis for a happy marriage!** Naturally, with time, passion and physical attraction change into a quieter form of love. However, two people who have truly felt passion for each other will always be happy to see that other person at the breakfast table. Mr. Rochester and Jane have different backgrounds and are from different social classes, but they are akin to each other in temperament and feelings and have similar ideas and interests.

⑦ Focusing on Words from the Academic Word List Use the most appropriate word from the box to fill in each of the blanks in the sentences taken from both sections of the reading in Part 2. Do NOT look back at the reading right away; instead first see if you can remember the vocabulary. Then check your answers with the text, if necessary.

convinced	expanded	similar
corresponding	medium	undertake

1. "I have already heard of a place that I think will suit; it is to _____ the education of the five daughters of Mrs. O'Gall of Bitternnutt Lodge, Connaught, Ireland."

2. "Because," he said, "I sometimes have a queer feeling with regard to you, especially when you are near me, as now; it is as if I had a string somewhere under my left ribs, tightly and inextricably knotted to a _____ string situated in the _____ quarter of your little frame."

3. "I have talked, face to face, with what I reverence; with what I delight in, with an original, a vigorous, and _____ mind. I have known you, Mr. Rochester…"

4. "I am not talking to you now through the _____ of custom, conventionalities, or even of mortal flesh; it is my spirit that addresses your spirit…"

5. "Am I a liar in your eyes?" he asked, passionately. "Little skeptic, you *shall* be _____."

Building Vocabulary Skills
Extensive vocabulary exercises introduce language that is encountered in everyday life.

Strategy

Presenting a Formal Reading of a Scene from a Story
In order to do a good formal reading, follow these steps:

1. Prepare in advance by reading through the text that you are going to present. Read it aloud *at least three or four times*. Make sure that you *pronounce all the words correctly*. Ask for advice from your instructor if you have any doubts.

2. As you read aloud, think about the character in the story who is speaking. *What emotions is he or she feeling?* Try to project those emotions into your voice (for example by laughing, sobbing, or shouting).

3. Remember that for a formal reading you need to read *slowly and distinctly*. Do not speak the way you normally do. Do not mumble. Do not speak too softly. *Don't be afraid to exaggerate*. After all, you are playing a role! Be an actor!

⑧ Presenting a Formal Reading of a Scene from *Jane Eyre* Imagine that Radio Station KBZ has organized a program about Charlotte Brontë's classic novel. Work in a group of three to prepare and present a formal reading of one of the scenes from Jane Eyre for the program.

One person plays the role of Jane, another plays the role of Mr. Rochester, and the third acts as the stage manager who introduces the reading by telling briefly what is happening or why it is important. He or she also presents any necessary sound effects (such as the wind blowing or the nightingale singing) and acts as narrator, reading any words that are not part of the conversation (such as Jane's thoughts that the author describes). The actor playing Jane reads the exact words that are in quotation marks and the actor playing Mr. Rochester reads the exact words (also in quotation marks). The stage manager may give advice to the actors if there is a rehearsal (practice) in advance.

First choose a part of the text (approximately 300–500 words long), or ask your teacher to assign a part for you to prepare. Then follow the steps in the strategy box. Good luck!

FOCUS ON TESTING

TOEFL® iBT

Answering Vocabulary Questions on Tests
Vocabulary questions in the reading section of the TOEFL® Internet-Based Test (iBT) are multiple-choice. You are presented with a vocabulary word or phrase. Then you are given four possible answers and asked to choose the one closest in meaning to that word or phrase. Often the four possible answers include:

• one item that is completely wrong and may even be the opposite of the target vocabulary word or phrase

Focus on Testing Students learn how to prepare for both typical college exams and international assessments.

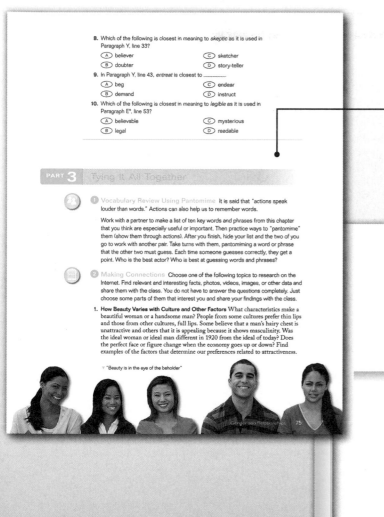

8. Which of the following is closest in meaning to *skeptic* as it is used in Paragraph Y, line 33?

  (A) believer   (C) sketcher

  (B) doubter   (D) story-teller

9. In Paragraph Y, line 43, *entreat* is closest to _____.

  (A) beg   (C) endear

  (B) demand   (D) instruct

10. Which of the following is closest in meaning to *legible* as it is used in Paragraph E*, line 53?

  (A) believable   (C) mysterious

  (B) legal   (D) readable

PART 3   Tying It All Together

1 Vocabulary Review Using Pantomime It is said that "actions speak louder than words." Actions can also help us to remember words.

Work with a partner to make a list of ten key words and phrases from this chapter that you think are especially useful or important. Then practice ways to "pantomime" them (show them through actions). After you finish, hide your list and the two of you go to work with another pair. Take turns with them, pantomiming a word or phrase that the other two must guess. Each time someone guesses correctly, they get a point. Who is the best actor? Who is best at guessing words and phrases?

2 Making Connections Choose one of the following topics to research on the Internet. Find relevant and interesting facts, photos, videos, images, or other data and share them with the class. You do not have to answer the questions completely. Just choose some parts of them that interest you and share your findings with the class.

1. **How Beauty Varies with Culture and Other Factors** What characteristics make a beautiful woman or a handsome man? People from some cultures prefer thin lips and those from other cultures, full lips. Some believe that a man's hairy chest is unattractive and others that it is appealing because it shows masculinity. Was the ideal woman or ideal man different in 1920 from the ideal of today? Does the perfect face or figure change when the economy goes up or down? Find examples of the factors that determine our preferences related to attractiveness.

▽ "Beauty is in the eye of the beholder"

Gender and Relationships   75

2. **Why Jane Eyre Is Alive and Well and Living on the Internet** How does the character of Jane Eyre, invented by Charlotte Brontë in the 1800s, influence people today? Look up Jane Eyre clubs, discussion groups, movies, ballets, radio and TV shows, videos, plays, or comics. What are Gothic novels and what influence does Brontë's heroine have on them? How does she affect other writers of today? How does she influence clothing and cosmetics? Why do you think her character remains so powerful more than 150 years after her creation? What can Jane Eyre teach us today?

3. **What is the hidden secret in the scene presented in the reading?** Did you get the feeling that one of the two characters was hiding something? If so, you are right! One of the two characters has a secret that will have great importance for the plot (action) of the novel. Who is hiding something and what is the truth? Read Jane Eyre and find out. In what ways will this secret influence what happens in the novel and how the story ends?

Responding in Writing

FOCUS

Writing Tip: Writing Down the Key Points in a Summary

To do a *summary* of a reading, write down its *key* (most important) ideas. No opinion of your own is expressed in a summary.

3 Writing a Summary Write a summary of the reading selection from Part 1 of this chapter or of an article that your teacher assigns to you, following these steps:

Step 1: Write down as your title:

My Summary of _____
(Fill in the title of the article in this space. Be sure to put it in quotation marks to show it is the title of something that has been published.)

Step 2: Skim the article and make a list of the important ideas.

Step 3: Think about what the author is trying to say. Decide what his or her main idea is and write it down *in your own words*. This is your first sentence.

Step 4: Then write a sentence for each of the other key ideas and put them in the order in which they appear.

Step 5: Read what you have written. Ask yourself: Is this in my own words or have I simply copied the sentences of the article? Of course, you can include words taken from the article, but not complete sentences. (If you find that you have copied long phrases and whole sentences from the article, immediately change what you have written. Say the same thing in different words.)

Step 6: Is your summary clear? Is it short enough? A summary should be no longer than 20–30% of the original article. If your summary is too long, cut words that are not necessary and the parts that are not so important.

76   CHAPTER 3

Part 3: Tying It All Together Students learn to apply their reading and writing skills to a variety of practical interaction.

Results for Students A carefully structured program presents and practices academic skills and strategies purposefully, leading to strong student results and more independent learners.

Scope and Sequence

Chapter	Reading Selections	Reading Skills and Strategies

Critical Thinking Skills	Vocabulary Building	Focus on Testing
Interpreting cultural differences concerning meeting and greeting Analyzing the title of a reading Synthesizing group discussion and reporting on it Synthesizing Internet content: Taking notes and presenting results Writing Tip: Using details to support your ideas	Understanding the meaning of words from context Understanding compound words (with and without hyphenation) Analyzing words with prefixes and suffixes Building new words with suffixes and prefixes Identifying common phrases and idioms and their meanings Focusing on words from the Academic Word List	**TOEFL iBT** Analyzing points of contrast on tests (Reading: *Two Different Styles of Democracy: A Personal Viewpoint*)
Using a graphic organizer (chain of events diagram) to identify the sequence of events Recognizing implied feelings Taking a stand for or against a proposal Synthesizing Internet content: Taking notes and presenting results Writing Tip: Describing people by using adjectives	Figuring out idiomatic expressions and specialized terms Learning sports-related vocabulary Inferring the meaning of words from context Understanding metaphors Using compound adjectives Inferring meaning of words as synonyms or antonyms Focusing on words from the Academic Word List	**TOEFL iBT** Using strategies to correctly answer multiple-choice questions
Choosing one point of view over another and defending your choice Making inferences about a relationship from dialogue Synthesizing Internet content: Taking notes and presenting results Summarizing a group opinion Writing Tip: Writing down the key points of an article in a summary	Matching phrases to their meanings Identifying words from the same family Focusing on words from the Academic Word List Reviewing vocabulary through pantomime	**TOEFL iBT** Answering vocabulary questions on tests

Critical Thinking Skills	Vocabulary Building	Focus on Testing
Using a graphic organizer (a continuum) to rank items	Getting meaning from context	
Taking a stand by agreeing or disagreeing	Recognizing synonyms	Analyzing compound words on vocabulary tests
Analyzing points of view	Scanning for vocabulary	
Using a Venn diagram to compare answers from an interview	Focusing on words from the Academic Word List	
Reaching a group consensus and writing an opinion statement		
Synthesizing Internet content: Taking notes and presenting results		
Writing Tip: Structuring an argument to support an opinion		
Filling out a chart for comparison	Inferring the meaning of expressions from context and vocabulary	
Comparing opinions	Inferring the meaning of specialized terms	Using a computer effectively on tests
Choosing a favorite theme-related item and researching it	Understanding compound words	
Creating a study outline	Analyzing compound adjectives with hyphens	
Interviewing and using a graphic organizer (Venn diagram) to compare answers	Focusing on words from the Academic Word List	
Synthesizing Internet content: Taking notes and presenting results		
Writing Tip: Selecting strong examples to support a point of view		
Comparing opinions	Recognizing word families	TOEFL iBT
Synthesizing Internet content: Taking notes and presenting results	Getting the meaning of words from context	Reading between the lines in reading comprehension tests
Analyzing the actions and outcomes of a situation and presenting an alternative solution through a skit	Focusing on words from the Academic Word List	
Solving problems related to the theme		
Writing Tip: Making a cluster diagram to help organize ideas		

Scope and Sequence

Chapter	Reading Selections	Reading Skills and Strategies
7 Remarkable Individuals p152  	*Confucius, 551 B.C.E.–479 B.C.E.* by Michael H. Hart *Courage Begins with One Voice* by Kerry Kennedy	Skimming for the general idea Identifying key terms Previewing to determine organization Identifying the voices in a reading
8 Creativity p172  	*Pure Genius* by Michael Michalko *"I Don't Do Nice"* by Jonathan Glancey	Scanning for compound words Recognizing nouns and verbs by definition and context Inferring character from actions Previewing an interview for organization and key ideas
9 Human Behavior p196	*Ethnocentrism* by John Friedl *A Clean, Well-Lighted Place* by Ernest Hemingway	Skimming for the main idea Scanning for development of the main idea Finding support for main ideas Previewing for characters and plot Expressing the theme
10 Crime and Punishment p220 	*Hooked on Crime* by Ken MacQueen *Eye Witness* by Ed McBain	Identifying the interviewees in an article Understanding the setting Identifying narrative elements Scanning for specific terms Reading and interpreting charts

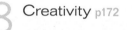

Critical Thinking Skills	Vocabulary Building	Focus on Testing
Supporting or disproving a general statement with facts Expressing an opinion Using a graphic organizer (a continuum) to rank leaders Comparing ideas Synthesizing Internet content: Taking notes and presenting results Writing Tip: Using a Venn diagram to compare and contrast two topics	Figuring out meaning from structure clues: compound words, prefixes and suffixes Forming new words from the same word family Matching words to their definitions Using expressive synonyms Creating new words using noun suffixes Focusing on words from the Academic Word List	**TOEFL® iBT** Understanding sentence-insertion questions on tests (Reading: *The Most Dangerous Jobs in the U.S.*)
Understanding the power of pictorial language Summarizing group discussions and reporting them to the class Synthesizing Internet content: Taking notes and presenting results Writing Tip: Making a plan before beginning to describe an object or invention	Matching set phrases or expressions to their context Guessing the meaning of words from structure and context Focusing on words from the Academic Word List	**TOEFL® iBT** Thinking twice about tricky test questions
Comparing opinions Analyzing love poems (Readings: three poems) Making inferences about characters Synthesizing Internet content: Taking notes and presenting results Writing Tip: Creating a dialogue	Using prefixes to build new words Scanning for words with clues Focusing on words from the Academic Word List Getting the meaning of words from context	**TOEFL® iBT** Answering questions on tests about an author's purposes or attitudes (Reading: *Gestural Ethnocentrism*)
Reporting opinions Using a graphic organizer (storyboard) to summarize the plot Interpreting a scene from the plot in a group skit Synthesizing Internet content: Taking notes and presenting results Writing Tip: Using a summary of an event to connect to a personal viewpoint	Getting the meaning of specialized terms from context Inferring the meaning of adjectives from context and structure Focusing on words from the Academic Word List Identifying spelling variations Matching descriptive adverbs to their context	**TOEFL® iBT** Understanding prose summaries on tests (Reading: *Privatized Prisons*)

1 New Challenges

> "We don't remain good if we don't always strive to become better."

Gottfried Keller
Swiss writer

In Chapter 1, we look at the challenges that cities face because of overpopulation. The first reading selection talks about megacities (cities with a population of over 10 million) and how they are coping with the massive migration of people from lesser-populated areas. Then we look at climate change. The second selection deals with how climate change affects the tourist industry. This chapter also offers a section on a personal challenge— how to meet and greet people from different countries and backgrounds.

Connecting to the Topic

1. Look at the photo of Seoul, Korea, one of the world's largest cities with a population of over 25 million. What are some of the problems of such huge cities?

2. Many people believe that the temperature of Earth is rising. Has there been much climate change recently in the place where you live? Explain. Do you think there are positive effects of this global warming? What could they be?

3. Look at the quote on the previous page. What do you think *to strive* means? Do you agree with the idea expressed in this quote? Why or why not?

Overpopulation Fuels Megacities, for Better or Worse

Strategy

Reading Without Knowing Every Word

The articles in this book contain many words that you know and also some words that you might not know. This is not surprising. Scholars tell us that, for historical reasons, English is one of the languages that have a very large vocabulary. However, it is not necessary to know every word in a reading to understand it. Practice the important skill of reading without knowing the meaning of every word by following these three steps:

- Look at the title, the headings, and any photos or illustrations and try to get a general idea of what the article is about.

- Read the article rapidly for the main ideas. Certain words have been highlighted for you to work on later, but for now, skip them and any other words you don't know. Keep on going to the end. Then, go back and read the article a second time.

- Do the exercises, referring back to the article and rereading all or parts of it as necessary. Two or three quick readings are better for comprehension than one slow one.

1 **Reading Without Knowing Every Word** Look over the article on pages 5–6 quickly. Then, by yourself or with a partner, answer the following questions.

1. The first and third words of the title are *compound words* because each contains two smaller words. *Overpopulation* contains *over* and *population*. Do you think it means "too many people" or "too few people"? Why? *Megacities* contains *mega* and *cities*. If you think of *megabytes* in computer programs, can you guess what *mega* means? What kind of cities are *megacities*?

2. The second word, *fuel*, is generally used as a noun when referring to something that gives power, like gasoline for a car. Here, *fuel* is not used as a noun. What part of speech is it? What do you think it means in this context? What does the whole title mean?

3. Look at the three section headings. What do you expect to learn in each section? If you want to find out about solutions to urban problems, in which section should you look?

Introduction

The population of planet Earth is exploding and its people are on the move. Where are we going? What are we leaving behind? How are our lifestyles changing? The following article discusses these questions and the good and bad consequences that may lie ahead in the future.

Overpopulation Fuels Megacities, for Better or Worse

A   In October of 2011, the world population hit an estimated seven billion for the first time in history. Not only are more babies being born, but people in the 21st century are healthier and they are living longer than ever before. Will we have the resources—food, water, energy—to sustain this ever-growing population? Where are all of these people going to live?

The Urban Explosion

B   Well, not in the countryside. The speed of urbanization—the rate at which the rural population of the world is moving to larger cities—is amazing. In 1950, only one in three people lived in urban areas, while the rest lived on farms or in towns and small communities. At the same time, only two cities in the world—Tokyo and New York City—were considered megacities: cities with a population of over 10 million. Now, there are 26 megacities and more are being added yearly. Over 180,000 people a day migrate from rural areas to cities. The number of megacities is expected to double over the next ten to twenty years.* Already well on their way to becoming megacities are Belhai in China, Palembang in Indonesia, Chittagong in Bangladesh, Toluca in Mexico, and Ghaziabad, Surat, and Faridabad in India.

C   The traditional pattern has been that industrial revolutions prompt people to abandon the countryside. North America and Europe experienced their industrial revolutions in the 1800s. This was a time when new machines for farming and manufacturing changed human life forever. Farming became more mechanized and this mechanization meant that fewer people were needed to run a farm. Many country dwellers moved to cities in search of better jobs, higher wages, and an easier life.

New Problems in Many Places

D   In China, the recent industrial revolution is the most rapid the world has ever seen. The Chinese economic explosion brought millions of people to the big cities. In January of 2012, China officially announced that more than half

5

10

15

20

25

of its population was now urban: 51%, or 690.79 million, were living in cities, compared to 656.56 million residing in rural areas. Chengdu, for instance, a smaller city that previously had been almost unknown except for its panda bears and teahouses, is now a thriving industrial and business center of 14 million inhabitants and moving rapidly toward the 20-million mark.

E   Rapid urbanization creates problems related to housing, education, jobs, clean water supply, sewage treatment, and crime. Infrastructure—such as roads, railroads, trains, and metros—needs to be built or enlarged to move the ever-increasing population from place to place. Slums have sprung up around many of the great cities of the world—Rio de Janiero, Mexico City, Cairo, Mumbai, Beijing, Johannesburg—just to name a few places. An estimated 1 billion people—almost one-seventh of the world's population—live in shanty towns mainly in Africa, Latin America, and Asia.

F   The highest rate of urban migration is in Sub-Saharan Africa. Due to armed conflicts among different groups, failing crops, droughts, and floods, people are fleeing to cities at twice the rate of other countries. Because they are not economically sound, these cities are unable to incorporate the huge populations moving into them. Richard Kollodge, editor of the United Nations Population Fund report released in October 2011, noted that many countries in Sub-Saharan Africa have high birth rates but low economic growth rates. "The population is growing faster than the government's ability to meet the need for services, education, and health. Economic growth isn't keeping up with population growth," said Kollodge. The result is that the countries are rapidly becoming poorer.

Looking to the Future

G   Is there any hope for the future? Experts in many fields are working on the problems of overpopulation and overcrowded cities. The two problems are closely tied. Education of women and access to birth control can lead to fewer and healthier children. City planners and architects can devise cities that make optimal use of the finite land of the earth. Engineers can work on ways to develop new water sources and improve the infrastructure of cities and the public transportation. Scientists are finding new types of clean energy and ways to reduce carbon emissions. Agricultural expertise can help grow the food to feed the masses. All of this will take international cooperation and vast sums of money.

H   And how does all of this relate to megacities? Joel Cohen, a professor of population studies at Columbia University in New York, suggests that well-designed smaller cities of about 1 million could provide a better future for urban life. But at the rate the population is growing now, Cohen said, "We are going to need to construct a city of a million people every five days for the next 40 years."

Source: "Overpopulation Fuels Megacities, for Better or Worse" (Miki Knezevic)

* The statistics in this paragraph are taken from "The Challenges Facing an Urban World," by Mark Kinver, BBC News, 6/13/2011.

2 **Recalling Information** Mark each statement with *T* (for true) or *F* (for false). Then correct the false statements to make them true. Remember to read the article (or parts of it) again if necessary. If you can do this activity successfully, then you have read well enough for your present purpose.

1. __F__ In the year 2011 the world population reached seven billion, which means that fewer people are being born now than in the past.

   It's the opposite. More people (not fewer people)
   are being born now than in the past...

2. _____ In 1950 there were only two megacities, but now there are over 25, almost all of them in Europe and North America.

3. _____ Traditionally, an industrial revolution causes people to leave rural areas and go to live in the cities.

4. _____ What is happening now in China is the most rapid industrial revolution that the world has known.

5. _____ More than half of the Chinese population now lives in the countryside.

6. _____ Rapid urbanization creates a great need for infrastructure to be built, such as roads and subways.

7. _____ In Sub-Saharan Africa today, people are not moving to the cities but are staying in the rural areas and practicing agriculture.

8. _____ When the population is growing very fast and the economy is not, a country becomes poor.

9. _____ Some solutions that experts are working on for the problem of overpopulation are educating women, developing new water sources, and improving public transportation.

Strategy

Finding the Main Idea of a Reading

It is often useful to find the main idea (the most important concept) of an article. Sometimes the main idea is expressed right at the beginning in a topic sentence. Then the rest of the article gives details to support the idea or explanations or subordinate (secondary) ideas that relate to it. Usually, however, the main idea is not stated in one sentence, and you have to read through the whole article to find it. Do not confuse the main idea with a subordinate idea that relates to only one part of the article.

3 **Finding the Main Idea of a Reading**   Look at the following statements. Then choose the one that you think best expresses the main idea of *Overpopulation Fuels Megacities, for Better or Worse*, and mark it with *M* for Main Idea. Two of the statements express secondary ideas; mark those with *S* for Secondary. One of the statements expresses an idea that is not included in the article at all; mark that one as *NI* for Not Included.

1. _____ Because of armed conflicts and bad weather conditions, many people in Africa and other parts of the world are leaving rural areas and going to live in cities that can not support them.

2. _____ The urbanization now happening in China is a great success because the country is industrializing very fast, and so its cities have no slums around them and offer good jobs for everyone.

3. _____ In recent years the world's huge population is going through a time of rapid urbanization that in many places is presenting new problems that need to be solved for the good of humanity.

4. _____ In 1950, there were just two "megacities" (cities with more than 10 million inhabitants) on the planet, New York and Tokyo; now there are at least 26 and every year more are added.

Strategy

Understanding the Meaning of Words from Context

The *context* of something is its surroundings or situation. The context of a word is what goes before it and after it. You can often guess the meaning of a new word by reading past it to the next sentence. If the meaning is still unclear, read the sentence before the word. If necessary, read the whole paragraph. Then go back and try to understand the word again.

4 **Understanding the Meaning of Words from Context**   Choose the best definition or synonym for each of the italicized words. If necessary, go back to the article and re-read the word in its larger context. If you are unsure, try putting the synonym you have chosen into its place in the sentence and see if it makes sense.

1. _____ In October of 2011, the world population hit *an estimated* seven billion... (**Hint:** How do people get a number like this?)

    Ⓐ a calculated   Ⓒ a large

    Ⓑ an exact   Ⓓ an imaginary

2. _____ Will we have the *resources*—food, water, energy—to sustain this ever-growing population? (**Hint:** Items inside of dashes are often examples.)

    Ⓐ books   Ⓒ materials

    Ⓑ knowledge   Ⓓ money

3. _____ The traditional pattern has been that industrial revolutions prompt people to *abandon* the countryside.

(A) appreciate   (C) fear

(B) dislike   (D) leave

4. _____ In January of 2012, China officially *announced* that more than half of its population was now urban...

(A) denied   (C) reported

(B) discovered   (D) understood

5. _____ *Slums* have sprung up around many of the great cities of the world...
(**Hint:** Look for a synonym in the next sentence in the article.)

(A) vegetable gardens on very small parcels of ground

(B) free government housing developments

(C) high-tech companies offering low salaries

(D) extremely poor unplanned neighborhoods

6. _____ Due to armed conflicts... , failing crops, *droughts,* and floods, people are fleeing to cities... (**Hint:** Notice that in a list the items belong to the same category and also, often two items of opposite meaning are placed side by side to give a contrast.)

(A) bad politics and corruption

(B) times of confusion

(C) times with no rain

(D) unemployment

7. _____ Because they are not economically *sound,* these cities are unable to incorporate the huge populations...

(A) crowded   (C) strong

(B) designed   (D) weak

8. _____ City planners... can devise cities that make optimal use of the *finite* land of the earth.

(A) extended   (C) unlimited

(B) limited   (D) wild

9. _____ Engineers can... *improve* the infrastructure of cities...

(A) defend   (C) learn about

(B) destroy   (D) make better

10. _____ Agricultural *expertise* can help grow the food to feed the masses.
(**Hint:** Think about the meaning of the smaller word inside of expertise.)

(A) knowledge   (C) machinery

(B) labor   (D) wealth

Understanding Compound Words

Some English words are called *compound words* because they are composed (made up) of smaller words joined together. Sometimes the smaller words are linked by hyphens, but most of the time they aren't. If you don't know whether to use a hyphen or not, look the word up in a dictionary or online.

To understand the meaning of compound words, break them into their smaller parts and look at the context. Then you can usually guess their meaning. You already saw two examples of compound words in the title of the article: *overpopulation* and *megacities*. Here are some more examples.

Examples

self-help (books): these are books that show you how to help or improve yourself

crosswalk: a place marked off where you cross a street by walking

underpaid: a description of someone who is not receiving enough money for his or her work

---

5 **Understanding Compound Words** The compound words, written in italics, are taken from the reading selection. Guess the meaning of each word by breaking it into the smaller words inside of it. If necessary, go back to the reading and look for clues to the word's meaning in its context. (The letter of the paragraph is given for each word to help you to locate it.) Write the meaning in the blank.

1. Will we have the resources… to sustain this *ever-growing* population? (A)

   Here "ever" means always and "growing" means getting bigger so this is a
   population that is always getting bigger.

2. The traditional pattern has been that industrial revolutions prompt people to abandon the *countryside*. (C)

   _____

   _____

3. Chengdu… previously had been almost unknown except for its panda bears and *teahouses*… (D)

   _____

   _____

4. Infrastructure—such as roads, *railroads*, trains, and metros—needs to be built… (E)

   _____

   _____

5. … needs to be built or enlarged to move the *ever-increasing* population from place to place. (E)

_____

_____

6. An estimated 1 billion people—almost *one-seventh* of the world's population… (E)

_____

_____

7. Experts… are working on the problems of overpopulation and *overcrowded* cities. (G)

_____

_____

8. … a professor… suggests that *well-designed* smaller cities… could provide a better future for urban life. (H)

_____

_____

Strategy

Analyzing Words with Suffixes and Prefixes

A **suffix** is a group of letters added to the *end* of a word to make a new word. For example, take the noun *accident* and add the suffix *-al* to it, and you get the adjective *accidental*, as in the sentence *It was an accidental mistake*. Take the verb *read* and add the suffix *-er* and you get the noun *reader*.

Sometimes there is a spelling change. For example, if the word ends in a silent *-e*, sometimes you drop the *-e* before adding the suffix. Sometimes you change the *-e* to *-i* before adding the suffix. Take the noun *finance* and add the suffix *-al*, and you get the adjective *financial*.

Here are examples of some common suffixes:

-al	comic + **-al** = comical; finance + **-al** = financial
-er	teach + **-er** = teacher; write + **-er** = writer
-tion	connect + **tion** = connection; educate + **tion** = education
-ation	specialize + **ation** = specialization; realize + **ation** = realization

A **prefix** is a group of letters added to the *beginning* of a word (rather than to the end, like a suffix). Like compound words, words with prefixes sometimes have hyphens and sometimes don't. Two prefixes occur in the reading: **sub-** and **un**.

Here are the meanings of these two prefixes:

sub-	*under, below*	**Sub-zero** *temperatures* means very cold temperatures *below* zero degrees.
un	*not*	She was **unconscious** for six hours after the accident.

6 Building New Words with Suffixes and Prefixes Make words used in the reading by adding suffixes from the list in the strategy box to the words in italics. In some cases you will have to make a noun plural or change a letter. Check your answers by finding the words in the reading.

1. In many places rural people want to *urbanize*, but this process of

   _____urbanization_____ often causes new problems.

2. In Europe, the *tradition* has been that people leave the farm and go to the city

   for a better life. But nowadays the _____ pattern does not

   always work.

3. In Europe and North America during the time of Queen Victoria of England,

   a great deal of *industry* was created. That's why this period is called the

   _____ revolution.

4. The invention of new machines caused farming to become *mechanized*, and this

   _____ ended the jobs of many farm workers.

5. Some people were happy to *dwell* in the countryside, but these country

   _____ had to move to the city when they could not feed

   their families.

6. Chengdu is a Chinese city *known* as a thriving business center, but it used to be

   _____ except for its panda bears and teahouses.

7. It is especially important to *educate* women because without _____

   they will not find employment.

8. The need to find work is one of the main reasons that rural people *migrate*, and

   their _____ is often to a megacity.

9. The area of Africa *below the Sahara* desert suffers from lack of water and armed

   conflicts; that is why _____ Africa is the part of the world with

   the highest rate of people leaving the countryside.

10. Thousands of migrants every day are *able* to find their way to the cities, but the

    cities are _____ to give them the jobs and security they need.

11. Many experts in *agriculture* are searching for new methods to feed the masses,

    but will this _____ expertise be enough for the population of

    the future?

12. The governments of many nations will have to *cooperate* because only with

    this _____ will the world as we know it survive.

7 **What's Your Opinion?** Work with a partner to answer the following questions. Then be prepared to explain to the class what you and your partner decided and why.

1. Of all the cities in the world, which would you like to visit most? Why? How long would you want to stay there? What would you see and what activities would you enjoy?

2. Is urban life always better than rural life? What advantages are there to living in the country? Would it be nice to live in a small town where you know everyone and everyone knows you? Why or why not?

3. Would you like to live for a while in different places? If so, where and for how long? If not, why not? After all, there is a saying: "Variety is the spice of life."

8 **Around the Globe** Working with a classmate, look at the photos in each section below to find out more about customs in the United States and around the world. Take turns reading aloud the descriptions that accompany the photos. Then follow the directions and answer the questions after each section.

A. Meeting and Greeting

A   In some cultures, such as the Japanese and Korean cultures, people bow to each other when they meet. In others, they put their palms together in front of their faces and incline their heads. (This is called *namaste* in India and *wai* in Thailand.) In Russia, France, Italy, and many other parts of Europe, as well as in Latin America, people touch each other when they meet, embracing (hugging) and often exchanging a quick kiss on one or both cheeks.

B   Muslims greet each other with a *salaam* greeting. This can be with or without bowing, perhaps shaking right hands or even hugging and kissing

▼ Namaste

(men with other men and women with other women). They say "Salaam Alaikum!" or a similar phrase wishing peace to each other. (*Salaam* means *peace*.) In the English-speaking world (for example, Australia, Canada,

▲ Handshake

New Zealand, the United Kingdom, Ireland, and the U.S.), the usual custom is to shake hands, but sometimes people don't, preferring to just nod and smile. A casual "Hi" or "How ya' doin'?" or "Hello, there" often takes the place of a formal handshake, but it means the same thing. If a person extends her or his hand in greeting, then it is polite to shake hands.

Hug ▶

Look at the photos on pages 13–14 and discuss the following:

1. What is happening in each photo? Where is the greeting taking place?

2. What do you think of these ways of greeting?

3. Is one of the ways of greeting above similar to the customs in your culture?

4. With your partner, practice greeting each other as they do in English-speaking cultures, and also in some other way. Introduce yourself by saying, "My name is _____. What's your name?" This is acceptable and often appreciated in English-speaking cultures. After learning the name of a person, say "Pleased to meet you!"

B. Social Distance

A   The "comfort zone," or the distance people stand from each other when they talk, varies among different cultures. Asians stand quite far apart when they talk. Greeks, many Arabs, and South Americans stand quite close together. Often, they move closer as the conversation heats up. Americans and Canadians are somewhere in the middle. Studies show that they feel most comfortable in conversation when standing about 21 inches apart from each other.

Look at the photos above and discuss the following:

1. What are the people doing and where do you think the conversation is taking place?

2. How far apart do people usually stand when having a conversation in your culture?

3. Stand up and play the role of two people talking about the weather. First, pretend you are in an Asian country, then in Greece, and then in the United States. Which distance feels most comfortable to you? Why?

9 Asking Personal Questions What questions are polite for a first meeting? This varies greatly depending on where you live. Look at the following questions and decide which ones would be polite and which would be impolite for a first meeting in your culture(s). Three of these questions would often be considered impolite in U.S. or Canadian culture, and a fourth one also, under certain circumstances. Can you guess which ones?

1. Where are you from?
2. How much did you pay for your jacket?
3. What do you do for a living?
4. How much do you earn?
5. Are you married?
6. How old are you?
7. Do you have any children?
8. What is your religion?

How much money do you make?

Go with the Floe: Adventure Travel's Love-Hate Relationship with Climate Change

Before You Read

Strategy

Analyzing the Title of a Reading

In general, a title has two purposes: to give us an idea of what the article is about and to motivate us to read it by provoking our interest or curiosity. A good title is both informative and interesting, and helps to set the stage (prepare our mind) for a good reading. So, before you start, analyze the title by following these steps.

1. Look at the title to see what information it gives about the reading. What points or themes are mentioned? What parts aim to provoke interest or curiosity in the reader?

2. Decide what words or phrases you don't understand and try to clarify them (make them clear). Sometimes they depend on *prior knowledge* (what a reader should already know). In that case you may have to go to another source (dictionary, phrase book, Internet) to get the meaning.

3. Finally, *paraphrase* the title (expressing it in your own words).

1 **Analyzing the Title of a Reading**   By yourself or with a partner, analyze the title of the article on page 19 by filling in the following blanks.

1. Write down the title. The article talks about a connection, or relationship, between two main themes. Circle the two main themes in the title.

   _____

2. What do you think a "love-hate relationship" is? Can you imagine a friend, family member, celebrity, or character in a movie or TV show who has a love-hate relationship with another person? Is it possible to have a love-hate relationship with a job, sport, or video game? Describe an example of this.

   _____

3. What reasons might cause people to feel a love-hate relationship between the two themes you circled in #1 above?

   _____

4. Write the first four words of the title. The last word *floe* is a *homophone*,[2] a word that sounds exactly like another word—in this case, *flow*—but has a completely different meaning. These first four words are a joke because the common saying *go with the flow*, which means "don't resist the movement around you, be laidback and flexible," has been changed to *Go with the Floe. Floe* means "a sheet of floating ice." Why do you think that the author changed *flow* to *floe* here? Which of the two themes does it refer to? Or, does it refer to both? Explain.

   _____

   _____

2 **Identifying Compound Words**   Look back at the Strategy box in Part 1 called "Understanding Compound Words" (page 10). Then read the article (pages 18–20) quickly to get the main idea. Then go back to the beginning of the article and find each compound word described below and write it in the blank. Remember that some compound words have hyphens and some do not. The words are presented here in the order of their appearance in the article.

1. a description of the age of a man from Scotland (Paragraph A)

   _____*55-year-old*_____ (professional)

2. a description of the length of a journey (Paragraph A)

   _____ (journey)

3. an area in rivers, lakes, or oceans through which boats may pass (Paragraph B)

   _____

4. a view of the visible aspects of an area including fields, mountains, etc. (Paragraph C)

   _____

[2]Other examples of homophones are *flour*, the kind used for making bread, and *flower*, the kind that grows in your garden; or *break*, to ruin or destroy (something), and *brake*, a stopping mechanism for a car. Jokes based on homophones are called *puns* and are very common in English.

5. the description of a industry that involves both excitement and tourism (Paragraph C)

_____ (industry)

6. a reference to the length of time one cruise will last (Paragraph C)

_____ (cruise)

7. a reference to the kind of diving that many scuba divers want to do (Paragraph C)

_____ (diving)

8. the kind of animal-watching that many tourists want to participate in (Paragraph C)

_____ (watching)

9. the season of the year when many travelers do nature walks (Paragraph E)

_____

10. an area completely covered with snow (Paragraph E)

_____

11. the group of animals that live far away from towns and cities (Paragraph F)

_____

12. an animal living in the mountains of Canada and the U.S. that tourists want to catch sight of (Paragraph F)

_____ (sightings)

Read

Introduction

The following article is from *Time*, the world's largest weekly news magazine with a global distribution of 25 million.* *Time* is famous for its unique (different-from-all-others) style of writing that began with its first editor, Britton Hadden, in 1923. *Time* often includes unusual or surprising details, even inventing new words. Several of these have become part of the English language, like *tycoon*, meaning "a wealthy and powerful business person." *Time*'s style has been called lively, zippy, distinctive, quirky, excessive, and strange, but it has never been called dull or boring. This article from *Time* explores the connection between one section of the tourism industry, adventure-travel, and the recent phenomenon of global warming—the fact that the overall temperature of Earth is getting warmer and warmer.

* *Time's* distribution numbers may go down since the appearance of Internet news services is now reducing the sales of almost all magazines and newspapers.

Go with the Floe: Adventure Travel's Love-Hate Relationship with Climate Change

A In late July, Jock Wishart, a 55-year-old professional adventurer from Scotland who has been to the magnetic North Pole so many times that he has lost count, took off for the top of the world once again. This time, however, he packed a paddle for the 450-mile (725-km) journey. Why are Wishart and his crew attempting to become the first to row there? Because, rather suddenly, they can. 5

B Climate change has finally melted enough ice and opened enough waterway for boats to reach that far north. "Ten years ago, we never would have thought this was remotely possible," says Wishart.

C His chilling quest is calling attention to the stunning things tourists 10 can do and see, thanks to the earth's changing landscape. Global warming hasn't exactly led to a boom in the adventure-travel industry. Those exotic trips are expensive—one 26-day cruise across the Northeast Passage costs $14,750—and tourists are feeling the economic strain. Plus, climate change has had an adverse effect on activities like coral-reef diving and 15 polar-bear watching.

D But as evidenced by Wishart's extreme row to the pole, new adventures are emerging. "The reality is that there are more opportunities for travelers to disembark," says Jorge Rodriguez, a marketing manager for Cruceros Australis, which operates cruises from the southern tip of South America. 20 "It's just easier to get to places."

▼ People kayaking in glacial water

E   Take hiking, for example. The Adventure Travel Trade Association, which offers resources to tourists, points out that even those who aren't super physically fit are doing springtime hiking in Greenland and eastern Tibet on mountain trails that had been covered in snow until summer. New trails are opening up in South America. "Due to the rapid glacial recession in the Andes of southern Peru, we are now doing treks over 17,000-ft. [5,000-m] passes on routes which until five years ago were snowfield," says Peter Robertson, president of Andean Treks, an operator based in Watertown, Mass.

F   Climate change is also making it easier to see wildlife in some regions. At Glacier National Park in Montana, mountain guide Laurie Barnard reports more frequent bighorn-sheep sightings; with milder conditions, she suspects, the sheep can roam at higher elevations. Whale- and dolphin-gazing trips are becoming more popular in Ireland and South Africa, places where scientists think warmer waters could be increasing sightings. And in Antarctica, a massive wall that for years had been an obstacle to whale watchers receded in 2010 to reveal a shallow channel full of feeding humpbacks. With the wall gone, says Troy Glennon, founder of Go South Adventures, his group's inflatable boats got within 10 yd. [9 m] of the whales. "They were so close to us, it was ridiculous," he says. "Everyone's heart was swelling."

▲ Whale-watching

G   But he and other adventure operators get a bit defensive when discussing climate change's impact on their business. They want you to know, often before you even bring it up, that they're in no way rooting for global warming. "We have a love-hate relationship with climate change," says Glennon. "It gives you access to places unseen and places unforeseen. But the loss of biodiversity, the loss of species—therein lies the hate."

H   Yes, there's a lot to loathe about climate change. But if Wishart wants to promote a product after rowing to the pole, it's O.K. to cheer a little. He and many other adventurers are adapting to a changing world.

Source: *Time Magazine* (Sean Gregory)

3 Checking Your Comprehension Underline the correct phrase in parentheses that best completes each statement about the article.

1. The professional adventurer Jock Wishart and his crew are attempting to be the first ones to reach the magnetic North Pole (by dogsled / in a rowboat).

2. Jock and his crew could not do this ten years before because (there was too much ice / they didn't have enough money).

3. Global warming has had an adverse effect on some activities, such as (hiking in the high mountains of Tibet / scuba diving in the coral reefs).

4. New trails have opened up in the Andes mountains of South America because the glaciers have become (larger / smaller).

5. In Antarctica, a massive wall of ice melted down to reveal (humpback whales feeding in a channel of water / the ruins of an ancient city unknown to modern man).

6. Adventure travel operators want everyone to know that they (have / do not have) an unconditional love of climate change.

7. Climate change is now making the earth (warmer / cooler).

8. There is a lot to loathe (hate strongly) about climate change, for example: the loss of (access to places unseen and places unforeseen / certain kinds of plants and animals).

Strategy

Identifying Common Phrases and Idioms

Learning to identify common phrases and idioms in English is a good way to improve your comprehension and fluency. A *common phrase* is a group of words often used together, such as *if all goes well* or *to be as busy as a bee*. Some common phrases are also idioms. An idiom is a group of words that means something completely different from the literal meaning of each word; for example: *We have to go to town on this project if we want to finish on time!* The idiom go to town doesn't mean to go anywhere; it means "to work very hard." Another example is that someone says, *I'm in a bind about whether to go to the party or not.* The idiom to be in a bind means "to have a problem with no easy answer."

Pay attention when you read to groups of words that are frequently used together to express a meaning. Look at the context they occur in and try to connect them to the idea they represent.

4 **Identifying Common Phrases and Idioms** Fill in the blanks with the appropriate idiom or common phrase from the article that is listed in the box. The meaning of each item is in parentheses after the blanks.

get defensive	(to be) rooting for
has lost count of	take off
in no way	top of the world
lead to a boom	

1. The travelers will soon ____take____ ____off____ *(leave)* for a high mountain in Greenland.

2. The leader has gone on this expedition so many times that he _____ _____ _____ _____ *(can't remember)* them all.

3. When some of the group complain about the high price of this expedition, the leader begins to _____ _____ *(react too strongly when it isn't necessary)* and asks them, "Could any of *you* plan a cheaper expedition?"

4. He wants everyone to know that he is _____ _____ _____ *(not at all)* happy about how expensive the trip is.

5. All the members of the expedition have already traveled with him to the _____ _____ _____ _____ *(North Pole)*.

6. This time their goal is to climb a very challenging mountain and they may not succeed, but all their friends are _____ _____ *(encouraging and supporting)* them.

7. If they succeed and return safely, the news about their trip may _____ _____ _____ _____ *(cause a big increase in the popularity)* in this kind of adventure travel.

5 **Focusing on Words from the Academic Word List** Read the excerpts below taken from the reading in Part 2, and fill in each blank with the most appropriate word from the box. Do NOT look back at the reading right away; instead, try to choose the correct words from the context or your memory. Then check your answers on pages 19–20.

access	channel	evidenced	impact	reveal
adapting	emerging	founder	resources	routes

But as _____evidenced_____ by Wisehart's extreme row to the pole,
                    1
new adventures are _____... Take hiking, for example. The
                          2
Adventure Travel Trade Association, which offers _____ to
                                                        3
tourists, points out that even those who aren't super physically fit are doing
springtime hiking in Greenland and eastern Tibet... New trails are opening
up in South America. "Due to the rapid glacial recession in the Andes of
southern Peru, we are now doing treks over 17,000-ft. [5,000 m] passes on
_____ which until five years ago were snowfield," says Peter
        4
Robertson... And in Antarctica, a massive wall that for years had been an
obstacle to whale watchers receded in 2010 to _____ a shallow
                                                      5
_____ full of feeding humpbacks. With the wall gone, says
        6
Troy Glennon, _____ of Go South Adventures, his group's
                    7
inflatable boats got within 10 yd. [9 m] of the whales... But he and other
adventure operators get a bit defensive when discussing climate change's
_____ on their business... "We have a love-hate relationship
        8
with climate change," says Glennon. "It gives you _____ to
                                                          9
places unseen and unforeseen... But if Wishart wants to promote a product
after rowing to the pole, it's O.K. to cheer a little. He and many other
adventurers are _____ to a changing world.
                      10

6 **Guided Academic Conversation** In small groups, discuss three of the following four topics. Make sure that everyone in the group contributes to the discussion. Choose one person for every selected topic to report the group's ideas to the class.

1. **The Impact of Urbanization.** Would you like to live in one of the world's 26 megacities? Why or why not? Which one would you choose as the best place to live, and why? Could you be happy living in the countryside? Explain. In general, what impact is rapid urbanization having on people today? Which areas of the world are benefiting the most and which ones are suffering the most? What are the reasons for this?

2. **The Attraction of Adventure Travel.** Why do you think adventure travel is popular even though it is dangerous and expensive? Who are these travelers? Are they mostly men? Where are they from? Do some cultures have a tradition of adventure travel? If you receive a prize some day and can go on any adventure trip you want, what will you choose? What wildlife would you like to see?

3. **The Humor in Language.** *Time* magazine isn't the only place to find playful language such as the pun on the homophones *flow* and *floe*.* Many jokes in English are based on puns. Here is an old one:

    — *That doctor will never be a success.*

    — *Why not?*

    — *Because he always loses his patience (patients)!*

    Do you understand this joke? When and where do people in your culture tell jokes? Are some of them based on puns? Try to describe a joke from your culture in English. Try to find another joke in English based on a pun and tell it to the group.

4. **Bringing the World Together.** Many people think that the biggest threat to the world is not climate change but war and conflict between cultures. What can be done to decrease this terrible possibility? In your opinion, does aid to poor countries from rich countries and the UN help or not? Explain. Do you think that more urbanization will bring more cooperation, or will it cause more conflict? Why? What about adventure travel? In your opinion, what is the best way to achieve world peace?

FOCUS ON TESTING

Analyzing Points of Contrast on Tests

The TOEFL® iBT often asks questions about points of contrast in a reading. These contrasts are usually between two ideas. Questions might also be about differences between events, styles, or groups of people.

To analyze points of contrast:

1. Fix firmly in your mind the two things that are being considered.

2. Look carefully for the ways in which the two are different. These are the points of contrast.

3. For each point, ask yourself exactly how the two things are different from each other.

4. Try to see how the many points of contrast add up to an overall idea.

TOEFL® is a registered trademark of Educational Testing Service (ETS). This product is not endorsed or approved by ETS.

Analyze the points of contrast in the following paragraph written by a U.S. citizen who moved to Canada as an adult.* Read the paragraph. Then, on page 26, mark an ✗ to indicate whether each point relates to Canadian or American society.

Two Different Styles of Democracy: A Personal Viewpoint

After moving to Canada from the U.S., I was surprised to discover a system of government quite different from that of my homeland. First of all, there is a Monarch, currently Queen Elizabeth ll of England, who functions as a figurehead but has no real power, although her face appears on Canadian currency. Also, instead of just two major parties, there are usually three or four parties of importance. Instead of a Congress composed of Congressmen and Congresswomen, there is a Parliament, made up of MPs (short for Members of Parliament). Like the U.S., Canada has a Senate, but it is only an advisory body, not the powerful institution I was accustomed to, that can vote in or veto laws. Perhaps most strikingly, there is no President; the most important person, the Executive, is the Prime Minister. These differences, however, go deeper than just having distinct names because in Canada people actually vote for the party, not the person, and the leader of the party that gets the most MPs automatically becomes Prime Minister. The result? You never have the situation that so often plagues and paralyzes any attempts at new laws and reform in the U.S. when the President is from one party and the majority in the House of Representatives and the Senate are from another. As a consequence of this difference, there is more possibility of change in the Canadian style of democracy. Is this better or worse? That is something I am still trying to figure out!

▼ The Royal Canadian Mounted Police (RCMP) is a visible and important force for upholding the law in Canada.

*Written by Brenda Wegmann.

	Canadian	American
1. ceremonial Monarch	_____	_____
2. Parliament made up of MPs	_____	_____
3. powerful Senate	_____	_____
4. Executive is the President	_____	_____
5. Congressmen and Congresswomen	_____	_____
6. usually only two parties of importance	_____	_____
7. Executive is the Prime Minister	_____	_____
8. Senate with little power	_____	_____
9. money with a royal face on it	_____	_____
10. Executive and Congress can be from different parties	_____	_____
11. Executive and the largest group in Parliament are from the same party	_____	_____
12. more possibility for change	_____	_____

9 What Do You Think? Read the paragraph below and in small groups discuss the questions that follow.

Choosing a Career to Save the World

The world has many challenges and problems, including economic, health, environmental, and educational. If you were to choose a job or career to help solve the problems, what would you choose? Would you be a politician, health-care worker, businessperson, or social worker? Would you be a teacher or scientist? An engineer or a city planner? Which field would you go into and why? Could you make a living in this field? Would you be satisfied with this type of job?

▼ What problems do architects and city planners solve?

▲ What problems does a scientist solve?

1. If you wanted to find out about training or education in your chosen field, where would you look?

2. In your native country, is it easy to change your job or profession? Is it easy or hard to open your own business? Explain.

3. In the future, which jobs do you think will be in the greatest demand? Explain.

1 Making Connections Read the questions below and choose one that interests you. Work by yourself to answer the questions by finding facts and opinions on the Internet or from other sources. Report your findings to your instructor or to the class. Be sure to write down your sources.

1. Choose a country in which English is widely spoken, other than the United States or Canada; for example, Australia, the U.K, India, Ireland, New Zealand, or Australia, and find information about urban life in that country. Are there many big cities? Where are they located? Is there a lot of poverty, and if so, where? What kind of jobs do most of the people have? Are some cities wealthier than others? If so, why?

2. Choose one of the countries listed in question 1 and describe rural life in that country. What percentage of the population lives in rural areas? What kinds of jobs do they have? How well are they doing economically? Are certain regions doing better than others? If so, why? How many people in rural areas are living in poverty? Is there a large migration now from the countryside to the cities?

3. Research and describe the Industrial Revolution that occurred in England from approximately 1760 to 1850. Was it a good time or a bad time for most people, or was it both good *and* bad? Explain. How is the industrialization that is now taking place in China similar? How is it different?

   Or, choose a different Asian or Latin American country that is now passing through a time of industrialization and tell how it is similar to or different from the Industrial Revolution that occurred in England.

4. Look up the famous British author Charles Dickens. Several of his novels present a vivid picture of what London was like during the Industrial Revolution. What is the title of one of these novels and how does it show the challenges and difficulties caused by rapid industrialization?

F⊙CUS

Writing Tip: Using Details To Support Your Ideas

Details are small points. They serve as examples or illustrations of a larger idea and make it more convincing and understandable. For example, if you say, *Tornados can be very destructive*, you can then describe houses that have fallen down and trees with their roots in the air. These details support your main idea

2 **Writing a Paragraph Using Details** Write a clear paragraph in English about something you have learned in either Part 1 or Part 2 of this chapter. Follow these steps.

Step 1: Choose *one* of the following beginnings (depending on which part of the chapter you prefer to write about).

A. From what I have learned in Part 1 of this chapter, I believe that urbanization is causing many problems in the world today because...

B. From what I have learned in Part 2 of this chapter, I believe that climate change is having a positive impact on adventure travel because...

Step 2: Complete the sentence you chose by stating the *main reason* or *reasons* why you think that urbanization is causing problems, or that climate change is having a positive impact on adventure travel, depending on the part of the chapter that you have chosen.

Step 3: Go back to the selection you are writing about and reread it quickly, making a list of the *details* (small points) that illustrate or give examples of your reason or reasons.

Step 4: Choose the three or four details that are the most interesting or convincing.

Step 5: Write a sentence about each one.

Step 6: Check over what you have written. Do all the sentences support your main idea? Change any that do not seem right.

Step 7: Look at the spelling, grammar, and vocabulary. Make your paragraph as correct, clear, and interesting as you can.

Self-Assessment Log

Read the lists below. Check (✓) the strategies and vocabulary that you learned in this chapter. Look through the chapter or ask your instructor about the strategies and words that you do not understand.

Reading and Vocabulary-Building Strategies

☐ Reading without knowing every word
☐ Finding the main idea of a reading
☐ Understanding the meaning of words from context
☐ Understanding compound words
☐ Analyzing words with suffixes and prefixes
☐ Analyzing the title of a reading
☐ Identifying common phrases and idioms

Target Vocabulary

Nouns

▨ access*
▨ channel*
▨ cooperation*
▨ countryside
▨ drought
▨ engineer
▨ expertise*
▨ founder*
▨ impact*
▨ infrastructure*
▨ landscape
▨ mechanization
▨ megacities
▨ migration
▨ overpopulation
▨ resources*
▨ routes*

▨ slums
▨ top of the world
▨ urbanization

Verbs

▨ abandon*
▨ adapting*
▨ emerging*
▨ evidenced*
▨ improve
▨ migrate
▨ promote*
▨ reveal*
▨ sustain*
▨ take off

Adjectives

▨ agricultural
▨ defensive
▨ estimated*
▨ finite*
▨ industrial
▨ overcrowded
▨ traditional*

Adverb

▨ in no way

Expressions

▨ has lost count of
▨ lead to a boom
▨ (to be) rooting for

* These words are from the Academic Word List. For more information on this list, see www.victoria.ac.nz/lals/resources/academicwordlist/

2 Teamwork and Competition

> "Two heads are better than one."
>
> English proverb

This chapter focuses on two important areas of world culture: sports and business. In sports and business, values that seem in some ways to be opposites—teamwork and competition—are in fact both crucial to success. In the first reading, the world-famous soccer player David Beckham describes the competition and teamwork that bring him success when he moves from England to join the Real Madrid soccer team in Spain. The second reading looks at how Kim Ssang Su, a talented Korean businessman, builds a globally competitive company by creating a sense of teamwork among his employees.

Connecting to the Topic

1. Look at the photo and read the title of this chapter. Why do you think it's important for these people to work together as a team? Explain.

2. The paragraph above states that both teamwork *and* competition are crucial to success in sports and business. Do you agree or disagree? Explain.

3. In what other areas of life do you think teamwork and competition play important roles? Why?

Beckham: An Autobiography

Before You Read

Strategy

Figuring Out Idiomatic Expressions and Specialized Terms

An *idiomatic expression* is a group of words with a meaning that is different from the meaning of each individual word, such as *get the drift* of something, which means to "understand the general idea of something." Learning expressions like these will help you to understand conversations and read informal writing in English.

Specialized terms are the words associated with a particular area of knowledge; for example, in this chapter, sports terms. Readings and discussions relating to sporting events include their own specialized vocabulary. For example, you might hear this in a soccer game: *go for goal,* which means to "try and kick the ball in the net and get a goal, or a point."

Often you can figure out the meanings of these words from their context.

1 **Getting the Meaning of Idiomatic Expressions from Context** In the first reading, David Beckham and his coauthor use a number of common idiomatic expressions. Read the sentences below from Beckham's autobiography and try to figure out the closest meaning for the underlined idiomatic expression in each sentence. Use the hint below each sentence to help you

1. I <u>took a knock or two</u> during my first year in Madrid.
   Hint: Usually to *knock* means to hit something, or it refers to the noise made when you hit something hard, such as *knocking on a door.* So, for someone to *take a knock or two* means:

   Ⓐ to leave quickly and with a lot of noise

   Ⓑ to knock on many doors, asking for help

   Ⓒ to have a hard time and to have problems

   Ⓓ to hit back at all the people who attack you

2. With the standards set by the club, you could never say you were <u>in a comfort zone</u> at Manchester United (the name of the team Beckham had played with before).
   Hint: A *zone* means a particular area or space. So, to be *in a comfort zone* means:

   Ⓐ to feel safe and relaxed   Ⓒ to be in the right part of the city

   Ⓑ to feel nervous and worried   Ⓓ to be on the wrong side of the field

3. Now I'd been <u>whisked off</u> to a new club in a new country…
   Hint: *Whisk* means to move rapidly in a brushing or whipping motion, as when you are cooking and you *whisk* the eggs with a special wire utensil. To be *whisked off* means:

   (A) to brush yourself off and get ready for something new

   (B) to decide to leave everything behind and go far away

   (C) to be told to accept a new position

   (D) to be moved to a new place very quickly

4. Now I'd been whisked off and <u>didn't really have a clue</u> what was coming next.
   Hint: When a detective tries to solve a murder, he or she looks for *clues* that will lead to a solution. To *not have a clue* means:

   (A) to feel positive about the future

   (B) to not know what to do

   (C) to understand that life is always a mystery

   (D) to search hard for the answer to a question

5. I was <u>bracing myself</u> for the challenge…
   Hint: A *brace* is a device for keeping something firmly in place, such as a metal frame used to hold the pieces of a chair together while it is being glued, or a device for someone with a back problem to hold his or her back straight. To *brace oneself* means:

   (A) to stop thinking about the future

   (B) to stop thinking about the past

   (C) to find a way to escape

   (D) to prepare for something unknown or difficult

6. I'm confident in my own ability but, that summer morning at the training ground, there was a little <u>twist in the pit of my stomach</u>: it felt as though I'd arrived in Madrid with something to prove.
   Hint: To *twist* means to turn or bend. So, a *twist* is something that has been turned or bent. The *pit* here means the deepest part. So, you may imagine from the context of the phrase above that to have a *twist in the pit of one's stomach* means:

   (A) to feel very sick after eating some bad food

   (B) to be in good shape and have strong stomach muscles

   (C) to feel very nervous and uncomfortable

   (D) to be happy and feel confident

7. The next day, I didn't need to understand the articles to <u>get the drift</u> of the headlines.
   Hint: To *drift* means to be moved in one direction by a current, as in a river or ocean, and *get* means to grab or catch. To *get the drift of* something, then, means:

   (A) to understand the general idea

   (B) to understand completely

   (C) to change the meaning of something

   (D) to read a newspaper article

8. Almost from kick-off you could tell it was going to be our night.
   Hint: Notice that the use of "our" in the expression implies *belonging*, meaning that the night will belong to our team. From the context, it was going to *be our night* means:

   (A) it was going to be late before the game would end

   (B) it was going to get dark very soon

   (C) we were going to lose that game

   (D) everything was going to go well for us

9. I celebrated with a new set of teammates who'd already done everything they could to make me feel at home…
   Hint: Usually people feel relaxed and at ease in their own homes. So, to make someone *feel at home* means:

   (A) to cause someone to think about childhood

   (B) to help someone to feel comfortable

   (C) to force someone to think about returning home

   (D) to influence someone to be good

2 **Getting the Meaning of Specialized Terms from Context** Read the sentences and phrases from the reading in the column on the left. Match the underlined phrase with the correct definition in the column on the right.

1. __e__ Carlos took me off ten minutes into the second half.	**a.** hit the ball with my chest
2. _____ Almost from kick-off you could tell it was going to be our night.	**b.** hit, when the player connects with the ball in any way
3. _____ Ronaldo got away down the left wing…	**c.** kick the ball across the field
4. _____ I was thinking: he'll not cross it here.	**d.** move in front of other players
	e. removed me from the game
5. _____ He's bound to cut in…	**f.** the center of the playing field
6. _____ and go for goal.	**g.** left side of the field when facing the other team's net
7. _____ He swung it over, through, and I could tell it was going to miss out Guti…	**h.** player in charge of defending the net
8. _____ at the near post.	**i.** side of the net nearest to the player
9. _____ I could see the goalkeeper coming to challenge…	**j.** the start of the game
10. _____ My first touch of the game,…	**k.** to not reach
11. _____ I chested the ball off…	**l.** try to put the ball in the net
12. _____ to someone in midfield…	

③ **Reading Without Knowing Every Word** As you read "Beckham: An Autobiography," pay attention to the key vocabulary words in bold blue type and use them in the activities that follow.

Introduction

The following reading passage is from the autobiography of David Beckham, from England, one of the world's most famous soccer players at the beginning of this millennium. He and his wife, Victoria Caroline Adams Beckham ("Posh Spice" of the musical group *The Spice Girls*) have three sons and a daughter: Brooklyn (born 1999), Romeo (born 2002), Cruz (born 2005), and Harper Seven (born 2011). In this selection, he has just moved from England, where he had been playing for ten years on the Manchester United soccer team, to Spain to play on the Real (pronounced ray-AL) Madrid team. The Real Madrid players have the nickname "galacticos" (a Spanish word deriving from "galaxy," and so implying *huge*) because almost every player on the team is a world star. The story is written in British English and describes how Beckham and his new team competed in the seasonal soccer tournament in Spain. (Beckham now plays for the Los Angeles Galaxy.)

• How do you think Beckham was feeling after moving to a new team in a new country? Why?

David Beckham ▶

Beckham: An Autobiography

A   I took a knock or two during my first year in Madrid. [...] With the standards set by the club [...], you could never say you were in a comfort zone at Manchester United. But for fifteen years, Old Trafford (Stadium) had been home for me, as a soccer player at least. I knew how things worked [...] and understood exactly what was expected of me. Now [...] I'd been   5
whisked off to a new club in a new country and didn't really have a clue what was coming next. I was bracing myself for the challenge: unfamiliar

surroundings, a different language, and another way of life. Soccer's soccer wherever you're playing it, of course, but I was pretty sure that training at Real [...] would be very different to what I'd grown used to back home. How much of what I'd learnt so far, as a player and as a person, was going to be of any use to me here?

B   It didn't help matters that I'd had some of the Spanish paper talk translated for me. Although I got the feeling that, in England, people wanted me to do well, some of the pundits here were saying that Florentino Perez had just signed me to help the club shift replica shirts.* I'm confident in my own ability but, that summer morning at the training ground, there was a little twist in the pit of my stomach: it felt as though [...] I'd arrived in Madrid with something to prove. For a start, I had the prospect of lining up alongside the *galacticos* [...]

C   [...] I was still pretty nervous when the balls came out and we got down to training. Was it because of what other people might have been saying or was it me feeling a bit unsure of myself? [...]

D   We had a *friendly*† against Valencia at the Mestella (Stadium) that didn't go well for me or the team. Then [...] we were away to Real Mallorca (Stadium) and just never found a shape or pattern. Worse for me, Carlos‡ took me off ten minutes into the second half. The next day, I didn't need to understand the articles to get the drift of the headlines. Basically, people were saying: *Is that it? If it is, what's he doing in Spain?* [...]

◀ The Real Madrid soccer team

*The word *pundits* refers (somewhat humorously) to journalists who think they know everything. They are suggesting that the manager Florentino Perez has brought Beckham to the team only because he is famous and his name will help sell T-shirts with the team name on them.
†A *friendly* is British slang for a match that does not count as part of the season's competition.
‡Carlos Queiroz, the coach of Real Madrid at the time.

E   Everything that had gone wrong in Mallorca seemed to come right at the Bernebeu (Stadium). Almost from kick-off you could tell it was going to be our night. Raul and Ronaldo both scored and then, about a quarter of an hour from the end, Ronaldo got away down the left wing. I was on my way forward but I was thinking: *He'll not cross it here. He's bound to cut in and go for goal.* He swung it over, though, and I could tell it was going to miss out Guti at the near post. As I jumped, I could see the goalkeeper coming to challenge and just concentrated on keeping my eyes open. It was a fantastic cross. I was in the right place for the ball to hit me on the head and go in, without me having to direct it at all. I could hardly believe it was happening. *My first game at the Bernebeu and I've just scored my first goal for Real Madrid.*

F   The other players all rushed over towards me. Roberto Carlos hugged me and lifted me up off the ground. I think the rest of the team understood what the moment meant to me […]. The Real crowd had been great with me all night, never mind what doubts I'd had beforehand. My first touch of the game, I chested the ball off to someone in midfield—a simple touch to a team-mate—and the fans were all up on their feet clapping and cheering. […]

G   I'd been so unhappy during my last few months at Old Trafford […]. Now, in those few seconds as I celebrated […] with a new set of team-mates who'd already done everything they could to make me feel at home […], I knew for sure that, by moving to Madrid, I'd done the right thing.

Source: "Futbol, La Vida" from *Beckham: Both Feet on the Ground: An Autobiography* (David Beckham with Tom Watt)

After You Read

Strategy

Using a Graphic Organizer to Follow the Sequence of Events

One important element of any story is the plot, a series of events (or chain of events) that lead to the story's conclusion. Following the various events in the order (sequence) they occur is necessary for an overall understanding of the story. In Activity 4, you will use a graphic organizer called a *chain of events diagram* to take notes on key events from David Beckham's autobiography.

4 Finding the Sequence of Events Read the sentences below about the events described by Beckham in his autobiography. Then look through the reading to find the sequence (order) in which they occur. Write the letter for each event in the chain of events diagram below, in the order in which it appears in the story. Write one letter in each box. Using a graphic organizer of this type helps to organize and retain information.

Key Events in the Selection from Beckham's Autobiography:

A. Beckham plays a great game at the Bernebeu stadium.

B. Public opinion seems to be asking what Beckham is doing in Spain, based on his poor performance so far.

C. A *friendly* [a non-official game] against the Valencia team at the Mestella stadium goes poorly for Beckham and his team.

D. Beckham leaves England and arrives in Spain to work with the Real Madrid team.

E. The crowd loves Beckham, and the fans clap and cheer for him.

F. The Spanish newspapers suggest that the team manager only signed on Beckham in order to sell more replica shirts (i.e., team merchandise).

G. A game at the Real Mallorca stadium goes poorly for Beckham and his team.

Chain of Events Diagram

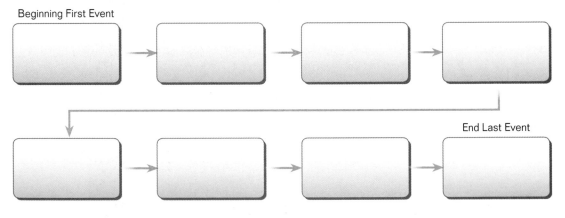

Beginning First Event

End Last Event

5 Guided Academic Conversation: The Inside Story Now you have a clear picture of the sequence of events in Beckham's autobiography. He also describes his reactions to these events, what he is feeling inside.

Work with a classmate and follow the steps below.

1. Discuss Beckham's moods and emotions and how they change.

2. Number from 1 to 7 on a piece of paper and make a list of the seven events (in brief form) from Activity 4, leaving space between them.

3. After each event, write a brief description of how Beckham feels and why. Use words and expressions from the article as much as possible.

4. Finish up with a concluding sentence about the overall change in this man.

5. After you finish, compare your list with those of other classmates.

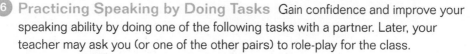

6 Practicing Speaking by Doing Tasks Gain confidence and improve your speaking ability by doing one of the following tasks with a partner. Later, your teacher may ask you (or one of the other pairs) to role-play for the class.

1. *"Madrid Tonight"…and Three Months Later*

   You are scriptwriters for the popular Spanish radio show *Madrid Tonight*. Make up two sets of interview questions for Beckham: (1) for when he first began with the Real Madrid soccer team and (2) for three months later. One person then plays the role of the radio announcer and the other the role of Beckham for the first interview. Change roles for the second interview.

2. *Only for Sports Fans: The Quick Draw*

   This activity is for those who have some knowledge about soccer or have a very analytical mind. Pretend you are a coach, and draw a diagram of the field, players, goal, etc. on a sheet of paper to illustrate what happened in the play a quarter of an hour from the end of the game at the Bernebeu that was so important to Beckham. (See lines 41–49.) Then explain out loud in your own words to a partner what happened, pointing to the parts of your illustration as you give your explanation of this play. The partner then gives an explanation, using his/her drawing. Compare your drawings. Are they the same? Were your explanations similar?

3. *Tell Us Your Story!*

   Have you ever felt that something (a sports game, a social event, a school assignment, or something else) was not going in your favor only to succeed in the end, as Beckham did here? Tell the story. This is the basis for the Spanish TV show, *Tell Us Your Story!* and you are the guest. (If nothing like this has ever happened to you, you can make up a story.) Be sure to tell about your emotions as well as the events, and don't be afraid to be "dramatic." Your classmate will be the TV host who introduces you and asks you questions. After you finish, reverse roles and start over.

▲ "Fight, team, fight!"

The Olympics

▲ "The Olympic Games are based on an ancient ritual that started in Greece.

A   The Olympic Games originated in Ancient Greece during the eighth century B.C.E. (Before Common Era, referring to the year 1). These games featured athletes from rival city-states competing in sporting events showcasing their physical prowess (skill) including boxing and a pentathlon, which involved skills in five events (*penta* means "five"): jumping, discus and javelin throws, a foot race, and wrestling. The Ancient Olympics were not without their religious significance; those who competed also participated in ritual sacrifice to honor Zeus, the father of the gods.

B   The Modern Olympic Games began in 1896 and, except for one cancellation during World War II, they continued to be held every four years through 1992. At that time, it was decided that the Games would be held every two years, alternating between the Summer Olympics and the Winter Olympics.

C   The Olympic Games are an international experience: athletes from all over the globe compete for the highest medals in a display of great athletic skill, while citizens from across the world gather in the host nation to view these events in person, and millions watch them on television. Yet the Olympics are not without their controversial aspects, including boycotts, the use of performance-enhancing drugs, bribing of officials and judges as well as acts of terrorism, leading to the questions concerning the value of the games for the international community and security issues for both participants and audience members.

1. In what country did the Olympic Games begin? What was the reason for their creation?

2. How long have the Modern Olympic Games been held? How often are they held?

3. Why do you think many countries want to host the Olympic Games? What are the benefits? What are some possible drawbacks?

4. Should the Olympic Games continue to be held when they are, or should they occur less often? Do you think the controversies surrounding the Games should be considered in possibly ending the Games for good?

Outward Bound

Before You Read

1 **Using the Context to Infer the Meanings of Words** Guess the meanings of the words in the sentences on pages 41–42 from their context or from clues within the words themselves. Mark the correct answer.

Guess the meanings of the words in the sentences on pages 41–42

> **Language Tip**
>
> Learning the specialized terms related to business can help you when you read or have discussions about business.

1. Kim Ssang Su is CEO of LG Electronics, Inc.

   Ⓐ the owner

   Ⓑ an outstanding employee

   Ⓒ the chief executive officer

   Ⓓ an assistant accountant

2. The managers seem happy that Kim has spent the day lecturing and rallying them.

   Ⓐ organizing and encouraging

   Ⓑ insulting and blaming

   Ⓒ boring

   Ⓓ complaining about

3. Kim Young Kee is a V.P. of LG Electronics.

   Ⓐ coordinator of prices

   Ⓑ Very Important Person

   Ⓒ admirer

   Ⓓ Vice President

4. LG's revenues jumped 18% last year, to $17 billion, and net profits rose 33%, to $556 million.

   Ⓐ interest on their debts

   Ⓑ earnings before expenses and taxes are deducted

   Ⓒ earnings after expenses and taxes are deducted

   Ⓓ salaries for employees

5. LG's revenues jumped 18% last year, to $17 billion, and net profits rose 33%, to $556 million.

   Ⓐ interest on their debts

   Ⓑ earnings before expenses and taxes are deducted

   Ⓒ earnings after expenses and taxes are deducted

   Ⓓ salaries for employees

6. Kim wants to lift LG up to the level of the biggest companies that have <u>global brands</u>.

   (A) huge buildings and equipment

   (B) more than 10,000 employees on their payroll

   (C) names and symbols known around the world

   (D) giant computer networks

7. The advanced Korean market provides a <u>testing ground</u> for new technologies.

   (A) a large amount of soil for planting

   (B) a group of skilled scientists and technicians

   (C) a laboratory for creating new inventions

   (D) a place to try out the latest products

8. Kim grew up on a farm and admits to being more comfortable visiting <u>factories</u> than in his spacious office in Seoul.

   (A) manufacturing plants where products are built

   (B) places where products are stored

   (C) centers where ad campaigns are planned

   (D) administration offices

Strategy

Scanning

Scanning is reading quickly to find particular bits of information. When you read for business, numbers are important. You can pick up information about business by scanning for numbers and seeing what they mean. To scan, follow these steps:

- Think of what you are looking for.
- Move your eyes quickly through the text until you find it. Do not pay attention to anything else.
- Stop and record the information.

2 **Scanning for Numbers** Scan the reading on pages 43–45 for the numbers needed to fill in the blanks below.

1. Kim Ssang Su is _____ years old.

2. He began his career _____ years ago.

3. LG Electronics' revenues for last year were _____

dollars, and its net profits were _____ dollars.

4. Samsung Electronics, LG's biggest competitor, had revenues of

_____ dollars.

5. In Korea, _____ % of households using the Internet have high-speed access.

6. Kim took over LG's appliance business in the year _____.

7. Under his guidance, sales in LG's appliance business reached _____ dollars last year.

8. Kim likes to hold breakfast meetings for top executives at _____ A.M. every morning.

Read

Introduction

Just like sports, the world of business also runs on teamwork and competition. The following selection tells the story of a Korean businessman who used some very unusual methods to inspire his team of workers and to create a strongly competitive company. You may be surprised to find where he comes from and interested to learn how he and his company moved outwards and expanded toward global success.

- What methods can you think of to inspire people to work together?
- For you, personally, what inspires you to work with others?

Outward Bound
Call Kim Ssang Su a Man of the People

A   On a chilly night in the mountains south of Seoul, Kim, CEO of LG Electronics, Inc.,* holds a paper cup filled with *soju*, a clear, sweet Korean drink with a vicious bite. Surrounding him are a dozen of the 300 LG suppliers' managers whom Kim has spent the day lecturing and rallying. They have also been hiking up a snow-covered mountainside—necessary training, he says, for the grand plans he has for South Korea's second largest electronics firm. At the end of the day, he treats a group of employees to an outdoor barbecue of grilled pork and bowls of fiery red kimchi. "Great people! Great company!" he barks. "Great company! Great company!" they chant back.

B   When dancing girls in short skirts and blond wigs start jiggling to earnumbing Korean pop music, the tireless Kim, 59, cavorts in a mosh pit† of workers near a stage. Later he ascends the stage himself, microphone in

---

* Kim Ssang Su was CEO of LG Electronics until 2007.
† A mosh pit is an area right beside the stage where music is performed and where audience members "slamdance," a type of dancing where people bump into each other in time to the music.

hand, to croon out a popular oldie called *Nui* (Sister). "We love our CEO," says Kim Young Kee, an LG executive V.P. "He shows us a good time."

C   CEOs rarely stoop to carouse with the common man in an Asia dominated by secretive business clans. But Kim is no ordinary Asian boss. He began his career 35 years ago as a nondescript engineer at an LG refrigeration factory, climbed the ranks and claimed the CEO post in October. Now he aims to duplicate the same feat with LG—lifting a company little known outside Asia into the stratosphere of global brands with Sony, Panasonic, and Samsung. "I want to go down in LG history," says Kim. "After death, a tiger leaves its skin. A man leaves his name."

D   LG seems well on its way. Revenues jumped 18% last year, to $17 billion, and net profits rose 33%, to $556 million. Last year, LG was the world's largest seller of mobile phones operating on the CDMA standard, which allows more people to use a network at the same time. It makes dazzling flatscreen TVs and other leading-edge gadgets.

E   LG faces plenty of competition. Its biggest rival at home and abroad, Samsung Electronics, whose revenues of $36.4 billion are two times as large as LG's, has already hit the U.S.— and scored big successes. Samsung is also ahead of LG in developing a truly global brand.

▲Kim Ssang Su lecturing and inspiring his employees.

F   In this new digital world, LG has a distinct advantage in its ultra-wired South Korean home base. The demanding Korean market, where an amazing 84% of households using the Internet have high-speed access, propels LG to develop more advanced products and provides a testing ground for new technologies. LG has outpaced Nokia and Motorola in cramming the hottest new features into its mobile phones. Its latest model, the SC8000, combines a PDA, an MP3 player, a digital camera, and a camcorder.

G   It may seem odd that LG has turned over its top job to a farm boy from a tiny village in eastern South Korea. Kim Ssang Su spent his childhood knee-deep in the family's rice paddies. He admits to being more comfortable visiting factory floors than in his spacious office overlooking Seoul's Han River.

H   It would be wrong, though, to underestimate Kim, who has become near legend in Seoul for the turnaround he engineered at LG's appliance business. When he took over in 1996, LG was making washing machines and refrigerators for low-cost Chinese companies. Kim sliced costs by moving production of low-end products to China. He proved there is room for innovation, introducing, for example, appliances like air conditioners that can be controlled from the Internet. The result: sales reached $4.7 billion last year, more than twice the number when Kim took control.

I   Kim is infusing LG's other businesses with the same vigor. Called a "commander in the field" by executives, he storms about LG's factories and offices poring over details, issuing commands and spurring on the staff by giving them what he terms "stretch goals." Awake at 5:30 each morning for a brisk walk, he openly prefers "morning people" and holds 7 A.M. breakfast meetings with top executives. "I don't like the expression 'nice,'" Kim says, "I don't want LG to be perceived as nice. None of the great companies in the world are nice."

Source: "Outward Bound" *Time Magazine* (Michael Schuman) Time, Inc. All rights reserved. Reprinted by permission.

For the complete article, see pages 246–248.

After You Read

3 Selecting the Main Idea   Circle the number of the statement below that you think best expresses the main idea of "Outward Bound." Why is it better than the other two?

1. LG Electronics is South Korea's second largest electronics firm and now seems to be increasing its revenues at a rate that is much faster than that of its competitors.

2. Kim Ssang Su rose from being a farm boy in a tiny village to CEO of LG Electronics, and his unique character and skills are mainly responsible for this company's growing success.

3. Kim Ssang Su provided a great inspiration for the managers of his 300 suppliers at the rally and party he organized for them, as well as giving them food, drink, entertainment, and personal contact.

Understanding Metaphors

Another aspect of readings that presents a challenge in a second language is the metaphor. A metaphor is an implied (suggested) comparison made by using a word or phrase associated with one thing to describe something completely different. For example, in the reading, *soju* is described as a "Korean drink with a vicious bite." A drink does not bite, of course. But the taste of the drink is similar to the strength of a bite by a person or a wild animal. Personification, presenting a thing with the qualities of a person, is one type of metaphor. Metaphors add interest and sometimes humor to writing. <u>The taste of a drink is</u> being compared to <u>the bite of a wild animal</u>.

▲ *Soju* is a Korean drink with a vicious bite.

4 **Understanding Metaphors** Metaphors are often implied (suggested) through the verb in a sentence. Below are examples of sentences showing the common usage of certain verbs. These verbs are also used as metaphors in the reading selection. Work alone or with a partner and find the examples from the reading selection using this same verb as a metaphor. Look for the meaning in the surrounding sentences. Then explain what is being compared to what. The first one is done as an example.

1. common usage of *barks*: The dog ___barks___ as people pass the yard.

   Usage in the article: _"Great people! Great company!" he barks_. (see line 8)

   metaphor: _The way Kim shouts_ is being compared to _the barking of a dog_.

2. common usage of *jumped*: The horse <u>jumped</u> over the fence.

   usage in the article: _____. (see line 23)

   metaphor: _____ is being compared to _____.

3. common usage of *chant*: The people in the temple <u>chant</u> religious songs.

   usage in the article: _____. (see line 9)

   metaphor: _____ is being compared to _____.

4. common usage of *cavorts*: The young calf cavorts in the field. [cavort = leap and prance around]

usage in the article: _____. (see line 11)

metaphor: _____ is being compared to _____.

5. common usage of *sliced*: The boy sliced (cut with a knife) some cheese for his sandwich.

usage in the article: _____. (see line 60)

metaphor: _____ is being compared to _____.

6. common usage of *to storm*: As it was storming outside, we stayed in the house, listening to the thunder and rain.

usage in the article: _____. (see line 66)

metaphor: _____ is being compared to _____.

F☉CUS

Using Compound Adjectives

English has many compound adjectives: words made up of two smaller words connected by a hyphen. Usually you can guess the meaning by breaking the word into the two smaller words. The article about Kim uses several compound adjectives. For example, it talks about *leading-edge gadgets*. A *gadget* is a small device or object. This phrase is related to the idea of competition. Can you guess what kind of a gadget is a *leading-edge* gadget*?

*The adjective *cutting-edge* is often used with the same meaning.

5 **Using Compound Adjectives** Match each compound adjective on the left to the noun it is modifying on the right. You can scan the article to find each compound adjective and noun. Be prepared to explain the meaning if called upon.

1. _____ ear-numbing   **a.** access

2. _____ flat-screen   **b.** Chinese companies

3. _____ high-speed   **c.** TVs

4. _____ knee-deep   **d.** products

5. _____ low-cost   **e.** pop music

6. _____ low-end   **f.** mountainside

7. _____ snow-covered   **g.** in rice paddies

6 **Inferring Meaning: Same or Opposite?** The following words in Column 1 are from the article on pages 43–45. Each is followed by a word or phrase in Column 2 that is a synonym (almost the same in meaning) or an antonym (almost the opposite). Check the box for either *Synonym* or *Antonym* in Column 3. For a word you are not sure about, scan the reading and use the context to infer its meaning.

Words from the Article	Other Words	Synonym or Antonym?	
1. ascend	move down	☐	☑
2. chilly	cold	☐	☐
3. croon	scream	☐	☐
4. duplicate	copy	☐	☐
5. goals	objectives	☐	☐
6. innovation	same old thing	☐	☐
7. nondescript	ordinary	☐	☐
8. oldie	new song	☐	☐
9. spur on	discourage	☐	☐
10. stoop	bend over	☐	☐
11. stratosphere	underground	☐	☐
12. tireless	lazy	☐	☐
13. turnaround	complete change	☐	☐
14. vicious	cruel and nasty	☐	☐
15. vigor	weakness	☐	☐

7 **Focusing on Words from the Academic Word List** Use the most appropriate word from the box to fill in each of the blanks in the paragraphs taken from Part 2. Do NOT look back at the reading right away; instead, first see if you can remember the vocabulary. Then check your answers on pages 44–45.

goals	odd
job	perceived
innovation	underestimate
issuing	

G It may seem _____ that LG has turned over its top
1
_____ to a farm boy from a tiny village in eastern South Korea.
2
Kim Ssang Su spent his childhood knee-deep in the family's rice paddies.
He admits to being more comfortable visiting factory floors than in his
spacious office overlooking Seoul's Han River.   5

H It would be wrong, though, to _____ Kim, who has
3
become near legend in Seoul for the turnaround he engineered at LG's
appliance business. When he took over in 1996, LG was making washing
machines and refrigerators for low-cost Chinese companies. Kim sliced
costs by moving production of low-end products to China. He proved there   10
is room for _____, introducing, for example, appliances like
4
air conditioners that can be controlled from the Internet. The result: sales
reached $4.7 billion last year, more than twice the number when Kim took
control.

I Kim is infusing LG's other businesses with the same vigor. Called a   15
"commander in the field" by executives, he storms about LG's factories and
offices poring over details, _____ commands and spurring on
5
the staff by giving them what he terms "stretch _____." Awake
6
at 5:30 each morning for a brisk walk, he openly prefers "morning people"
and holds 7 A.M. breakfast meetings with top executives. "I don't like the   20
expression 'nice,'" Kim says, "I don't want LG to be _____ as
7
nice. None of the great companies in the world are nice."

8 Guided Academic Conversation In small groups, discuss three of the following four topics. Write a group opinion statement about them.

1. **Kim, the Man**
   What kind of a man is Kim? How is he different from the bosses at many firms? Where did he grow up? How have his circumstances changed during his life? What do we know about his tastes and preferences? What animals are mentioned or suggested in the article in reference to his actions? What do others call him or say about him?

2. **Kim's Leadership Style**
   Would you describe Kim's style as strong or weak? Explain. Why does he make his managers hike up a mountainside and call it "necessary training" for his plans for the company? And why the party afterwards? What tactics does he use, according to the article, that have helped him make LG Electronics more competitive?

3. **Kim and his Company**
   Write down a list of all the different devices LG Electronics makes that you can find listed in this article. What is the function of each of these items? Which one of these would you most like to receive as a present and why? How does LG have a competitive edge with each of the devices you listed? How did Kim cause a turnaround in LG's appliance business?

4. **Your Personal Reaction to Kim**
   Kim said in the article, "After death, a tiger leaves its skin. A man leaves his name." How do you think Kim wants people to think about his name? Is it important for people to leave a name for themselves in the world? How would you want people to remember you in the future? Why doesn't Kim like the word "nice"? Do you agree with him? What actions of his do you admire? Are there any of his actions that you dislike? Would you like to work in a company run by Kim? Why or why not? Explain.

PART 3 Tying It All Together

1 End-of-Chapter Debate Competition over teamwork? Teamwork over competition? Which of these is more important in the selection "Outward Bound"? Think about this for a couple of minutes. Your teacher will write *Competition* on one side of the board and *Teamwork* on the other side. Then you and your classmates will take a stand, literally. You will walk over and stand beside the word that you consider indicates the more important factor. Once there, your teacher may ask you why you chose the way you did. What will you say?

Now, think back to the first selection of the chapter, "Beckham: An Autobiography." If asked the same question, will you stay where you are or will you move? Why?

2 Making Connections Do some research on the Internet and take notes on one of the following topics. Type in key words. Visit two or more sites. Share your results with the class or in a small group.

1. How has David Beckham's life changed since this autobiography was written in 2004? How is he doing now and how does the press view him?

2. Who is Zinedine Zidane, and what is his connection to the Real Madrid team? What was his role in the 1998 World Cup Championship? What was his role in the 2006 World Cup Championships? What is he doing now and how does the world press view him?

▲ Zinedine Zidane was instrumental in the outcome of the 1998 World Cup and helped lead the French team to the finals in 2006.

3. What is new with Kim Ssang Su? Is he still the CEO of LG Electronics? What can you find out about him, his family, and his life in general?

4. Who are the CEOs of some of the other successful electronics companies? Are there any women among them? What is their average age? Do any of them have unusual or interesting styles of management?

Responding in Writing

FOCUS

Writing Tip: Describing People By Using Adjectives

You can describe a person with adjectives that represent his or her most outstanding qualities. Then you illustrate each of these with one or more concrete examples.

Example

Ellen is a very generous person. She donates to several charities and volunteers twice a week at a local hospital.

3 Writing and Using Adjectives Write a paragraph that describes Kim Ssang Su or David Beckham. This is like painting a portrait (a picture of a person) in words. Follow these steps.

Step 1: Write down the name of the person you are going to describe. Look back at the article about him and make a list of his most important qualities (characteristics).

Step 2: Begin by writing *is* after his name plus three or four adjectives that express his main qualities or characteristics. (You may find these adjectives in the article or you may have to think them up for yourself after you read about the actions and words of the person you are describing.)

Step 3: Reread the article and find at least one detail that illustrates each of the adjectives you mentioned.

Step 4: Scan the selection for the words and phrases that are in boldface and try to use them in your sentences.

Step 5: Check over what you have written to catch and correct any mistakes.

Step 6: Think of a clever, funny, or interesting title and write it at the top of the page.

FOCUS ON TESTING

TOEFL iBT

General Testing Practice

Many standardized tests include multiple-choice questions. There are strategies you can use when taking a multiple-choice test.

1. Read the answers first.

2. Look for an answer that seems right and completes the question smoothly. For example, if the question asks why something happened, then the answer must indicate a cause.

3. Try to eliminate any answers that are clearly wrong.

4. Notice the wording of questions. Look for qualifying phrases such as "which of the answers below is not true."

5. Statistically, the least likely correct answer on a multiple-choice question is the first choice.

6. When in doubt, pick the longer of two answers.

7. Always choose an answer, even if you're not sure which one is correct.

The following sample includes two sections from a test on reading comprehension.

They are similar to sections on standardized exams given at many universities. You may find this test tricky. Most people can improve their scores on this kind of exam through practice. After finishing, correct your work. Try to understand why you made the mistakes that you did.

Practice Section 1 (Questions 1–7)

The questions in this part are based on two paragraphs about historical events. Choose the one best answer, and fill in the correct oval. Answer all questions according to what is stated directly or implied in the paragraph.

Paragraph 1:

An Augustinian monk named Gregor Mendel was the first person to make precise observations about the biological mechanism of inheritance. This happened a little over 100 years ago in an Austrian monastery, where Mendel spent his leisure hours performing experiments with pea plants of different types. He crossed them carefully and took notes about the appearance of various traits, or characteristics, in succeeding generations. From his observations, Mendel formed a set of rules, now known as the Mendelian Laws of Inheritance, which were found to apply not only to plants but to animals and human beings as well. This was the beginning of the modern science of *genetics*.

1. The importance of Gregor Mendel is that he was the first person to
_____.

- (A) imagine that there existed a precise mechanism for inheritance
- (B) approach the problem of inheritance scientifically
- (C) think about why animals and plants inherit certain characteristics
- (D) invent the word genetics

2. When did Mendel perform his experiments?

- (A) in ancient times
- (B) in the 1680s
- (C) in the 1860s
- (D) at the beginning of last century

3. Why did Mendel do this work?

- (A) He formed a set of rules.
- (B) He enjoyed it.
- (C) He lived in Austria.
- (D) He was paid for it.

4. The Mendelian Laws of Inheritance describe the transmission of biological traits in _____.

- (A) plants
- (B) animals
- (C) human beings
- (D) all of the above

Paragraph 2:

The magnificent warship Wasa, which sank after a maiden "voyage" of some 1,500 yards, was salvaged and restored, after lying at the bottom of Stockholm's harbor for over 330 years. The ship now rests in the National Maritime Museum of that city.

5. The Wasa sank around the year _____.

- (A) 1330
- (B) 1500
- (C) 1650
- (D) 1960

6. Which of the following statements about the Wasa is probably not true?

    Ⓐ It met with a catastrophe shortly after being built.

    Ⓑ It carried many soldiers and cannons.

    Ⓒ It was a veteran of many hard-fought battles.

    Ⓓ It was raised by modern salvaging techniques.

7. The Wasa ship appears to be _____.

    Ⓐ Swedish

    Ⓑ Dutch

    Ⓒ American

    Ⓓ British

Practice Section 2 (Questions 8–10)

In questions 8–10, choose the answer that is closest in meaning to the original sentence. Notice that several of the choices may be factually correct, but you should choose the one answer that is the closest restatement of the given sentence.

8. No hour is too early or too late to call Jenkins Plumbing Company.

    Ⓐ Jenkins Plumbing Company does not answer calls that are too early or too late.

    Ⓑ Jenkins Plumbing Company accepts calls at any hour of the day or night.

    Ⓒ Whether you call early or late, Jenkins Plumbing Company will come in one hour.

    Ⓓ If you call at an early hour, Jenkins Plumbing Company will never be late.

9. When TV first became available to large numbers of Americans in the 1950s and 1960s, most producers ignored its possibilities as a tool for education.

    Ⓐ In the 1950s and 1960s, there were not many educational programs on American TV.

    Ⓑ Until the 1950s and 1960s, most of the TV programs in the United States were tools for education.

    Ⓒ After the 1950s and 1960s, most American producers did not see the educational possibilities of TV.

    Ⓓ During the 1950s and 1960s, educational programs first became available to Americans.

10. In spite of the high interest rates on home loans, the couple did not change their plans to buy a new house.

    Ⓐ High interest rates caused the couple to change their plans about buying a house.

    Ⓑ The couple did not buy the house because of the high interest rates.

    Ⓒ Since interest rates were no longer high, the couple bought the house.

    Ⓓ Although the interest rates were high, the house was bought by the couple.

Self-Assessment Log

Read the lists below. Check (✓) the strategies and vocabulary that you learned in this chapter. Look through the chapter or ask your instructor about the strategies and words that you do not understand.

☐ Figuring out idiomatic expressions and specialized terms
☐ Using a graphic organizer to follow the sequence of events
☐ Using the context to infer the meanings of words
☐ Scanning
☐ Selecting the main idea
☐ Understanding metaphors
☐ Using compound adjectives
☐ Inferring meaning: same or opposite?

Target Vocabulary

Nouns

- CEO
- factories
- global* brand
- goalkeeper
- goals*
- innovation*
- job*
- mountainside
- net profits
- oldie
- revenues*
- stratosphere
- testing ground
- turnaround
- vigor
- V.P.

Verbs

- ascends
- barks
- cavorts
- chant
- croon
- duplicate
- issuing*
- jumped
- perceived*
- rallying
- sliced
- stoop
- storms
- underestimate*

Adjectives

- chilly
- ear-numbing
- flat-screen
- high-speed
- knee-deep
- leading-edge
- low-cost
- low-end
- nondescript
- odd*
- snow-covered
- tireless
- vicious

Idioms and Expressions

- to be our night
- bracing myself
- to chest a ball
- cross it
- cut in
- didn't (don't) really have a clue
- feel at home
- get the drift
- go for goal
- in a comfort zone
- kick-off
- left wing
- midfield
- miss out
- (the) near post
- spurring on
- took (take) a knock or two
- took (take) me off
- touch
- twist in the pit of my stomach
- whisked off

*These words are from the Academic Word List. For more information on this list, www.victoria.ac.nz/lals/resources/academicwordlist/

Gender and Relationships

"Life is no longer one's own when the heart is fixed on another."

Hindustan proverb

Many roads can be taken to find love and a compatible partner with whom to share one's life. From an arranged marriage by parents to a worldwide hunt on the Internet, the search for love is never-ending. The first selection deals with tips on how to attract a potential partner. The second selection is an excerpt from a famous novel called *Jane Eyre,* by Charlotte Brontë. In this passage, two people from different economic and social backgrounds declare true love for one another despite the many obstacles in their path.

Connecting to the Topic

1. Look at the proverb on the previous page. What does it mean? Do you have a similar saying in your culture?

2. How do two people find each other in this crowded world? Could it be a chance meeting, an introduction by a friend, or communication on the Internet? What are some characteristics that humans look for in potential mates?

3. When two people are in love, they often marry. At the end of some wedding ceremonies, as shown in the photo on these pages, the bride throws her bouquet of flowers to a group of single women. What do you suppose this ritual means?

Being Beautiful or Handsome is Easier Than You Think!

Before You Read

Strategy

Skimming for the General Idea

You can find the general idea of a reading selection quickly by skimming. To skim, follow these three steps.

1. Look first at the title, headings, photos, and captions to see what subject matter is being presented.

2. Move your eyes rapidly over the whole article, paying special attention to the first and last sentences of each paragraph and key words and phrases that are repeated.

3. Try to express briefly (in a sentence or two) the main idea or general message of the reading, using your own words.

1 Skimming for the General Idea Skim the reading selection that starts on page 59. Then work with a partner to answer these questions: What does the title tell us about the subject of the selection? What smaller topics do we learn about from the section headings? Which phrases or sentences seem especially important? Why? Together, write a brief description of the general idea of the article.

2 Matching Phrases to their Meanings Match each phrase on the left with the correct definition on the right. If you are unsure, find the phrase in the reading and use its context to guess the meaning. The first one is done for you as a model.

1. __f__ feature clusters   **a.** worry over constantly

2. _____ good grooming   **b.** examination of data and information

3. _____ opposite sex   **c.** good posture

4. _____ physical features   **d.** do too much or try too hard

5. _____ standing up straight   **e.** a person's shape of face, and height

6. _____ statistical analysis   **f.** femininity, masculinity and pleasantness

7. _____ be shooting for   **g.** males if you are female, or females if you are male

8. _____ go overboard   **h.** neat hair, regular showering and nice clothing

9. _____ obsess about   **i.** be trying to get

Introduction
This article is taken from the popular magazine *Psychology Today*. Which group of readers do you think would be most interested in an article like this one: teenagers, young adults, middle-aged people, or senior citizens (those over age 65)? Why? Would they be likely or unlikely to change their habits or attitudes after reading it? Explain your opinion.

Being Beautiful or Handsome is Easier Than You Think!

How to Be Attractive and Improve Your Appearance

A   When I was young, I often obsessed about what I looked like. Perhaps this happens to everyone, more-or-less. It is common to be a bit dissatisfied with parts of our body, our appearance, and our level of attractiveness. This dissatisfaction and concern especially comes out when we think about dating and becoming passionate with a partner.   5

B   As I studied attraction further, however, I came to understand that physical appearance was not the only aspect of ourselves that was attractive. Our personalities can influence how others see us. In addition, our confidence and social skills can spark attraction, passion, and intrigue in potential lovers.   10

C   Eventually, I also discovered that those "unchangeable" parts of our looks were not driving attraction anyway! Contrary to popular belief, a symmetrical nose, the perfectly proportionate figure, or a classic face are not nearly as important as the aspects of yourself that are easy to change. The little things under your control are the most attractive characteristics of all.   15
Read on for the research…

Research on Physical Appearance and Attractiveness

D   Mehrabian and Blum (1997) began their research with a simple idea— they wondered what physical features were most attractive to the opposite sex. More particularly, they wanted to discover the relative importance of stable features (e.g., body type and height) versus changeable features (e.g.,   20
grooming and clothing) in physical attractiveness. In essence, they wondered what combinations really made someone "attractive."

E   To answer that question, they presented 117 male and female university students with pictures of 76 partners of the opposite sex, varying in different physical features. They had the students rate the attractiveness of the people   25
pictured and also measured their emotional responses. Then, through statistical analysis, the researchers figured out who was attractive—and why.

F   Their shocking finding was that, by far, the most attractive features fell under the category of "self care." These features were changeable aspects like good grooming, neat hair, nice fitting and quality clothing, good posture, and healthy weight. Essentially, the most attractive features about a person (male or female) is that they put forth some effort to shower, groom, select some nice clothes, stand up straight, and manage their diet a bit. No plastic surgery, major gym time, or extensive overhauling required.

G   Coming in at only one-third as important as "self care" were three other feature clusters —"masculinity," "femininity," and "pleasantness."

H   Masculinity, somewhat attractive to women, was comprised of some of the stable features (depending on your gym time) of muscularity, shoulder width, larger chest, and a bigger jaw.

I   Femininity, somewhat attractive to men, contained more changeable features of wearing makeup, longer hair, and greater femininity (in posture, body language, etc.).

J   Finally, pleasantness, somewhat attractive to both men and women, was all about being happy, positive, and friendly in attitude.

K   Overall, the VAST majority of features important to attractiveness are relatively easy to change. Just grooming, standing up straight, getting a decent wardrobe, and staying relatively healthy makes you attractive! Beyond that, being positive, pleasant, and friendly makes you truly alluring. Finally, if guys want to spend a bit of time in the gym, or if women want to grow their hair and put on some makeup, then they can have the whole package. Again, no implants, Botox, nose jobs, or facelifts required…

What This Means for Your Love Life

L   Being attractive is easier than you think. Just keep up with as many of these changeable features as you can.

M   **1. Grooming**—by far, the most important feature. Take some time to care for yourself. Shower, style your hair, and shave or trim where you need to. Be clean, neat, and smell good, too. Grooming alone can make (or break) your attractiveness—and all it takes is a bit of time, effort, and a toothbrush!

N   **2. Clothing**—also an important and a relatively easy fix is your style. The research says that three aspects of clothing are required to be attractive—neat, well-fitting, and more formal. Put plainly, your clothes need to be clean, pressed, and well maintained. They also need to fit you well and flatter your shape. Finally, they should be a little classy. Don't be chronically "under-dressed"... buy some dressier gear. Also, the color red is a good choice.

O   **3. Posture**—practice standing up straight. Hold your head up. Put your shoulders back. Buy some sensible shoes, a good desk chair, or a corset if you need to. Good posture is sexy. It also contributes to the right body language for dating and relating.

P   **4. Attitude**—remember to put on a happy face. Smile. Be pleasant, positive, and friendly. Heck, a good personality can even overshadow other physical issues you may have. So, be happy… and get a date or keep a lover.

▲ Is he attractive? Why or why not?

▲ Is she attractive? Why or why not?

Q **5. Fitness**—granted, this isn't as easily "changeable" as the others. But, the research is not talking about the "perfect butt" or "washboard abs" anyway. Essentially, we're shooting for "relatively healthy" (e.g., not super obese, no severely protruding stomach, etc.). So, no need to obsess and go overboard. But, do your best to eat well, move around a bit, and care for your health. Good grooming, the right clothes, and standing up straight can go a long way towards minimizing what diet and exercise don't do!

R **6. Gender**—generally, try to look masculine or feminine (depending on who you want to attract). To be more masculine, muscle up your shoulders and chest (or wear a nice, padded, sport coat). Grow a goatee, chin-strap, or beard to hide a weak jaw. To be more feminine, learn to properly apply makeup—accentuating your eyes and lips. Also, grow your hair longer (or just get extensions).

Source: *Psychology Today,* "The Attraction Doctor"
(Jeremy Nicholson, M.S.W, Ph.D.)
Blog: www.psychologytoday.com/blog/the-attraction-doctor

After You Read

3 **Identifying Words from the Same Family** Many words are members of a word family because they have the same root and differ one from the other because of a prefix or suffix. Fill each blank with a word from the reading that is in the same family as the word in italics. The first sentence is done for you as a model.

1. Young people often have an *obsession* with their physical appearance. When they get older, they realize that they _____obsessed_____ about being too heavy or too thin when it wasn't really necessary.

2. It is common to be *dissatisfied* with parts of our body and this _____ can make us feel miserable at times.

3. If we have a *passion* for a certain kind of music or book, we will occasionally become _____ when we speak about it and this *passion* can attract people to us.

4. In general, which physical features *attract* people of the opposite sex and which ones do not? Which combinations are the most _____?

5. Scientific *research* from the field of psychology may be able to give us answers to these questions. Mehrabian and Blum are two _____ who decided to study this topic.

6. Everyone knows that a good personality can spark *attraction*, but are the stable (unchanging) features the most important in determining physical _____ in people?

7. These scientists came to the shocking conclusion that the stable *unchanging* features like body type and height were not as important as the _____ features like grooming and clothing!

8. It was also shown that in general, people who are *pleasant* attract the opposite sex and this quality of _____ can be developed by smiling and acting in a positive way.

4 Recalling Information   Underline the correct word or phrase in parentheses to complete the following sentences about the article.

1. According to the article, in order to be attractive, a perfectly proportionate figure or a classic face is (more / less) important than certain aspects of ourselves that are easy to change.

2. The scientific study by Mehrabian and Blum determined that one of the most attractive features of a person was (high quality clothing / plastic surgery / an advanced level of fitness).

3. In both men and women good posture is recommended, which means essentially (getting a decent wardrobe / working out in the gym / standing up straight).

4. In the feature cluster called "masculinity," the stable features of muscularity, larger chest and bigger jaw were considered to be (somewhat attractive / unattractive) to women.

5. In the feature cluster called "femininity," the changeable features of wearing makeup and wearing longer hair were considered to be (somewhat attractive / unattractive) to men.

6. Overall, the article states that to be more attractive, the most important feature of all is (attitude / Botox / grooming).

5 Guided Academic Conversation: Presenting Your Ideas   Talk about two or three of the following topics with your partner. Then compare your opinions with those of your classmates.

1. **A Shocking Finding** What exactly was the "shocking finding" of the two researchers? Do you find this shocking or even surprising? Why or why not? What features do you find are the most attractive in a person of the opposite sex?

2. **Love at First Sight: True or False?** When a man or a woman meets someone and instantly falls in love, it is called *love at first sight* in English. It is described differently in some other cultures; for example, as a "lightning bolt" *(coup de foudre)* in French or a "blow from an arrow" *(el flechazo)* in Spanish. How is it described in your culture? Do you believe that love at first sight is possible? Or do you think it takes time to fall in love? Explain.

3. **Different Kinds of Love** In many places in the world the law now permits marriage between two people of the same sex (gay men or lesbians). Do you think that the research mentioned in this article would also apply to them? Is it is easier or harder for gay men or lesbians to find a dating or marriage partner than it is for the rest of the population? Or is it basically just the same?

4. **With a Little Help from Your Surgeon** The article states "no implants, Botox, nose jobs, or facelifts required," but does that mean that these are never beneficial? What do you think of plastic surgery or other interventions that many people have? Are they dangerous? Can they be helpful or even necessary for people who need to improve their self-esteem?

6 **What Do You Think?**   Read the paragraph below and in small groups discuss the questions that follow.

Online Dating

Online dating services are popular worldwide and offer people who ordinarily wouldn't meet a chance to get to know each other through the Internet. Sometimes, after exchanging ideas and photos online, people decide to meet in person to see if they wish to carry the relationship further. There are positive and negative aspects to the process. Although online dating can bring love and even marriage, sometimes it can be dangerous.

1. What are positive aspects of dating online?

2. What trouble could a person get into by having an online relationship?

3. What do you think the advantages and disadvantages of dating online are for women? For men?

4. Would you consider online dating? Why or why not? What if the online site was sponsored by your religion? Or by an organization for people of your ethnic background? Or your hobby or profession? Why would that be a better (or worse) way of finding a mate?

Looking for love online ▶

Jane Eyre (Extract from the classic English novel)

Introduction to *Jane Eyre*

Jane Eyre is a famous British novel published in 1847. It has been immensely popular ever since and has served as the basis for ballets, musicals, radio adaptations, TV shows, and more than 15 movies (including one in 2011). The story is told in the first person (using "*I*") as if it were an autobiography, and in fact, some parts really do reflect the true experiences of the author, Charlotte Brontë.

▲ Charlotte Brontë

The main character is an orphan (a person whose parents die when he or she is a child) named Jane Eyre, who suffers great difficulties in her childhood from poverty to physical and emotional abuse by relatives and some teachers. Nevertheless, Jane manages to do well in school and gains employment at a wealthy estate called Thornfield Hall as a governess (private female teacher) for a young girl who is being raised by the eccentric owner, a widower named Edward Rochester. The owner does not abuse or look down upon Jane for being poor; instead, he spends time with her, conversing about interesting subjects and sharing ideas and opinions. Jane enjoys this and becomes strongly attracted to her employer. Then she finds out something that threatens to change everything!

One reason for the continuing appeal of this novel is the remarkable character of Jane. Jane Eyre burst onto the literary world of the 19th century as a new kind of heroine (female protagonist). Up to that point, female characters in novels were usually *damsels in distress*: lovely, weak, and helpless creatures in need of rescue by a hero (a tradition that persists today in many adventure movies). In contrast, Jane is strong and self-reliant and speaks her mind. Some critics suggest that Jane Eyre represents an early version of the feminist woman.

Before You Read

1   **Scanning for Words with a Specific Meaning**   Be a word detective and read the clues below about nine key words in the first section of the reading selection. Review the scanning strategy (Chapter 2, Part 2) if necessary and use it to find those words. Write each word in the blank beside its description. The words are asked for in the order of their appearance in the text.

1. a word that begins with *b* and means "a man who is going to be married soon"

   _____ bridegroom _____

2. a word meaning "employee" that begins with *d* _____

3. a word beginning with *b* that means "an obstacle or difficulty that is in the way"

   _____

4. a word beginning with *s* that means "crying in a loud or noisy way"

   _____

5. a descriptive word that starts with *a* and means "similar in thoughts and feelings" _____

6. a word beginning with *n* that is the name of "a European bird known for its beautiful song" _____

7. a word that begins with *o* and means "a vow or serious promise declared with God as a witness" _____

8. a word beginning with *a* that means "a robot or machine that acts like a person but has no emotions" _____

9. an action word that starts with *s* and means "express disdain or contempt (looking down on someone as worthless and inferior)" _____

Strategy

Making Inferences about a Relationship from Dialogue

By reading the exact words two people speak to each other, it is possible to make inferences (draw conclusions) about their relationship. Do they talk to each other as equals, or is one dominant (superior) and the other subordinate (inferior)? Are they both involved in the conversation, or is one person interested and the other indifferent? As you read, look for words that show what emotions each person feels. For example, do they express fondness, admiration, love, hatred, annoyance, or disdain (looking down on someone)?

2 **Making Inferences about a Relationship from Dialogue** Read the following excerpts (parts) from the conversation between the young governess Jane Eyre and her middle-aged employer Mr. Rochester. Choose the correct options from the words in parentheses, and complete the statements that follow.

1. (Jane speaking) "It is a long way off, sir."
   "No matter—a girl of your sense will not object to the voyage or the distance."
   "Not the voyage, but the distance; and then the sea is a barrier—"
   "From what, Jane?"

   This shows that the two characters are (equal / not equal) socially because

   Jane Eyre calls Mr. Rochester "_____" and he calls her

   "_____." Therefore, in the society of that time Jane is

   (dominant / subordinate) and Mr. Rochester is (dominant / subordinate).

2. (Mr. Rochester speaking) "… especially when you are near me, as now; it is as if I had a string somewhere under my left ribs, tightly and inextricably knotted to a similar string situated in the corresponding quarter of your little frame. And if… two hundred miles or so of land come between us… that cord… will be snapped; and… I should take to bleeding inwardly. As for you, you'd forget me."

"That I *never* should, sir—."

This shows that Mr. Rochester feels there is a (connection / barrier) between Jane and him like a string which goes from one (head / heart) to the other. However, he believes that once they would be apart, he would (be happy / suffer) and Jane would _____ him, but she says that she _____ should (forget him).

Read

Introduction

This reading has been divided into two sections because of its length. Read the first section and check your comprehension afterwards with *Recalling Information 1*. Then read Section 2 and work out *Recalling Information 2* and the rest of the exercises. Section 1 begins with a conversation between Jane and her employer, Mr. Rochester, after Jane has found out that he is planning to get married soon to a rich lady named Miss Ingram and that she, Jane, will have to leave Thornfield Hall forever.

▲ Actress Joan Fontaine in a movie version of *Jane Eyre*

Jane Eyre
(Extract from the classic English novel)*

Section 1

A "In about a month I hope to be a bridegroom," continued Mr. Rochester; "and in the interim, I shall look out for employment for you."

B "Thank, you sir; I am sorry to give—"

C "Oh, no need to apologize! I consider that when a dependent does her duty as well as you have done yours, she has a claim upon her employer for assistance. I have already heard of a place that I think will suit; it is to undertake the education of the five daughters of Mrs. O'Gall of Bitternutt Lodge, Connaught, Ireland.

D "It is a long way off, sir."

E "No matter—a girl of your sense will not object to the voyage or the distance."

F "Not the voyage, but the distance; and then the sea is a barrier—"

G   "From what, Jane?"

H   "From England; and from Thornfield; and—"

I   "Well?"

J   "From *you*, sir."

K   I said this almost involuntarily; and my tears gushed out. I did not cry so as to be heard, however; I avoided sobbing. The thought of Mrs. O'Gall and Bitternutt Lodge struck cold to my heart; and colder the thought of all the brine and foam, destined to rush between me and the master, at whose side I now walked; and coldest at the remembrance of the wider ocean—wealth, caste, custom,—between me and what I loved.

L   "It is a long way," I again said.

M   "It is, to be sure; and when you get to Bitternutt Lodge, I shall never see you again, Jane; that's certain. I never go over to Ireland. We have been good friends, Jane, have we not?"

N   "Yes, sir."

O   "And when friends are on the eve of separation, they like to spend the little time that remains to them close to each other. Come, we'll talk over the voyage and the parting quietly, half an hour or so, while the stars enter into their shining life up in heaven; here is the chestnut tree: here is the bench at its old roots. Come, we will sit there in peace to-night, through we should never more be destined to sit there together." He seated me and himself.

P   "It is a long way to Ireland, Janet, and I am sorry to send my little friend on such weary travels; but if I can't do better, how is it to be helped? Are you anything akin to me, do you think, Jane?"

Q   I could risk no sort of answer by this time; my heart was full.

R   "Because," he said, "I sometimes have a queer feeling with regard to you, especially when you are near me, as now; it is as if I had a string somewhere under my left ribs, tightly and inextricably knotted to a similar string situated in the corresponding quarter of your little frame. And if that channel, and two hundred miles or so of land, come between us, I am afraid that cord of communion will be snapped; and then I've a notion I should take to bleeding inwardly. As for you, you'd forget me."

S   "That I *never* should, sir—".

T   "Jane, do you hear that nightingale singing in the wood? Listen!"

U   In listening, I sobbed convulsively; for I was shaken from head to foot with acute distress. When I did speak, it was only to express an impetuous wish that I had never been born, nor come to Thornfield.

V   "Because you are sorry to leave it?"

W   The vehemence of emotion, stirred by grief and love within me, was asserting a right to predominate—to overcome, to live, rise at last; yes, and to speak.

X   "I grieve to leave Thornfield; I love Thornfield; I love it, because I have lived in it a full and delightful life. I have not been trampled on. I have not

---

* This extract is taken directly from the novel. It has been shortened by omitting a few phrases and sentences, but it has not been adapted or simplified; not one word has been added or changed.

been buried with inferior minds. I have talked, face to face, with what I reverence; with what I delight in, with an original, a vigorous, and expanded mind. I have known you, Mr. Rochester; and it strikes me with terror and anguish to feel I absolutely must be torn from you forever. I see the necessity of departure; and it is like looking on the necessity of death."

Y   "Where do you see the necessity?" he asked, suddenly.

Z   "Where? You, sir have placed it before me."

A*   "In what shape?"

B*   "In the shape of Miss Ingram; a noble and beautiful woman, your bride."

C*   "My bride! What bride? I have no bride!"

D*   "But you will have."

E*   "Yes; I will! I will!" He set his teeth.

F*   "Then I must go; you have said it yourself.

G*   "No; you must stay! I swear it, and the oath shall be kept."

H*   "I tell you I must go!" I retorted, roused to something like passion. "Do you think I can stay to become nothing to you? Do you think I am an automaton?—a machine without feelings? Do you think, because I am poor, obscure, plain, and little, I am soulless and heartless? You think wrong! I have as much soul as you, and full as much heart! And if God had gifted me with some beauty, and much wealth, I should have made it as hard for you to leave me as it is now for me to leave you. I am not talking to you now through the medium of custom, conventionalities, or even of mortal flesh; it is my spirit that addresses your spirit; just as if both had passed through the grave, and we stood at God's feet, equal—as we are!"

I*   "As we are!" repeated Mr. Rochester—"so," he added, enclosing me in his arms, gathering me to his breast, pressing his lips on my lips; "so, Jane!"

J*   "Yes, so, sir," I rejoined; "and yet not so; for you are a married man, or as good as a married man, and wed to one inferior to you—to one with whom you have no sympathy—whom I do not believe you truly love; for I have seen and heard you sneer at her. I would scorn such a union; therefore I am better than you—let me go!"

After You Read

3 **Recalling Information (Section 1)** Underline the correct phrase in parentheses to complete the following sentences about Section 1 of the reading.

1. Mr. Rochester informs Jane that he has found employment for her (with a rich family that lives nearby / with a lady who lives across the sea).

2. Jane begins to cry because (she does not want to be separated from her employer / she loves England and hates the idea of leaving it).

3. Mr. Rochester tells Jane that they (have a good working relationship / have been good friends).

4. He suggests that they can have a talk together (at the dining room table / outside under the stars).

5. Jane expresses the wish that she had never come to Thornfield Hall because (she is now very sad about leaving it / she has always hated being there).

6. She describes the mind of her employer as (inferior and not open to communication / original, strong and expanded).

7. Jane insists that it is necessary for her to leave Thornfield because (she can not be happy if Mr. Rochester's bride lives there / she wants a better job that pays more).

8. She tells Mr. Rochester that she is better than he is because (she would never get married to someone she did not truly love as he plans to do / she has a greater intelligence than he has, even though she did not have his wealth and position).

Before You Read

4 Matching Phrases to their Meanings Before reading Section 2, try to guess the meanings of some key phrases. Match each phrase on the left to the correct definition on the right. If you are unsure, find the phrase in the reading and use its context to guess the meaning. The first one is done for you as a model.

1. __d__ speak your mind   **a.** by taking one long step

2. _____ play a farce (on someone)   **b.** beg (someone) to say yes

3. _____ be still   **c.** absolutely not

4. _____ with a stride   **d̸.** express your real thoughts

5. _____ writhe from (someone's) grasp   **e.** examine the expression on a face

6. _____ not a whit   **f.** trick (someone) just for fun

7. _____ cause a rumor to reach (someone)   **g.** twist and turn to get free (from someone)

8. _____ entreat (someone) to accept   **h.** remain quiet and motionless

9. _____ read a countenance   **i.** tell someone a false story (about someone else)

Read

Section 2 The conversation continues.

A   "Where, Jane? to Ireland?"

B   "Yes—to Ireland. I have spoken my mind, and can go anywhere now."

C   "Jane, be still; don't struggle so, like a wild, frantic bird."

D   "I am no bird; I am a free human being with an independent will, which I now exert to leave you."

5

E Another effort set me at liberty, and I stood erect before him.

F "And your will shall decide your destiny," he said; "I offer you my hand, my heart, and a share of all my possessions."

G "You play a farce, which I merely laugh at."

H "I ask you to pass through life at my side—to be my second self, and best earthly companion"

I "For that fate you have already made your choice, and must abide by it."

J "Jane, be still a few moments; you are over-excited; I will be still too."

K A waft of wind came sweeping down the laurel-walk, and trembled through the boughs of the chestnut. I again wept. Mr. Rochester sat quiet, looking at me gently and seriously. Some time passed before he spoke; he at last said—

L "Come to my side, Jane, and let us explain and understand each other."

M "I will never again come to your side."

N "But, Jane, I summon you as my wife; it is you only I intend to marry."

O I was silent; I thought he mocked me.

P "Come, Jane."

Q "Your bride stands between us."

R He rose, and with a stride reached me.

S "My bride is here," he said, again drawing me to him, "because my equal is here, and my likeness. Jane, will you marry me?"

T Still I did not answer, and still I writhed myself from his grasp; for I was still incredulous.

U "Do you doubt me, Jane?"

V "Entirely."

W "You have no faith in me?"

X "Not a whit."

Y "Am I a liar in your eyes?" he asked, passionately. "Little skeptic, you *shall* be convinced. What love have I for Miss Ingram? None, and that you know. What love has she for me? None, as I have taken pains to prove; I caused a rumor to reach her that my fortune was not a third of what was supposed, and after that I presented myself to see the result; it was coldness. I would not—I could not—marry Miss Ingram. You—you strange—you almost unearthly thing! I love as my own flesh. You—poor and obscure, and small and plain as you are—I entreat to accept me as a husband."

Z "What, me!"

A* "You, Jane. I must have you for my own—entirely my own. Will you be mine? Say yes quickly."

B* "Mr. Rochester, let me look at your face; turn to the moonlight."

▲ Jane and Mr. Rochester in deep discussion

C*   "Why?"

D*   "Because I want to read your countenance; turn!"

E*   "There; you will find it scarcely more legible than a crumpled scratched page. Read on; only make haste, for I suffer."

F*   His face was very much agitated and flushed, and there were strange gleams in the eyes.   55

G*   "Oh, Jane, you torture me!" he exclaimed. "With that searching and yet faithful and generous look you torture me. Jane, accept me quickly. Say, Edward—give me my name—Edward, I will marry you."

H*   "Are you in earnest? Do you truly love me? Do you sincerely wish me to be your wife?"   60

I*   "I do; and if an oath is necessary, I swear it."

J*   "Then, sir, I will marry you."

After You Read

5 Recalling Information (Section 2) Underline the correct word or phrase in parentheses to complete the following sentences about Section 2 of the reading.

1. After Jane speaks her mind, she says that she (will stay at Thornfield / can go anywhere).

2. She explains to Mr. Rochester that she is (a free human being with an independent will / like a wild bird who struggles to fly away).

3. He then asks her to be his wife but Jane doesn't accept him because she (believes that he speaks falsely since he is promised to Miss Ingram / understands now that she is not really in love with him).

4. Mr. Rochester reveals that Miss Ingram no longer wants to marry him because (she has discovered that he is really in love with Jane / she believes the false rumor that he does not have very much money).

5. Then Mr. Rochester asks Jane to marry him, and also he makes another request: that she please call him (sir / Edward).

6. She (accepts / does not accept) his request to marry him, and then she calls him (sir / Edward).

6 Guided Academic Conversations The class divides into small groups. One "volunteer" from each group reads aloud the first of the *Two Points of View Concerning Marriage* in the following Focus box. Then a different volunteer reads aloud the second one. Afterwards, each member of the group in turn gives his or her opinion about the two points of view. Finally, a vote is taken. How many are in favor of #1? How many are in favor of #2? When your instructor says that "time is up (finished)," be prepared to report your group's opinions to the class. Which point of view is more popular? Do all of the groups agree? Why or why not?

Two Points of View Concerning Marriage

1. **Passion is not enough for a happy marriage!** In fact, it is not even necessary. Passion wanes (becomes weaker, diminishes) with time. Jane and Mr. Rochester are physically attracted to each other, but if they get married, they will have conflicts because their backgrounds are very different. For a marriage to be successful, husband and wife should be from the same social class and have a similar level of education. It's better to be practical than passionate.

2. **Passion is the basis for a happy marriage!** Naturally, with time, passion and physical attraction change into a quieter form of love. However, two people who truly have felt passion for each other will always be happy to see that other person at the breakfast table. Mr. Rochester and Jane have different backgrounds and are from different social classes, but they are akin to each other in temperament and feelings and have similar ideas and interests.

7 **Focusing on Words from the Academic Word List** Use the most appropriate word from the box to fill in each of the blanks in the sentences taken from both sections of the reading in Part 2. Do NOT look back at the reading right away; instead first see if you can remember the vocabulary. Then check your answers with the text, if necessary.

convinced	expanded	similar
corresponding	medium	undertake

1. "I have already heard of a place that I think will suit; it is to _____ the education of the five daughters of Mrs. O'Gall of Bitternnutt Lodge, Connaught, Ireland."

2. "Because," he said, "I sometimes have a queer feeling with regard to you, especially when you are near me, as now; it is as if I had a string somewhere under my left ribs, tightly and inextricably knotted to a _____ string situated in the _____ quarter of your little frame."

3. "I have talked, face to face, with what I reverence; with what I delight in, with an original, a vigorous, and _____ mind. I have known you, Mr. Rochester…"

4. "I am not talking to you now through the _____ of custom, conventionalities, or even of mortal flesh; it is my spirit that addresses your spirit…"

5. "Am I a liar in your eyes?" he asked, passionately. "Little skeptic, you *shall* be _____."

Presenting a Formal Reading of a Scene from a Story

In order to do a good formal reading, follow these steps:

1. Prepare in advance by reading through the text that you are going to present. Read it aloud *at least three or four times*. Make sure that you *pronounce all the words correctly*. Ask for advice from your instructor if you have any doubts.

2. As you read aloud, think about the character in the story who is speaking. *What emotions is he or she feeling?* Try to project those emotions into your voice (for example by laughing, sobbing, or shouting).

3. Remember that for a formal reading you need to read *slowly and distinctly*. Do not speak the way you normally do. Do not mumble. Do not speak too softly. *Don't be afraid to exaggerate*. After all, you are playing a role! Be an actor!

8 **Presenting a Formal Reading of a Scene from** *Jane Eyre* Imagine that Radio Station KBZ has organized a program about Charlotte Brontë's classic novel. Work in a group of three to prepare and present a formal reading of one of the scenes from Jane Eyre for the program.

One person plays the role of Jane, another plays the role of Mr. Rochester, and the third acts as the stage manager who introduces the reading by telling briefly what is happening or why it is important. He or she also presents any necessary sound effects (such as the wind blowing or the nightingale singing) and acts as narrator, reading any words that are not part of the conversation (such as Jane's thoughts that the author describes). The actor playing Jane reads the exact words that are in quotation marks and the actor playing Mr. Rochester reads the exact words (also in quotation marks). The stage manager may give advice to the actors if there is a rehearsal (practice) in advance.

First choose a part of the text (approximately 300–500 words long), or ask your teacher to assign a part for you to prepare. Then follow the steps in the strategy box. Good luck!

FOCUS ON TESTING

Answering Vocabulary Questions on Tests

Vocabulary questions in the reading section of the TOEFL® Internet-Based Test (iBT) are multiple-choice. You are presented with a vocabulary word or phrase. Then you are given four possible answers and asked to choose the one closest in meaning to that word or phrase. Often the four possible answers include:

• one item that is completely wrong and may even be the opposite of the target vocabulary word or phrase

- one item that is a "decoy"; it is similar in form to the target item but different in meaning
- one item that is close in meaning to the target word or phrase but not quite right
- one item that is correct

Vocabulary questions on the iBT come in two basic formats:

1. *Which of the following is closest in meaning to* _____ *(the target word or phrase), as it is used in Paragraph A (or B or C, etc.)?*

2. *In Paragraph A (or B, or C, etc.),* _____ *(the target word or phrase) is closest in meaning to...*

(The paragraph letters refer to a prior reading which has its paragraph labeled alphabetically from A to Z, and after that A* to Z*.)

Practice

Practice taking this kind of test by doing the following exercise. Look again at Selection 1, the reading from *Jane Eyre*, Section 2, on page 69. Then mark your answers to the following questions. After you finish, compare and discuss the answers with your classmates.

1. Which of the following is closest in meaning to *frantic* as it is used in Paragraph C, line 3?
   - (A) calm and peaceful
   - (B) extremely fragile
   - (C) loud and angry
   - (D) overly excited

2. In Paragraph F, line 8, *possessions* is closest in meaning to _____.
   - (A) ambitions
   - (B) belongings
   - (C) collections
   - (D) confessions

3. Which of the following is closest in meaning to *play a farce*, as it is used in Paragraph G, line 9?
   - (A) forget to tell the truth
   - (B) have fun with a strange game
   - (C) tell a joke to entertain me
   - (D) try to fool me with a silly lie

4. In Paragraph I, line 12, *abide by* is closest in meaning to _____.
   - (A) abandon
   - (B) accept
   - (C) object to
   - (D) turn away from

5. Which of the following is closest in meaning to *summon* as it is used in Paragraph N, line 20?
   - (A) call
   - (B) free
   - (C) insult
   - (D) reject

6. Which of the following is closest in meaning to *drawing* as it is used in Paragraph S, line 25?
   - (A) dropping
   - (B) pulling
   - (C) pushing
   - (D) representing

7. In Paragraph T, line 27, *writhed* is closest to _____.
   - (A) offered
   - (B) twisted
   - (C) wished
   - (D) wrinkled

8. Which of the following is closest in meaning to *skeptic* as it is used in Paragraph Y, line 33?

    (A) believer   (C) sketcher

    (B) doubter   (D) story-teller

9. In Paragraph Y, line 43, *entreat* is closest to _____.

    (A) beg   (C) endear

    (B) demand   (D) instruct

10. Which of the following is closest in meaning to *legible* as it is used in Paragraph E*, line 53?

    (A) believable   (C) mysterious

    (B) legal   (D) readable

PART 3   Tying It All Together

1 Vocabulary Review Using Pantomime It is said that "actions speak louder than words." Actions can also help us to remember words.

Work with a partner to make a list of ten key words and phrases from this chapter that you think are especially useful or important. Then practice ways to "pantomime" them (show them through actions). After you finish, hide your list and the two of you go to work with another pair. Take turns with them, pantomiming a word or phrase that the other two must guess. Each time someone guesses correctly, they get a point. Who is the best actor? Who is best at guessing words and phrases?

2 Making Connections Choose one of the following topics to research on the Internet. Find relevant and interesting facts, photos, videos, images, or other data and share them with the class. You do not have to answer the questions completely. Just choose some parts of them that interest you and share your findings with the class.

1. How Beauty Varies with Culture and Other Factors What characteristics make a beautiful woman or a handsome man? People from some cultures prefer thin lips and those from other cultures, full lips. Some believe that a man's hairy chest is unattractive and others that it is appealing because it shows masculinity. Was the ideal woman or ideal man different in 1920 from the ideal of today? Does the perfect face or figure change when the economy goes up or down? Find examples of the factors that determine our preferences related to attractiveness.

▼ "Beauty is in the eye of the beholder"

2. **Why Jane Eyre Is Alive and Well and Living on the Internet** How does the character of Jane Eyre, invented by Charlotte Brontë in the 1800s, influence people today? Look up Jane Eyre clubs, discussion groups, movies, ballets, radio and TV shows, videos, plays, or comics. What are Gothic novels and what influence does Brontë's heroine have on them? How does she affect other writers of today? How does she influence clothing and cosmetics? Why do you think her character remains so powerful more than 150 years after her creation? What can Jane Eyre teach us today?

3. **What is the hidden secret in the scene presented in the reading?** Did you get the feeling that one of the two characters was hiding something? If so, you are right! One of the two characters has a secret that will have great importance for the plot (action) of the novel. Who is hiding something and what is the truth? Read Jane Eyre and find out. In what ways will this secret influence what happens in the novel and how the story ends?

Responding in Writing

FOCUS

Writing Tip: Writing Down the Key Points in a Summary

To do a *summary* of a reading, write down its *key* (most important) ideas. No opinion of your own is expressed in a summary.

3 Writing a Summary Write a summary of the reading selection from Part 1 of this chapter or of an article that your teacher assigns to you, following these steps:

Step 1: Write down as your title:

My Summary of _____

(Fill in the title of the article in this space. Be sure to put it in quotation marks to show it is the title of something that has been published.)

Step 2: Skim the article and make a list of the important ideas.

Step 3: Think about what the author is trying to say. Decide what his or her main idea is and write it down *in your own words*. This is your first sentence.

Step 4: Then write a sentence for each of the other key ideas and put them in the order in which they appear.

Step 5: Read what you have written. Ask yourself: Is this in my own words or have I simply copied the sentences of the article? Of course, you can include words taken from the article, but not complete sentences. (If you find that you have copied long phrases and whole sentences from the article, immediately change what you have written. Say the same thing in different words.)

Step 6: Is your summary clear? Is it short enough? A summary should be no longer than 20–30% of the original article. If your summary is too long, cut words that are not necessary and the parts that are not so important.

Step 7: Write a final sentence to conclude your summary. This should not be your opinion, but the author's. Think again about what the author wants to say, and express that in a different way from the first sentence with the main idea.

Step 8: It is not easy to write a good summary, but it is a useful skill for university studies or business, and for almost any career. If you have time available in class, work in a group with two or three other students. Read all the summaries and talk about which one is the best (short, clear, complete, and interesting) and why. Then revise and improve your summary.

Self-Assessment Log

Writing down the key points in a summary. Read the lists below. Check (✓) the strategies and vocabulary that you learned in this chapter. Look through the chapter or ask your instructor about the strategies and words that you do not understand.

Reading and Vocabulary-Building Strategies

☐ Skimming for the general idea
☐ Identifying words from the same family
☐ Scanning for words with a specific meaning
☐ Making inferences about a relationship from dialogue
☐ Presenting a formal reading of a scene from a story

Target Vocabulary

Nouns		Adjectives	Idioms and Expressions
▪ appearance	▪ posture	▪ attractive	▪ be shooting for
▪ attraction	▪ researchers*	▪ convinced*	▪ go overboard
▪ automaton*	▪ skeptic	▪ corresponding*	▪ the opposite sex
▪ conventionalities		▪ frantic	▪ play a farce
▪ dependent	**Verbs**	▪ legible	▪ speak your mind
▪ dissatisfaction	▪ abide	▪ obscure	▪ statistical analysis*
▪ gender*	▪ drawing	▪ passionate	
▪ grooming	▪ entreat	▪ proportionate*	
▪ medium*	▪ sobbing	▪ similar*	
▪ obsession	▪ summon	▪ unchanging	
▪ pleasantness	▪ undertake*		
▪ possessions	▪ writhed		

* These words are from the Academic Word List. For more information on this list, see www.victoria.ac.nz/lals/resources/academicwordlist/

4 Health and Leisure

> " A good laugh and
> a long sleep are the
> best cures in the
> doctor's book. "
>
> Irish proverb

In this CHAPTER

People the world over are becoming increasingly interested in health and travel. Many spend their free time in gyms, on the tennis courts, in martial arts classes, and in health food stores in an effort to build up their bodies. Both young and old are journeying more and farther than ever before. The first reading selection in this chapter discusses the foods we eat and what effects they have on us. The second takes a look at some of the surprising effects that tourists have on the places they visit.

Connecting to the Topic

1. Look at the photo. What are the man and the boy doing? What do you think their relationship is to each other?

2. People all over the world are becoming increasingly interested in health. What have you noticed people doing in order to improve their health?

3. This chapter also discusses travel and tourism. How do you think tourists can be helpful to the places they visit? How can they be harmful?

Eat Like a Peasant, *Feel* Like a King

Strategy

Using Headings to Preview

Picking out the headings in an article is one form of previewing. It improves comprehension by helping you see the organization and major ideas. Headings are usually of two kinds: they present or illustrate the main idea of a section, or they give a small detail to catch the reader's interest. The ones that tell the main idea are the most helpful.

1 Using Headings to Preview The article on pages 81–84 begins by introducing its subject. Answer the questions about headings.

1. After the introduction, there are two headings. List them below.

   Introduction

   _____

   _____

2. In this story, which heading tells the main idea of the section?

3. Judging from the headings, what do you think you will read about in Sections 2 and 3?

2 Getting Meaning from Context Guess the meaning of words from their context by following these instructions.

1. The only uncommon word in the title is *peasant*. To infer its meaning, notice how it is in a parallel construction with the word *king*: "Eat Like a

   _____, Feel like a _____." A parallel construction is used either for comparison or for contrast. So *peasant* means either something very similar to *king* or something very different. With this clue in mind, read the sentence on lines 44 to 48, and tell what you think is meant by a *peasant diet*. How does this relate to the title?

   _____

2. Notice the context: "Eat simple foods, not elite treats." The word *not* tells you that *elite treats* are the opposite of *simple foods*. *Elite* is also used in line 2 to describe a group of people. Look at this context too; then in your own words, explain the meaning of *elite*.

_____

3. Look at the second word of the second paragraph: *eclectic*. It describes the menu that makes up the entire first paragraph. Read that paragraph and think about what is special and unusual about the grouping of foods described here. Then explain the meaning of the word *eclectic*.

_____

4. Scan the first two sections of the essay for the noun *affluence* and its related adjective *affluent*, which are used four times. From the contexts, guess its meaning and write it here. Can you also find a synonym for *affluence* in the fifth paragraph, beginning with the letter *p*?

_____

5. The word *cuisine* is used three times in the essay. Scan for it and, using the contexts, explain what you think it means.

_____

Introduction

"You are what you eat" is a popular American saying, and what you eat can contribute to improving or destroying your health. According to modern research, certain cultures have healthier diets than others. The following article from *American Health* magazine talks about the foods that can help to keep us healthy. Try to guess the answers to these questions which are discussed in the article:

- Which cultures have traditional diets that are good for our health?
- What foods should you choose to avoid cancer, hypertension, and heart disease?

Eat Like a Peasant, *Feel* Like a King

Research around the globe points to a recipe for well-being: Eat simple foods, not elite treats.

A   Start with miso soup, a classically simple Japanese recipe. For an appetizer, try a small plate of pasta al pesto. On to the main course: grilled chinook salmon, with steamed Chinese cabbage on the side. End with a Greek salad, sprinkled with olive oil, and a New Zealand kiwi fruit for dessert.   5

B   An eclectic menu, to be sure. But it could contain some of the world's healthiest dishes. Miso soup, according to recent Japanese research, may help prevent cancer, as may cabbage. Salmon, olive oil, and the garlic in pesto can all help fight heart disease. Even kiwi is rich in fiber, potassium, and vitamin C. In the last few years, nutritionists have been studying such international superfoods—dishes from around the globe that may hold the key to healthy eating. They're building on research that began in the '40s and '50s, when researchers first realized that a country's diet is intimately connected to the health of its people.

▲ A healthy meal has lots of vegetables

C   Since then, an explosion of medical studies has produced a flood of information on diverse human diets—from the Inuit of the Arctic to the Bushmen of Africa's Kalahari Desert. But the globe-trotting researchers have done more than discover the best features of each country's cuisine. They've also demonstrated broad nutritional principles that apply to people all over the world. And their clearest finding is a sobering one.

D   In many countries, they've found, the healthiest diet is simple, inexpensive, traditional fare—precisely the diet that people abandon as they move into affluence. Japanese immigrating from the high carbohydrate Pacific to high-fat America have a greater risk of heart disease the more Westernized their diet becomes. The same pattern holds for developing nations that emerge from poverty into prosperity. Poor people who can't get enough to eat are at risk, of course, whatever their diet. But as a country's food becomes richer, the scourges of poverty (infectious disease and malnutrition) are replaced by the "diseases of civilization" (arteriosclerosis, certain cancers, obesity).

▲ A "fast food" meal is often unhealthy.

E   The simple, ideal diet—often called the "peasant diet"—is the traditional cuisine of the relatively poor, agrarian countries. It's usually based on a grain (rice, wheat, corn), fruits and vegetables, small amounts of meat, fish, eggs or dairy products, and a legume.

F The advantages are obvious: low fat and high fiber, with most calories coming in the grains and legumes. "A low-fat, high-fiber diet is a preventive diet for heart disease, certain cancers, hypertension, adult-onset diabetes, obesity," says Dr. Wayne Peters, director of the Lipid Consultation Service of Massachusetts General Hospital.

Early Diets: Nuts and Plants

G According to Peters, "We evolved eating a low-fat diet, and that's what our genetic composition is really designed to handle." Studies of one of the world's most primitive diets—and one of the healthiest ones—back him up. In southern Africa's Kalahari Desert, some tribes still eat as early humans did, hunting and gathering.

▲ The !Kung people eat mongongo, an abundant nut.

H "Hunting and gathering may not have been such a bad way of life," says Richard Lee, an anthropologist at the University of Toronto who has studied the !Kung tribe since the 1960s. "The main element of the !Kung diet is the mongongo, an abundant nut eaten in large quantities. They routinely collect and eat more than 105 edible plant species. Meat is secondary."

I Another student of the !Kung, Stewart Truswell, a professor of human nutrition at Australia's University of Sydney, says their eating schedule is really continual "snacking" (the gathering) punctuated by occasional feasts after a successful hunt. They are nutritionally healthy, the only shortfall being fairly low caloric intake.

J Few people, though, would choose a !Kung diet—or even a simple peasant diet from western Europe (which is now much less common there). In an affluent society, it takes willpower to keep fat intake down to the recommended maximum: 30% of total calories. (The average American gets more than 40% of his or her calories from fat.) When a country reaches a certain level of affluence, as the U.S. and Japan, grain and beans give way to beef and butter.

K In India, for example, many middle-income people are now gaining weight on a rich diet—even though the poor half of the population still can't afford enough to eat. As the middle class has become more affluent, they've been able to indulge, and Indian doctors are reportedly seeing more obesity, hypertension, and heart disease. Very recently, though, Indians have gone for the diets and aerobics classes that are popular among the rest of the world's elite.

L   If it's just too difficult to stay with a really low-fat "peasant" diet, the alternative is to rehabilitate high-calorie dishes. Cut down on overall fat intake and substitute, in the words of one researcher, "nice fats for nasty fats." Americans have already been following this advice. In the past 20 years, the consumption of "nasty" saturated fats has declined, while we've taken in more of the polyunsaturated fats, such as corn and safflower oils, that can help lower blood cholesterol. This change may help explain the simultaneous 20% to 30% drop in heart disease in the U.S.

Why Socrates* Loved Olive Oil

M   An even better strategy for changing our fat intake may come from studying diets in the Mediterranean—Spain, Greece, and southern Italy. With some regional variation, people in these cultures eat small amounts of meat and dairy products and get almost all of their fat in the form of olive oil, says physiologist Ancel Keys, professor emeritus at the University of Minnesota School of Public Health and leader in international dietary studies.

N   Keys has noted that farmers sometimes quaff a wineglass of oil before leaving for the fields in the morning. Elsewhere in the Mediterranean, bread is dipped in olive oil. Salads are tossed with it. Everything's cooked in it.

O   Though people in some of these countries eat nearly as much total fat as Americans, they are singularly healthy, with very little heart disease. Now laboratory studies of olive oil help explain why. Unlike most other vegetable oils common in the West, olive oil consists mainly of "monounsaturated" fats. Recent research indicates that monounsaturates do a better job of preventing heart disease than the more widely touted polyunsaturates.

P   As Americans become ever more concerned with healthy eating, we're likely to pay more and more attention to world cuisines. The polyglot among nations, we've started to seek out ethnic flavors from everywhere. "Foreign" ingredients, from seaweed and bean curd to tortillas and salsa, are now readily available in large supermarkets. And Mexican and Asian restaurants have become more widespread than any other eateries except ice cream parlors, hamburger stands, and pizzerias, according to the National Restaurant Association.

▲ Olive oil is healthy for you.

Q   But the trick to finding healthy food, wherever it comes from, is to look carefully at each dish. No single cuisine is all good or all bad. Each has something to teach us.

Source: "Eat Like a Peasant, *Feel* Like a King" *American Health Magazine* (Andrew Revkin)

*Socrates was an ancient Greek philosopher. He is often used to represent a wise man.

3 Recalling Information Based on what you have read, match the food on the left to its description on the right.

Food

1. _____ a grain, a legume, fruits, vegetables and a bit of meat, eggs or fish

2. _____ garlic and salmon

3. _____ olive oil

4. _____ miso soup and cabbage

5. _____ kiwi fruit

Description

a. monounsaturate that seems to prevent heart disease

b. rich in fiber, potassium, and vitamin C

c. may help prevent cancer

d. the simple "peasant diet" that is good for you

e. can help fight heart disease

Strategy

Paraphrasing Main Ideas

Learn to express the main ideas from readings in your own words, simply and clearly. This is sometimes called *paraphrasing*. You can use words or short phrases taken directly from the author but not long phrases or sentences.

4 Paraphrasing Main Ideas Read and respond to the items below. Use your own words.

1. The main idea of the article is given in simple terms in the title and the italicized sentence that follows it. In your own words, what is the main idea?

_____

_____

2. Another key idea is the relationship between affluence, diet, and health. The article illustrates this by referring to several different societies. Explain how affluence changes diet and health, and refer to at least two cultures that illustrate it.

_____

_____

_____

_____

_____

_____

5 **Recognizing Synonyms** Match each vocabulary word from the reading to its *synonym* or definition in the right column. Can you use these words in a good English sentence?

Vocabulary Word	**Synonym**
1. _____ affluent	**a.** combining different influences
2. _____ cuisine	**b.** simple, from a farm
3 _____ eclectic	**c.** rich
4 _____ elite	**d.** wealth
5. _____ peasant (adjective)	**e.** upper class
6. _____ prosperity	**f.** style of cooking

6 **Ranking Foods on a Continuum** Work with a partner to rank the food items below from most healthy to least healthy. Write them on the continuum. Then compare your work with that of the rest of the class.

beans (legumes)	crackers	kim chee
beef	eggs	noodles
butter	fish	olive oil
cheese	fruit	pizza
chicken	guacamole	rice

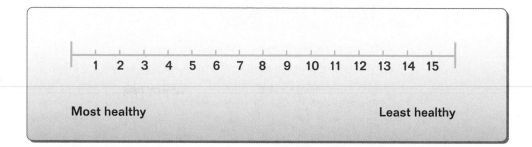

| | 1 | 2 | 3 | 4 | 5 | 6 | 7 | 8 | 9 | 10 | 11 | 12 | 13 | 14 | 15 | |

Most healthy   **Least healthy**

7 **Taking a Stand: Agree or Disagree?** Work in a small group. Read the following statements and choose two that you all agree upon (either *for* or *against*). With your group, write a list of reasons that support your stand on each of the two questions. Be prepared to defend your position to the class.

1. Tea is better for you than coffee.

2. Exercise is essential for mind and body, and the best exercise is running.

3. Fast food is junk food: no exceptions.

4. You can never be too thin.

5. It is more important to sleep well than to exercise.

6. Smoking four or five cigarettes a day does not harm your health.

7. It is always better to eat at home than at a restaurant.

8 **Guided Academic Conversation** Gain confidence and improve your speaking ability by doing one of the following tasks with one or more of your classmates.

1. **Become a Salesperson!** Choose a food mentioned in the article and make up a TV ad for it. First think of a *catchy phrase*—one that catches people's attention. For example, "Olive oil will make you live longer!" Then present it in a surprising or humorous way. For example, a group of people singing while they make a salad with olive oil. Finally, talk about the good qualities of your product. For example, "It's healthy, tasty, easy to use." Write out a script and perform your ad for the class or a small group.

2. **Create a Menu for a Healthy Restaurant.** Pretend that you have just opened a restaurant and want to attract health-conscious customers. Invent a catchy name for your restaurant and make up a menu of three courses (appetizers, main dishes, and desserts) and a list of beverages. Then show the menu to the class, tell them about each course, and explain why it is good for their health.

Analyzing Compound Words

As we saw in Chapter 1 (page 10), many English words are made up of two shorter words. These are called compound words, and they are usually adjectives or nouns. Some compound words are written with a hyphen between them, such as *low-fat*; others such as *wineglass*, are written as one word. Breaking apart compound words can help you understand their meaning. For example, look at the word *well-being* in the introductory quote in the reading selection "Eat Like a Peasant, *Feel* Like a King." What do you think it means?

When taking vocabulary tests, try breaking apart the compound words to help understand their meaning.

Practice

Choose the word or phrase that best explains the meaning of the underlined word or phrase. Refer back to the selection "Eat Like a Peasant, *Feel* Like a King" if necessary.

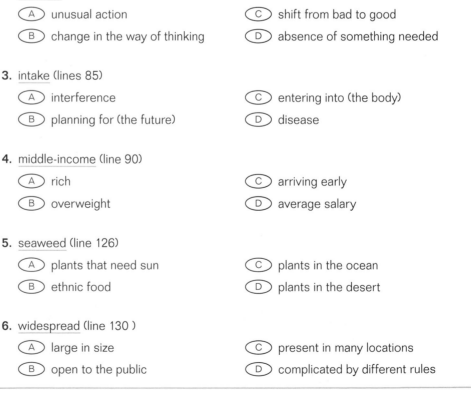

1. <u>globe-trotting researchers</u> (line 26).
   - (A) professors and students of geography
   - (B) investigators who travel around the world
   - (C) people who study the movement of the Earth
   - (D) experts in the benefits of exercise

2. <u>shortfall</u> (line 82)
   - (A) unusual action
   - (B) change in the way of thinking
   - (C) shift from bad to good
   - (D) absence of something needed

3. <u>intake</u> (lines 85)
   - (A) interference
   - (B) planning for (the future)
   - (C) entering into (the body)
   - (D) disease

4. <u>middle-income</u> (line 90)
   - (A) rich
   - (B) overweight
   - (C) arriving early
   - (D) average salary

5. <u>seaweed</u> (line 126)
   - (A) plants that need sun
   - (B) ethnic food
   - (C) plants in the ocean
   - (D) plants in the desert

6. <u>widespread</u> (line 130)
   - (A) large in size
   - (B) open to the public
   - (C) present in many locations
   - (D) complicated by different rules

What Do You Think? Read the paragraph below and then discuss the questions that follow.

Smoking

Medical evidence proves that smoking is a health risk. Smokers have a greater chance of developing cancer, emphysema, and heart problems. Second-hand smoke, which exposes nonsmokers to smokers' fumes, also increases the chances for nonsmokers of developing serious diseases. Yet, many smokers feel they have a right to smoke and that it is no worse than certain other practices, such as overeating or drinking too much alcohol.

1. Are the people you know who smoke smoking more or less nowadays?

2. What do you think about restrictions against smoking inside public buildings? Should it also be restricted outside? Explain.

3. Do you smoke? Why or why not?

10 **Discussing Information from a Chart** Look at the chart and the list of benefits below. Then answer the questions.

Some Benefits of Quitting Smoking	
Source: The U.S. Surgeon General's Report and the American Cancer Society	
20 minutes after quitting • Heart rate and blood pressure drop	**1 year after quitting** • Excess risk of coronary heart disease is half that of a continuing smoker's
12 hours after quitting • Carbon monoxide level in the blood drops to normal	**5 years after quitting** • Risk of cancer of the mouth, throat, esophagus, bladder, kidney, and pancreas decreases
2 weeks to 3 months after quitting • Circulation improves • Lung function increases	
1 to 9 months after quitting • Coughing and shortness of breath decrease • Cilia start to regain normal function in the lungs, increasing the ability to handle mucus, clean the lungs, reduce infection	**10 years after quitting** • Lung cancer death rate about half that of a continuing smoker's
	15 years after quitting • Risk of coronary heart disease is that of a nonsmoker's

1. What, according to this chart, are the benefits of quitting smoking? Can you think of other benefits that are not in the chart?

2. In your opinion, which three of the benefits from quitting smoking are the most important? Why?

3. Which benefits might be most likely to motivate people to stop smoking?

Here Come the Tourists!

Before You Read

Strategy

Understanding Point of View

A piece of writing presents ideas about a certain subject. It may also present a certain attitude or point of view about the subject. The point of view may be positive, in favor of the person, place, or thing being talked about. On the other hand, it may be negative, against it. The third possibility is a point of view that is somewhere in between and shows both positive and negative aspects of the subject.

1 Skimming for the Point of View It is obvious from the title that the following reading deals with tourism. But what point of view does it express about it? Skim the reading to identify its point of view. Then put a check in front of the statement below that best expresses the point of view of the article.

1. _____ Tourism has a good effect on the places visited.

2. _____ Tourism has a bad effect on the places visited.

3. _____ Tourism has both good and bad effects on the places visited.

2 Analyzing the Point of View Answer the questions about the point of view in the reading with a partner.

1. What do you think of this point of view?

2. Is it similar to your own attitude toward tourism?

3. Does the photo on page 93 illustrate the point of view of the selection? Explain.

3 Getting the Meaning of Words from Context Read the analysis below each of the following sentences from the reading to learn some new words and methods of figuring out meanings. Then fill in the best response.

1. It was hard to believe that the community began its ecotourism project in 1992 in order to protect natural resources. (lines 2–4)

The word *ecotourism* has only been in use for about the last 30 years. The first part, *eco-*, is taken from the word *ecology*, which means "the relationship between people and their natural surroundings or environment." In recent years, concern for a healthy ecology has become an important theme.

Judging from this, what kind of tourism do you think *ecotourism* is?

(A) tourism that does not cost much

(B) tourism for the very rich

(C) tourism that does not harm the environment

(D) tourism that uses the environment for adventure

2. Their repeated "requests" annoyed tourists. (line 5)

Quotation marks are sometimes used to show that a word does not have its usual meaning. Usually, a *request* is the action of asking for something politely. Here, an example of a typical "request" made to tourists is given in the first sentence. This gives you a clue about the meaning of *annoyed*.

What does it mean to *annoy* someone?

(A) to make someone happy   (C) to make someone confused

(B) to make someone sad   (D) to make someone angry

3. Some locals were more skilled and playful in their requests, others up-front and demanding. (lines 6–9)

Adjectives in English can often be used as nouns if a word like *the* or *some* is put in front of them. The word *local* is used that way here, and then made plural with an *s*. Scan the second paragraph and you will see it used in three other sentences.

What does the word *locals* mean?

(A) people from nearby   (C) beggars

(B) people from far away   (D) workers

The adjective *up-front* is a compound word, so the two short words that make it upcan give you some clue to its meaning. Also, it is paired with *demanding* and both words are put in contrast with *skilled* and *playful*. That means they mean something very different from *skilled* and *playful*.

What does *up-front* mean?

(A) tall   (C) smart

(B) direct   (D) funny

4. Indigenous people in the Andes demand compensation for having their photographs taken... (lines 31–32)

The word *indigenous* is followed by the word *peoples*. This gives you a clue about its meaning. These people live in the Andes mountains, and that gives you another clue.

What does *indigenous* mean?

(A) rude   (C) foreign

(B) courteous   (D) native

5. These young vacationers like to distinguish themselves as "travelers" not "tourists." (lines 50–51)

In this sentence, two words are put in quotation marks because they are direct quotes of what people say and also because they are used in a special way. The first is said to distinguish people from the second.

What does *distinguish* mean?

- (A) make similar
- (B) make different
- (C) go far away
- (D) come closer

6. But in "frontiers" like Kathmandu, Goa, and Bangkok, where a backpacking subculture has existed since it became part of the "hippie" routes in the 1960s… (lines 52–54)

Once again, we have a word in quotation marks because it is used with a special meaning that is not the usual one. The word *frontier* has two usual meanings: a place near the border of another country, or a new, unexplored area of the world or of knowledge.

What do you think the word *frontiers* means here?

- (A) very popular places for tourists
- (B) places where no tourists ever go
- (C) places where only adventurous tourists go
- (D) places where tourists may go in the future

The prefix *sub-* means "under" as in the word *submarine* (a vehicle that goes under the water) or "lesser in importance."

What does *subculture* mean in the phrase "a backpacking subculture"?

- (A) a group of people who are all very different
- (B) a group of people with similar customs
- (C) a group of people who are very wealthy
- (D) a small group of people with an excellent education

7. … such travelers have a reputation for *stinginess* and rude, hard *bargaining*. (lines 54–55)

The suffix *-ness* tells us this is a noun, the quality of being stingy. For clues to the meaning of *stingy* and *stinginess*, look at the examples of how the young vacationers and backpackers act in the sentences before and after this one.

What does *stinginess* mean?

- (A) practice of insulting people for no reason
- (B) attitude of kindness and humility
- (C) custom of not spending or giving money
- (D) habit of spending and giving money freely

Related to the word *stinginess* is the word *bargaining*. This is the gerund (*-ing* form) of the verb *to bargain*, which is used in line 55.

What do you think the verb *to bargain* means?

- (A) to look at something carefully before buying it
- (B) to try to make the price of something lower
- (C) to give away one thing in exchange for another
- (D) to sell something for very little money

Introduction

This selection is an excerpt taken from a book by Deborah McLaren called *Rethinking Tourism* and *Ecotravel*. The author is a journalist and director of the Rethinking Tourism Project, a nonprofit group that supports networking and indigenous self-development. She has lived and worked in various parts of Asia and the Americas and has her residence in St. Paul, Minnesota.

- What do you think tourists bring to the places they visit?
- What do they take away?
- Do you expect to learn something new about travel in this article? Why or why not?

Here Come the Tourists!

A   "Give me the t-shirt," the woman said to the tourist. The small village in the Amazon was almost filled with beggars. It was hard to believe that the community began its ecotourism project in 1992 in order to protect natural resources. The villagers had lost interest in the land and became enchanted by the things the tourists had. Their repeated "requests" annoyed tourists.   5 Some locals were more skilled and playful in their requests, others up-front and demanding. "They have money and many things," 10 said the woman asking for the t-shirt. "It's no problem for tourists."

▲ Tourists visiting the Amazon

B   It is easy for the locals to perceive tourists as 15 incredibly wealthy. The entire tourist experience revolves around money and purchases. The community itself is being purchased. Tourists are superconsumers who bring their 20 foreign languages and communications, strange and inappropriate clothing, and cameras into the community. In the context of a brief visit, sometimes an overnight, few real friendships are formed between tourists and locals. Tourists are eager for adventure, or at least the perfect photo opportunity. If the tourist becomes upset in the midst of the excitement, the local usually 25 pays the price. But these strange people sometimes give away token gifts to locals, even money. This results in begging, which becomes increasingly widespread as locals begin to see themselves as "poor" and tourists as "rich." The psychological pressure of viewing oneself as poor or backward can manifest itself in crimes not previously common in a community.

C   Indigenous people in the Andes demand compensation for having their photographs taken, saying it's intrusive. A woman in Otavalo, Ecuador, explained to me, "We see ourselves and our children on postcards and in books. We do not benefit from having our photos taken. A foreigner does. We demand part of the profits." In some indigenous communities, photography is taboo because it is believed to cause physical and spiritual harm to the person who is photographed. In India, young children have had limbs torn from their bodies to make them more pathetic and hence "better" beggars. Adults who commit this violence often have several children who work for them. Other forms of begging, sometimes found amusing by tourists, offend many locals. An indigenous leader from Panama told me, "It breaks my heart to see the young boys swimming after the coins the tourists throw in the water. We spent years acquiring our rights to these lands. Now with tourism, the people here do not care about the land anymore. They just want tourist dollars."

D   While tourists believe they can contribute to destination communities, locals don't always agree. Money spent by budget travelers—especially backpackers—may go into the local economy. They tend to stay in cheaper hotels and eat in cheaper restaurants owned by locals and so get closer to the local culture. These young vacationers like to distinguish themselves as "travelers" not "tourists." They live by budget travel guides and often flock to the same inexpensive areas of villages and cities. But in "frontiers" like Kathmandu, Goa, and Bangkok, where a backpacking subculture has existed since it became part of the "hippie" routes in the 1960s, such travelers have a reputation for stinginess and rude, hard bargaining. In Indonesia, I met a British bicyclist who was cycling around the world. He was proud that he had spent virtually no money on his trip. He lived with families that took him in every night from the road and ate what was offered to him by people he met along his way. He had not worked in any of the places he had visited. He was extremely happy that he had just bargained a local merchant down from the equivalent of ten cents to a penny for four pieces of bread. I thought it was rather odd that he was taking advantage of everyone he met and wouldn't even pay a fair price to a poor baker.

Source: "Here Come the Tourists!"
Excerpt from *Rethinking Tourism and Ecotravel* (Deborah McLaren)

▲ Children in the Amazon endanger wild animals by capturing them to show to tourists.

Strategy

Distinguishing Between Fact and Opinion

The distinction between fact and opinion often is not clear. Events taken to be common knowledge (Earth revolves around the sun), statements supported by scientific evidence (some studies show that vitamin C may be good for our health), or statements about something that can be confirmed (Bangkok is the capital of Thailand) are generally taken to be facts. Beliefs expressed by only one person are usually considered opinions, unless the person is judged to be an expert or authority on the matter. (Hamburgers are delicious.)

4 Distinguishing Between Fact and Opinion Which of the following statements from the reading do you think are facts and which ones are opinions? Why? Write *F* in front of the facts and *O* in front of the opinions. Compare your answers with those of your classmates. Line numbers are given so you can examine the contexts.

1. _____ The community began its ecotourism project in 1992. (lines 2–3)

2. _____ The villagers lost interest in the land. (line 4)

3. _____ The entire tourist experience revolves around money and purchases. (lines 16–19)

4. _____ Few real friendships are formed between tourists and locals. (line 23)

5. _____ If the tourist becomes upset, the local usually pays the price. (lines 25-26)

6. _____ Indigenous people in the Andes demand compensation for having their photographs taken. (lines 31–32)

7. _____ In some indigenous communities, photography is taboo because it is believed to cause physical and spiritual harm. (lines 35–37)

8. _____ Tourists believe they can contribute to destination communities. (line 46)

9. _____ Budget travelers… tend to stay in cheaper hotels and eat in cheaper restaurants. (lines 47–49)

10. _____ In Kathmandu, Goa, and Bangkok, a backpacking subculture has existed since the 1960s. (lines 52–54)

5 Scanning for Vocabulary Find the following words in the article, using your scanning skills and the clues given here. Words are asked for in order of their appearance in the selection. (If necessary, review instructions for scanning, page 42).

1. A two-word phrase meaning *things that a country has and can use to its benefit, such as coal and petroleum:* n_____ r_____

2. An adjective that starts with *e* and means *delighted, pleased as if by magic*:

   e_____

3. An adjective starting with the prefix *in-* and meaning *not correct for the occasion*: in_____

4. An adjective that came into English from the islands of Tonga and means *considered not acceptable and so forbidden*: t_____

5. A synonym for *getting* or *obtaining*: a_____

6. A verb that means *to move together in a group* (like birds): f_____

7. An adjective starting with the prefix *in-* and meaning *not costing very much*:

   in_____

8. A word in quotation marks that refers to the group of young people in the late 1960s who wore flowers and strange clothes, reacted against traditional values, and took mind-altering drugs: h_____

9. An adverb that means *almost completely, for the most part*: v_____

10. A verb starting with b that means to *negotiate and come to an agreement about something, particularly the price of something*: b_____

6 **Focusing on Words from the Academic Word List** Use the most appropriate word from the box to fill in each of the blanks below in the paragraph taken from Part 2. Do NOT look back at the reading right away; instead, first see if you can now remember the vocabulary. Check your answers on page 94.

acquiring	communities	found	physical
benefit	compensation	hence	

C   Indigenous peoples in the Andes demand _____ for having their photographs taken, saying it's intrusive. A woman in Otavalo, Ecuador, explained to me, "We see ourselves and our children on postcards and in books. "We do not _____ from having our photos taken. A foreigner does. We demand part of the profits." In some indigenous _____, photography is taboo because it is believed to cause _____ and spiritual harm to the person who is photographed. In India, young children have had limbs torn from their bodies to make them more pathetic and _____ "better" beggars. Adults who

commit this violence often have several children who work for them. Other ₁₀
forms of begging, sometimes _____ amusing by tourists,
                                        6
offend many locals. An indigenous leader from Panama told me, "It breaks
my heart to see the young boys swimming after the coins the tourists throw
in the water. We spent years _____ our rights to these lands.
                                          7
Now with tourism, the people here do not care about the land anymore. ₁₅
They just want tourist dollars."

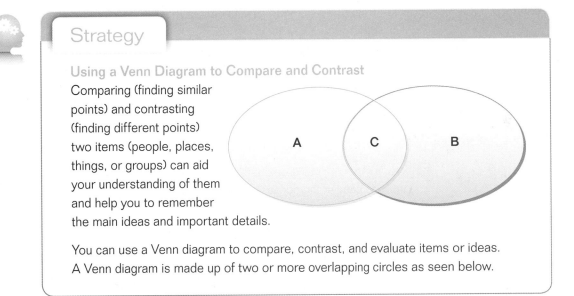

Strategy

Using a Venn Diagram to Compare and Contrast

Comparing (finding similar points) and contrasting (finding different points) two items (people, places, things, or groups) can aid your understanding of them and help you to remember the main ideas and important details.

You can use a Venn diagram to compare, contrast, and evaluate items or ideas. A Venn diagram is made up of two or more overlapping circles as seen below.

7 **Comparing and Contrasting with a Venn Diagram** Scan the article to find examples of the actions and attitudes of tourists. Write them in circle A. Then do the same for the actions and attitudes of the locals and write them in circle B. If there are actions and attitudes that you think both groups share, put those in the middle, part C, where the two circles intersect. Compare your diagram with the diagrams of others in the class and be prepared to explain your choices.

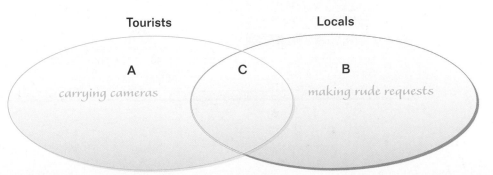

Guided Academic Conversations In small groups, discuss the first topic below. Then choose two others to discuss. Reach a group consensus (agreement by everyone) and write up a group opinion statement for each topic you discuss.

1. **Jobs and Tourism** Is tourism good or bad for the economy of a region? What kinds of jobs does tourism bring? Are these good or bad jobs? Who benefits from them? What places have you visited as a tourist and what did you observe about the people who lived and worked there?

2. **Begging** Does giving to beggars help or hurt the local people? Where is begging a problem? Is it wrong to pass by a beggar and not give anything, or is that the correct thing to do? Should you sometimes give to women and children who beg in the street, but not to men? Is there anything that you can give to beggars besides money?

3. **Taboos** Are taboos important cultural norms or just silly superstitions? Why is photography taboo in some communities? Do you ask permission before taking photos of strangers? Why or why not? Are there any actions that are taboo in your culture but are done by tourists?

4. **Different Kinds of Travelers** Which ones are good and which ones are bad? What is a "budget traveler" and why do such travelers sometimes bring money into the local economy? What do you think of the attitude of the British tourist who was cycling around the world? What actions and attitudes do you dislike in certain travelers?

9 **Reading Charts** Look at the three charts that follow and work together with a group to answer the questions about them.

1.

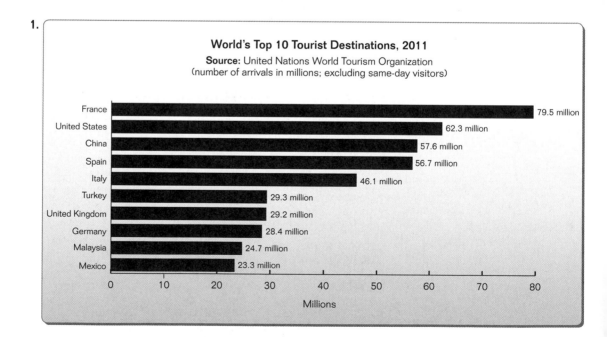

World's Top 10 Tourist Destinations, 2011

Source: United Nations World Tourism Organization
(number of arrivals in millions; excluding same-day visitors)

Country	Millions
France	79.5 million
United States	62.3 million
China	57.6 million
Spain	56.7 million
Italy	46.1 million
Turkey	29.3 million
United Kingdom	29.2 million
Germany	28.4 million
Malaysia	24.7 million
Mexico	23.3 million

2.

Top Countries in Tourism Earnings, 2011
Source: United Nations World Tourism Organization
International tourism receipts (excluding transportation)

Rank	Country	Receipts	Rank	Country	Receipts
1.	United States	$116.3 billion	6.	Germany	$38.8 billion
2.	Spain	59.9 billion	7.	United Kingdom	35.9 billion
3.	France	53.8 billion	8.	Australia	31.4 billion
4.	China	48.5 billion	9.	Macao (China)	27.8 billion
5.	Italy	43.0 billion	10.	Hong Kong (China)	27.2 billion

3.

Average Number of Vacation Days per Year, Selected Countries
Source: World Tourism Organization

Country	Days	Country	Days	Country	Days
1. Italy	42	4. Brazil	34	7. Korea	25
2. France	37	5. United Kingdom	28	8. Japan	25
3. Germany	35	6. Canada	26	9. United States	13

1. In Chart 1, what is meant by the "World's Top 10 Tourist Destinations"? On what basis are these countries *ranked* (put in order)? Which continent has the largest number of top countries? Do you think that this is due to its location or to other factors? Explain.

2. How is Chart 2 different from Chart 1? Which countries are in this chart that were not in the top ten in the first one? In your opinion, what qualities do these ten countries have in common that make them attractive to tourists?

3. What information do we learn from Chart 3? How much difference is there between the country ranked as number 1 and the country ranked as number 9? What effects do you think this has on production, on the health of workers, and on the general happiness of the populations? What do you consider the ideal number of vacation days per year? Why?

PART 3 Tying It All Together

1 End-of-Chapter Game Show Supplies: small pieces of paper on which to write questions, two bags, small prizes (candies or fancy pencils, etc.)

The class should divide into two equal-sized groups. Each group chooses a team name, and then works together to write ten questions on ten pieces of paper, covering material from Chapter 4. (These questions can cover vocabulary or content, such as, "What does the word *indigenous* mean?" or "Which foods may prevent heart disease?") Each team puts their pieces of paper into a bag.

Teams line up on different sides of the classroom in pairs. The instructor takes a question from team 2 and asks it to the first pair from team 1. If they answer the question correctly, team 1 gets a point. Then the instructor asks a question from team 1 to the first pair from team 2, and so on until all the questions have been asked. If a team's question doesn't ask about information from Chapter 4, the other team gets a point. When the game ends, the team with the higher number of points wins the prizes.

2 **Making Connections** Choose one of the topics about health below. Answer the questions about that topic by finding facts and opinions on the Internet. Report your findings to the class.

1. **Diets to lose weight** Which diet is more popular for losing weight: the low fat or the low carb? Which is more effective?

2. **Herbal teas** Are they really good for your health? Can they be dangerous?

3. **Exercise classes** What kinds are in fashion now? What types of people take them? Why?

4. **Vitamins** Why do many people take them every day? Can they help you to feel good or to live longer?

5. **Meditation** What is it? Can it really improve your health? Why or why not?

6. **Reiki** What is it? Does it help you or is it a fraud?

7. **Bathing at a spa** A spa is a place that usually has a hot tub, sauna, or steam room. Why do so many people do it? What are the different styles of enjoying water as a method of cleaning and relaxation? Which do you prefer?

8. **Acupuncture or Chiropractic** What is it? Can it cure illness? Explain.

9. **Junk food** Is it a big business? How is it affecting people's health around the world?

Responding in Writing

FOCUS

Writing Tip: Structuring An Argument To Support Your Opinion

First, think about a topic and form your opinion. Then structure an argument in favor of it by presenting your main point, listing details that support it, and finishing with a concluding statement.

3 **Writing a Paragraph that Expresses Your Opinion** Write a paragraph expressing your opinion on one of the following topics: 1) The Best Way to Improve Your Health; or 2) The Best Way to Travel. Follow these steps:

Step 1: Work with a partner and brainstorm to find all the ideas you can on the topic you have chosen and make a list of them, in any order.

Step 2: Choose the idea you like best, the main idea that expresses your opinion on the topic.

Step 3: Write one sentence that states this idea clearly.

Step 4: Look through your list and back through the chapter. Think of at least three examples that support or illustrate your main idea. Make up sentences about these in your own words.

Step 5: Write a final sentence that either repeats your idea in different words or makes a new personal comment about it.

Step 6: Invent a good title for your paragraph. Try to think of something that will catch people's interest and make them want to read it.

Self-Assessment Log

Read the lists below. Check (✓) the strategies and vocabulary that you learned in this chapter. Look through the chapter or ask your instructor about the strategies and words that you do not understand.

Reading and Vocabulary-Building Strategies

☐ Using headings to preview
☐ Getting meaning from context
☐ Paraphrasing main ideas
☐ Recognizing synonyms
☐ Organizing information using a continuum
☐ Understanding point of view
☐ Skimming for the point of view
☐ Distinguishing between fact and opinion
☐ Scanning for vocabulary
☐ Using a Venn diagram to compare and contrast
☐ Reading charts

Target Vocabulary

Nouns
- affluence
- bargaining
- begging
- benefit*
- cancer
- communities*
- compensation*
- cuisine
- diet
- ecotourism
- fiber
- frontiers
- grain
- heart disease
- hippies
- legumes
- locals
- monounsaturates
- natural resources
- peasant
- prosperity
- requests
- stinginess
- subculture
- tourists
- treats

Verbs
- acquiring*
- bargained
- distinguish
- flock
- found* (find)
- prevent

Adjectives
- affluent
- annoyed
- demanding
- eclectic
- elite
- enchanted
- inappropriate*
- indigenous
- inexpensive
- peasant
- physical*
- taboo
- up-front

Adverbs
- hence*
- virtually*

*These words are from the Academic Word List. For more information on this list, see www.victoria.ac.nz/lals/resources/academicwordlist/

5 High Tech, Low Tech

In this
CHAPTER

Technology keeps transforming our world, providing important solutions to global problems. The first article presents the benefits of the hybrid car as a compromise in a world with pollution problems that needs to slowly move away from dependence on gasoline. The second describes recent advancements in information and communication technology in developing countries and the great changes that technology can bring.

Connecting to the Topic

1. Look at the photo. Where is this man? What is he doing?

2. Today's technology allows people to be in contact from almost anywhere all of the time. What are the advantages and disadvantages of this?

3. In your opinion, what are our biggest global problems? How do you think technology is solving, or could help solve, these problems?

How Hybrid Cars Work

Before You Read

Reading Tip

Use what you already know about skimming to find the general idea of the reading. This will give you a context to help you understand the new vocabulary.

1 Skimming for the General Idea The word *hybrid* refers to something that has been produced by combining elements or characteristics from two very different sources. Skim the article.

This article focuses on _____.

a. the new types of cars on the market, including gasoline-powered, electric, and hybrid cars by different car companies

b. the hybrid car itself, how it combines features of gasoline-powered and electric cars, and the reasons for it being produced

c. the various ways to get better mileage from your car and how fuel tanks and batteries can be used to store energy

Strategy

Scanning for an Important Word in Context to Increase Your Understanding
When you see a word that seems important at the beginning of an article or in the title and you are not completely sure of its meaning, scan the article for the word in its different contexts to increase your understanding of it.

2 Scanning for an Important Word in Context Scan the beginning of the article (lines 1–20) for the word *hybrid* and answer the following questions.

1. Why are hybrid cars now considered important? _____

_____

2. What two different elements are combined in the hybrid car? _____

_____

Inferring Meaning

In Chapters 1 and 2, you practiced the skill of inferring the meaning of words from their context. Now, extend that skill by inferring the meaning of expressions, groups of words that have a special meaning when used together. Remember that an inference can also be called an "educated guess." You guess what something means based on what you know about the general idea or context behind it.

3 **Inferring the Meaning of Expressions from Context and Vocabulary** Now that you know the general idea of the article, read the statements below and try to infer (make an inference about) the meaning of the phrases or expressions in these questions. Use the hints to help you.

1. With so much emphasis being placed on the environment, hybrid cars have emerged as one of the leading ways that we as individuals can *do our bit*.
   Hint: Here the "environment" refers to the natural world that surrounds us and it's stated that the environment is somehow related to hybrid cars. In this sentence, *do our bit* means _____.

   Ⓐ find more options for transportation

   Ⓑ contribute positively to our surroundings

   Ⓒ understand the leading problems of urban life

2. In fact, hybrid cars have a lot more to offer than being more environmentally friendly and *reducing our carbon footprint*.
   Hint: The two qualities listed for hybrid cars are connected by *and*, which suggests that they are close in meaning. *Reducing our carbon footprint* here means _____.

   Ⓐ causing less damage to the environment

   Ⓑ causing more damage to the environment

   Ⓒ causing no damage to the environment

3. In a gasoline-powered car, gasoline is supplied to the engine by the fuel tank. This is then *ignited* and used to power the transmission…
   Hint: Think about what must happen to gasoline in order to convert it into movement. In this sentence, *ignited* means _____.

   Ⓐ added to water

   Ⓑ broken down

   Ⓒ lit on fire

4. An electric car *produces no emissions* because there is no combustion involved in the driving of the vehicle.
   Hint: Notice the reason given here is that there is no combustion (burning) in an electric car. So *produces no emissions* means _____.

   (A) sends out no smoke or gas

   (B) creates no light or sounds

   (C) causes no accidents or injuries

5. However, electrical batteries have a comparatively low capacity and *need regular recharging.*
   Hint: The prefix *re-* means *again.* The word *charge* can have many meanings, such as: *to accuse someone with a crime; to pay with credit;* or *to supply, fill, or load something.* In this sentence, *need regular recharging* means _____.

   (A) must be paid for again with credit

   (B) must be accused again

   (C) must be refilled often with energy

6. The standard car battery, though, is only required to recharge a *small portion of the components* in a gasoline car...
   Hint: When you have a *portion* of something, you have a part of it. *Components* are parts of a system or machine. Here, *a small portion of the components* means

   _____.

   (A) all of the parts

   (B) a few of the parts

   (C) small parts of a machine

7. A hybrid car combines electric motors and a gasoline engine *to give greater performance...* than an electric car.
   Hint: The word *performance* can refer to different situations. It can refer to a presentation (such as a concert), to how something functions or operates, or to an act or occurrence. In this sentence, which is related to a car, *to give greater performance* means _____.

   (A) to improve the function

   (B) to act in a great manner

   (C) to give a better concert

8. At the same time, it utilizes the electric batteries to greatly reduce emissions and *improve fuel consumption.*
   Hint: The word *consumption* is related to the word *consume,* which means *to use.* So *improve fuel consumption* means _____.

   (A) increase the amount of fuel used

   (B) use fuel to make better emissions

   (C) reduce the amount of fuel used

9. Combining an electric motor and a gasoline engine is not as easy as putting them both under the hood and *letting them do their own thing…*
Hint: *To do one's own thing* is an informal expression that means *to do what you want* or *to be independent*. Here, *letting them do their own thing* means _____.

    Ⓐ letting the motor and the engine work together

    Ⓑ letting the motor and the engine work individually

    Ⓒ letting the motor and the engine work very hard

Read

Introduction

Air pollution (air contaminated by smoke, waste, or chemicals) has become a growing concern in the global community, with agreements such as the Kyoto Protocol* aimed at reducing its devastating effect on the world. With more and more people driving all the time, the automotive industry has become one of the big targets of measures to reduce pollution. The following selection presents one result of this effort to revolutionize the automotive industry: the hybrid car. In this selection, you will learn terminology in English relating to the technology of automobiles, and you will also get to practice discussing the important issue of climate control.

- What do you think about air pollution? Is it a problem in the place where you live?
- In your opinion, what would the perfect car be like?

▲ A hybrid car is more fuel efficient. Although most hybrid cars use diesel or gas, alternative fuels such as ethanol are also used sometimes. In the U.S., corn is the primary stock used for making ethanol.
Source: wikipedia.org

* The Kyoto Protocol is an agreement of over 150 countries to reduce emissions of greenhouse gases between the years 2008 and 2012 by at least 5% from 1990 levels. It was adopted by the United Nations Framework Convention on Climate Change in 1997.

How Hybrid Cars Work

A   With so much emphasis being placed on the environment, hybrid cars have emerged as one of the leading ways that we as individuals can do our bit. In fact, hybrid cars have a lot more to offer than being more environmentally friendly and reducing our carbon footprint. The technology is now well-developed and is recognized as being a serious advancement.

How Gasoline and Electric Cars Work

B   To look at how hybrid cars work, we need to take a basic look at how gasoline and electric cars respectively are used to drive a car.

- In a gasoline-powered car, gasoline is supplied to the engine by the fuel tank. This is then ignited and used to power the transmission which then turns the wheels, giving the car motion. This is a very basic and simplistic explanation, but it covers the essential steps in a car's drive train method (how the transmission connects to the car's driving wheels) when using a gasoline engine.

- An electric engine uses batteries to provide power to the engine. The power is again sent to the transmission which drives the vehicle. An electric car produces no emissions because there is no combustion involved in the driving of the vehicle. However, electrical batteries have a comparatively low capacity and need regular recharging. They also produce less power than a combustion engine and provide a vehicle with less performance than a strictly gasoline-powered engine.

Electric Batteries and Car Engines

C   Electric engines tend to use the motion of the car to help recharge their batteries, in the same way that a gasoline car battery is recharged. The standard car battery, though, is only required to recharge a small portion

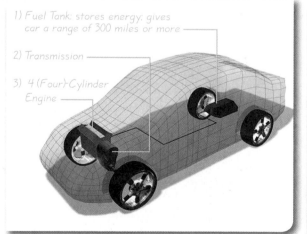

▲ **Figure 1** shows a gas-powered car. It has a fuel tank, which supplies gasoline to its four-cylinder engine. Gas car engines can operate at speeds of up to 8,000 rpm.

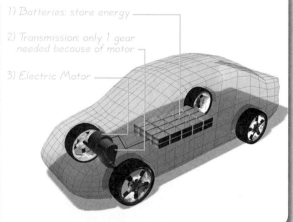

▲ **Figure 2** shows an electric car, which has a set of batteries that provides electricity to an electric motor. Batteries give the car a range of about 50–100 miles.

of the components in a gasoline car and is not required to drive the vehicle. This means a smaller battery can be used and the regular driving of the vehicle ensures that the battery remains charged and serviceable.

How Hybrid Cars Work to Combine Power Sources

D   A hybrid car combines electric motors and a gasoline engine to give greater performance and longer traveling distances than an electric car. At the same time, it utilizes the electric batteries to greatly reduce emissions and improve fuel consumption. The end result is a vehicle that is better for the environment but still offers a viable means of transport for the owner.

Methods of Combining Gas and Electric

E   Combining an electric motor and a gasoline engine is not as easy as putting them both under the hood and letting them do their own thing because they each require very different components to drive the transmission. Engineers and hybrid car manufacturers have developed a number of methods to get around this problem.

- The parallel hybrid offers the transmission power from both sources simultaneously. The transmission is connected directly to the gasoline engine and also to the electric motor so that when the car is driven it draws propulsion power from both these sources of energy.
- The series hybrid works very differently. The fuel tank is connected directly to a combustion engine where the gasoline is used to create combustion power. This power is not fed directly to the transmission as in a standard gasoline car. Instead, the engine is used to power a dual-purpose generator. The electrical power created by this generator can then be used to either recharge the batteries or to drive the transmission and provide the car with the propulsion power it needs.

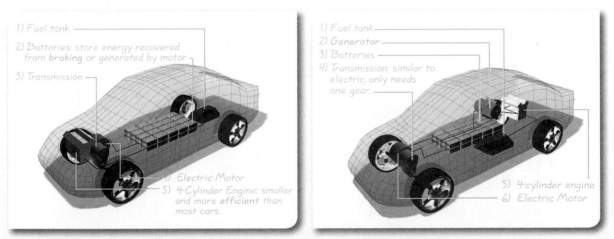

1) Fuel tank
2) Batteries: store energy recovered from braking or generated by motor
3) Transmission
4) Electric Motor
5) 4-Cylinder Engine: smaller and more efficient than most cars.

1) Fuel tank
2) Generator
3) Batteries
4) Transmission: similar to electric, only needs one gear.
5) 4-cylinder engine
6) Electric Motor

▲ **Figure 3** shows a typical parallel hybrid. You'll notice that the fuel tank and gas engine connect to the transmission. Its engine is smaller than that of most cars, but it is efficient. The batteries and electric motor also connect to the transmission independently. As a result, in a parallel hybrid, both the electric motor and the gas engine can provide propulsion power.

▲ **Figure 4** shows a series hybrid car that works with a generator. The generator can either charge the batteries or power the electric motor that drives the transmission. The batteries store the energy recovered from braking.

The Advantages of a Hybrid Engine

F   One of the biggest advantages in creating a hybrid car is that the gasoline combustion engine can be considerably smaller than the one in a standard gasoline car. This can mean fewer cylinders, lighter parts, and a more efficient engine load. This means that the car will use substantially less gasoline while being driven under normal circumstances, offering better fuel consumption and less-damaging emissions pumped into the atmosphere.

How Hybrid Cars Work to Use Different Energy Sources

G   • Generally, a hybrid car uses the gasoline engine for constant and ideal driving conditions such as steady and constant speeds. Because it is much smaller, this already means a reduction in emissions while providing a more than adequate amount of power necessary to drive the car under these conditions.

   • The electric motor will usually come into play when the car is put under extra pressure and requires a little extra assistance. Driving up hill, accelerating, and driving in difficult conditions will normally mean that the electric motor will give an additional push and ensure that the hybrid car has ample power to perform any task.

Hybrid Car Technology

H   Hybrid cars have advanced considerably in a relatively short space of time, and new techniques and processes are being evolved to further reduce both gas consumption and harmful emissions. Modern hybrid cars work in such a way that it is possible to greatly reduce your fuel consumption without having a detrimental effect on the performance or range of the car.

Source: "How Hybrid Cars Work" as appeared on www.howhybridcarswork.com. Courtesy of HybridKingdom.com

After You Read

Strategy

Learning Specialized Terms
Learning specialized terms about a topic can help you understand the reading. Specialized terms in the article "How Hybrids Cars Work" are words that you might use when talking about automobiles.

4 Inferring the Meaning of Specialized Terms Match each term on the left to the correct definition on the right. For a term you are not sure about, scan the article or diagrams for it, and use the context to infer its meaning.

Terms

1. _____ fuel tank [line 8]
2. _____ transmission [line 9]
3. _____ four-cylinder engine [Figure 1]
4. _____ parallel hybrid [line 37]
5. _____ components [line 24]
6. _____ electric motors [line 27]
7. _____ propulsion power [line 40]
8. _____ braking [Figure 4]
9. _____ efficient [Figure 3]
10. _____ series hybrid [line 41]
11. _____ combustion engine [line 19]
12. _____ generator [line 45]
13. _____ rpm [Figure 1]
14. _____ speeds [Figure 1]

Definitions

a. revolutions per minute (how fast something turns)

b. the slowing down of the car

c. a car where the gasoline engine's purpose is to recharge the batteries or drive the transmission

d. an engine driven by energy produced by burning of fuel

e. a machine that converts mechanical into electrical energy

f. how fast something moves

g. the storage place in a car for gasoline

h. a car with transmission power from an electric motor and a gasoline engine

i. a motor with four chambers in which pistons move

j. producing results with minimal effort

k. machines that convert electricity into mechanical energy or motion

l. parts that make up a whole

m. the force to move something

n. the vehicle part that transmits power from the engine to the wheels

Strategy

Using a Graphic Organizer Chart for Comparison

Creating a chart can often help you clearly see the similarities and differences between different objects or concepts. First, make a list of important factors or qualities on the left. Then put columns across the top with the name of the different objects or concepts, and fill in the specific numbers or descriptions for each. See the chart in Activity 5 for an example.

5 Filling Out a Chart for Comparison Look at the diagrams for the gas-powered car, the electric car, the parallel hybrid, and the series hybrid to try to understand the similarities and differences between these types of cars. Work together to fill in the chart on page 112, putting a check mark (✓) to indicate the cars that have the qualities described in the column on the left.

Quality	Gasoline Car	Electric Car	Parallel Hybrid	Series Hybrid
1. Has a fuel tank				
2. Has batteries to store energy				
3. Can operate at speeds of up to 8,000 rpm				
4. Has a range of 50–100 miles				
5. Runs only on electricity				
6. Has a generator				
7. Has a four-cylinder engine				
8. Has both a four-cylinder engine and an electric motor				
9. Has a four-cylinder engine in the trunk (back) area				

6 **Talking It Over** Discuss the following questions with a partner. Afterwards, compare your opinions with those of two other classmates.

1. Do you know anyone who owns a hybrid car? What is your opinion of hybrid cars?

2. Would it be better for society if more people owned one? Or should we all be encouraged to move to purely electric cars? Why or why not?

3. Should there be laws and regulations that push forward the manufacturing of hybrids? Why or why not?

4. How are the series and parallel types of hybrid cars different? Which is better, in your opinion, and why?

5. Can you think of possible ways to get consumers to buy hybrid or electric cars? Write down three persuasive things you could tell consumers that would get them to buy hybrid cars.

7 **Researching a Gadget** New technology is coming out all the time to provide us with new products that propose to make our lives easier or more enjoyable. Some of these products are large, like cars, but others are gadgets, small mechanical devices that we can carry around and use in our homes and at work. Look at the list below, and choose a gadget you'd like to research.

1. an e-Reader (Kindle [Touch, Fire], Nook, Kobo)

2. an iPhone® or other smartphone with wireless Internet access

3. an iPad® or other tablet

4. other: _____.

Find out everything you can about this gadget. What can it do? Why is it fun (or not fun) to have? How much does it cost? Where can you get it? You can talk about your own experience with the gadget, look it up on the Internet, or go to a store where the gadget is sold.

Take notes on your findings and come to class prepared to talk about it either to the whole class or in a small group. You may even want to bring your gadget if you already own one!

PART **2** Main Ideas and Details

Leapfrogging the Technology Gap

Before You Read

Strategy

Identifying the Pattern of Organization in a Reading
All professional writing has some set structure. Professional writers are careful in where they put their main points and how they organize their specific details. Understanding the logic behind this structure helps you understand better what is being communicated and also helps you improve your own ability to write well.

1 **Identifying the Pattern of Organization** Look at the title, illustrations, and instructions of the article on pages 117–118. What problem is being discussed? What solution is being offered?

Now that you know the topic, try to identify the way the article is organized. This can help you to read it more easily. First, look quickly at the following three common patterns. Then take a couple of minutes to skim the article. After you finish, read the three patterns with more care and tell which pattern best describes the article's organization.

Pattern 1: From General to Specific

- Description of a problem
- Description of the solution(s)
- History of why the problem exists
- Examples to illustrate the problem and solution

Pattern 2: From Specific to General

- Description of a number of specific examples of a larger problem
- Explanation of the problem and its history
- Solution(s)

Pattern 3: From Specific to General to Specific

- One specific example to attract readers' interest and introduce the topic
- Description of the problem
- Description of the solution(s)
- Further examples to develop and illustrate the problem and solution

2 **Outlining the Specific Details** The article uses detailed examples of the types of technology that can play an important role in underdeveloped countries, but these details come out most clearly in the specific locations used to illustrate them. Scan the article to identify which areas (cities and/or countries) the author uses to present examples and write the areas below:

I. _____

II. _____

III. _____

IV. _____

V. _____

3 **Analyzing the Main Point (Thesis) of an Article** Before reading the article, answer the questions below.

1. The following quotation presents the main point of the article: "Villages like Robib have been described as leapfroggers: communities or even whole countries in the developing world that are using information and communication technologies to leapfrog directly from being an agricultural to an information economy."

▲ Leapfrogging is not only for frogs.

From the quotation above, what does the term *leapfrog* mean? What two words make up this compound word? What metaphor (image of one thing representing another) do you get from this term? The image of a

_____ represents _____.

Explain how one thing could represent the other.

2. What do you think an *agricultural economy* is? What is an *information economy?*

3. Even before you read the article, do you know (or can you guess) what type of economy usually comes between an agricultural and an information economy that is being skipped over in these "leapfrogging" countries?

FOCUS

Understanding Compound Words

A number of words in this article, like the words *leapfrog* or *schoolchildren* in the second sentence are actually compound words. (See Chapter 1, page 10, to review what compound words are and how to guess their meaning.)

4 **Understanding Compound Words** Figure out the meaning of the compound words in the following sentences by breaking them up into parts or by looking at the context. Mark the letter of the phrase that best expresses the meaning of each underlined compound word.

1. Schoolchildren are seeing their country's most famous landmarks for the first time.

    A a monument, building, or other object that serves as a typical marker on the land

    B a plot of land marked out for a house to be put up

    C an important person, like a politician or police officer

2. And the village economy is taking off, fueled by the sale of its handmade silk scarves on the global market.

    A kept close at hand

    B made with a pattern of handprints

    C made by hand, not by a machine

3. Each vehicle [motorcycle] has a transmitter that allows it to upload and download email and data…

    A to move the computer mouse up and down while riding in a vehicle

    B to move information up [from vehicle to computer or server] and to move information back down [from server to vehicle]

    C to package and unpackage the computer before and after loading it in a vehicle that carries information to places that need it

4. … farm economies made room for craftsmen and artisans, who gave way to industrial production…

    A people who are sneaky and crafty

    B people who make crafts with their hands

    C workers in large industrialized factories

5. <u>Widespread</u> industrial development would still leave much of Africa, Asia, or Latin America a generation behind Europe and North America.

    (A) extending all over the globe

    (B) circulation in limited areas

    (C) widely recognized by many people

6. The Internet kiosks [booths or stands] that access a global <u>marketplace</u> can also be used to access political information or organize grassroots campaigns in emerging democracies.

    (A) a covered building used for trading food and clothing

    (B) meeting of representatives from different countries for the purpose of providing aid

    (C) place where ideas, as well as goods, are bought and sold

7. The Internet kiosks [booths or stands]… can also be used to access political information or organize <u>grassroots</u> campaigns in emerging democracies.

    (A) based on (rooted in) the needs of ordinary people

    (B) natural and friendly to the environment

    (C) occurring in areas that are full of grass, like fields

8. Pondicherry, India's information and communications technology development strategy traces back to a 1998 project that brought Internet-linked <u>telecentres</u> to the region's villages. (Note: Also spelled *telecenters*)

    (A) televisions for viewing programs and movies

    (B) meeting places for community activities, like team sports, shows, or political rallies

    (C) locations for long-distance communication by computer, telephone, telegraph, television, etc.

Read

Introduction

In the world today, there are many countries whose development and quality of life still lag behind that of the countries traditionally known as "first world." Moving from an agrarian economy to an industrialized economy and then to an information economy took many decades in Europe, Japan, the United States, and Canada. However, at the present time, some developing countries are bypassing the long route to development. They are "leapfrogging" into the information age by using combinations of high-tech and low-tech technology in creative ways. Read the following article to find out more about this new path to development.

- Have you ever seen a frog leap? What does it look like?
- Why are some developing countries now called "leapfroggers"?
- What technologies do you think you will read about in this article?

Leapfrogging the Technology Gap

A   In Robib, Cambodia, villagers are getting medical advice from the world's best doctors. Schoolchildren are seeing their country's most famous landmarks for the first time. And the village economy is taking off, fueled by the sale of its handmade silk scarves on the global market.

B   All these benefits are coming via motorcycle—Internet-enabled motorcycles. A wireless network links computers in the village to computer chips on each of the five motorcycles. Each vehicle has a transmitter that allows it to upload and download email and data as it passes by village computers. At the end of the day, the bikes return to a hub where they upload the information received. The next morning, they download email and data from the hub and take it out to the villages for transmission.

C   Villages like Robib have been described as "leapfroggers": communities or even whole countries in the developing world that are using information and communication technologies to leapfrog directly from being an agricultural to an information economy. It's a phenomenon that combines technology high and low in innovative ways, and is generating not only economic benefits but a new world of education, social, and political opportunities.

D   In highly developed countries, the information economy has emerged from a long evolution—farm economies made room for craftsmen and artisans, who gave way to industrial production, and manufacturing has yielded to the rise of an information and service-based economy.

E   Economists and development experts wonder whether the developing world can—or should—follow the same path. Widespread industrial development would still leave much of Africa, Asia, or Latin America a generation behind Europe and North America.

F   Of greater concern is the potential environmental impact of widespread industrialization: large-scale factory production in the developing world could greatly increase global energy consumption and pollution levels, particularly if factories use cheaper and dirtier production methods.

G   Information and communication technologies provide an alternative to this environmental and economic nightmare. The hardware, software, and networks that have propelled developed economies out of the industrial era and into the information age are now promising to take the developing world directly from agrarian to post-industrial development.

H   The same satellite networks that link remote villages to urban markets can bring classroom education to communities too small or poor to support secondary schools. The cell phone systems that power community businesses can connect patients or doctors, or disparate family members. The Internet kiosks that access a global marketplace can also be used to access political information or organize grassroots campaigns in emerging democracies.

I   Societies that place a high value on education, like Vietnam, are at an advantage, because a highly educated population is ready for work in a knowledge-based economy. Bangalore, India, is the best-case scenario.

Recognized as the Silicon Valley of the developing world, Bangalore has parlayed India's wealth of well-educated, tech-savvy, English-speaking programmers into a massive hive of interlocking programming shops, call centres, and tech companies.

J While Bangalore's technological, education, and linguistic advantages have given it a head start on leapfrogging, regions that lack those advantages stand to gain even more from the creative use of technology. Indeed, the countries that stand to benefit most from a leapfrogging strategy are those with limited infrastructure, limited education access, and limited literacy rates.

▲ Students using technology in the classroom.

K In Bolivia, a rural radio station uses the Internet to answer questions from listeners—like the farmer who wanted help dealing with a worm that was devouring his crops. Working online, the station found a Swedish expert who identified the worm and broadcast the information on pest control to the entire community.

L "The development community has placed a great emphasis on being able to meet basic development objectives," says Richard Simpson, the Director of E-Commerce for Industry Canada. "It is not about rich countries getting richer. It's not even about emerging economies. It's about countries at every stage of development using technology in a way that is appropriate to their needs." Needs like those of Nallavadu, a village in Pondicherry, India. A region in which many people live on incomes of less than one dollar a day, Pondicherry's information and communications technology development strategy traces back to a 1998 project that brought Internet-linked telecentres to the region's villages. Today, villagers routinely use the Internet to access information that helps them sell their crops at the latest commodity prices, obtain medical advice, and track regional weather and transport.

M How does that kind of technology affect daily life? Just look at what happened in the village of Nallavadu. Vijayakumar Gunasekaran, the son of a Nallavadu fisherman, learned of December's earthquake and tsunami [2004] from his current home in Singapore. When Gunasekaran called home to warn his family, they passed along the warning to fellow villagers—who used the village's telecentre to broadcast a community alarm. Thanks to that alarm, the village was evacuated, ensuring that all 3,600 villagers survived.

Source: "Leapfrogging the Technology Gap" from pipermail.org (Alexandra Samuel)

Strategy

Creating a Study Outline

To help you review an article or prepare for a test on it, you can create an informal outline. Write out a list of main points you want to remember, using roman numerals (I, II, III, IV, V, VI, VII, etc.); then put examples under each, using regular numbers (1, 2, 3, etc.). Use your outline when filling in exercises, preparing for class discussion, or reviewing for an exam.

5 Creating a Study Outline Complete the study outline below for the article "Leapfrogging the Technology Gap." In this case, it will be an outline of places that can be called "leapfroggers" with examples of the development in those places. First, fill in the locations, I–V, that you outlined in Activity 2 on page 114. Then write the main example (or examples) of the types of development occurring there. You can look back through the article to complete the outline.

I. Location: _Robib, Cambodia_

   1. _Motorcycles are Internet-enabled. They carry information between_

     remote villages and central computer hubs.

II. Location: _____

   1. _educated population can work in a_ _____ _economy_

III. Location: _____

   1. _shops_ _____

   2. _centers_ _____

   3. _____

IV. Location: _____

   1. _a rural_ _____ _use the_ _____ _to research information_ _____

V. Location: _____

   1. _____ _telecentres_

   2. _used as a community_ _____ _during the_ _____ _of 2004_

Understanding Compound Adjectives

Often when two or more words come before a noun and function together as an adjective (word that describes something), they are linked together by a hyphen (-).

6 **Analyzing Compound Adjectives with Hyphens** Analyze the meanings of the words in italics by looking at the shorter words that are connected by the hyphen and at the context. Write explanations in the blanks.

1. All these benefits are coming via motorcycle—*Internet-enabled motorcycles.*

   motorcycles that can access the Internet

2. Farm economies made room for craftsmen and artisans, who gave way to industrial production, and manufacturing has yielded to the rise of an information and *service-based economy.* **Hint:** *Service* here relates to jobs in which employees provide something nontangible rather than producing goods.

   _____

3. *Large-scale factory production* in the developing world could greatly increase global energy consumption and pollution levels.

   _____

4. Societies that place a high value on education, like Vietnam, are at an advantage, because a highly educated population is ready for work in a *knowledge-based economy.*

   _____

5. Bangalore, India, is the *best-case scenario.*
   Hint: *Scenario* here means a course of action that could happen.

   _____

6. Recognized as the Silicon Valley of the developing world, Bangalore has successfully parlayed India's wealth of *well-educated, tech-savvy, English-speaking* programmers into a massive hive of interlocking programming shops, call centres, and tech companies.

   a. *well-educated programmers* are _____

   b. *tech-savvy programmers* are
      Hint: "Savvy" comes from the Spanish word *sabe* which means "know."

   _____

7. Therefore, *well-educated, tech-savvy, English-speaking programmers* are

   _____

8. Pondicherry's information and communications technology development strategy traces back to a 1998 project that brought *Internet-linked telecentres* to the region's villages.

   _____

7 **Focusing on Words from the Academic Word List** Use the most appropriate word from the box to fill in each of the blanks in the paragraph taken from Part 2. Do NOT look back at the reading right away; instead, first see if you can remember the vocabulary. One word will be used twice. Check your answers on page 117.

benefits	data	global	network	vehicle
computers	economy	medical	transmission	via

A   In Robib, Cambodia, villagers are getting _____ 1 advice from the world's best doctors. Schoolchildren are seeing their country's most famous landmarks for the first time. And the village _____ 2 is taking off, fueled by the sale of its handmade silk scarves on the _____ 3 market.

B   All these _____ 4 are coming _____ 5 motorcycle—Internet-enabled motorcycles. A wireless _____ 6 links _____ 7 in the village to computer chips on each of the five motorcycles. Each _____ 8 has a transmitter that allows it to upload and download email and _____ 9 as it passes by village computers. At the end of the day, the bikes return to a hub where they upload the information received. The next morning, they download email and _____ 10 from the hub and take it out to the villages for _____ 11 .

Talking It Over

8 **Discussing Information Technology** In a small group, discuss the following questions. Then compare your answers with those of another group.

1. The article mentions various solutions for getting information technology into developing communities. What solutions are mentioned? Which solution do you consider the most creative and/or effective? Why?

2. Do you think that companies could make money providing this type of service or would it be purely charity work on their part? Is it possible to fulfill both of these goals at once?

3. Can you think of other countries where this type of revolution in technology is happening or should happen? Explain.

4. Besides the advantages (educational programs, medical and crop advice, warning systems, etc.) of communications technology offered here, what other advantages can you think of? In your opinion, will there be disadvantages, too? Explain.

9 **What Do You Think?** Read the paragraph below and discuss the questions that follow.

Using Cellular Phones

Millions and millions of people around the world now own cell phones. This means that any time of day or night, these people can call or be called if the phone is on. Their phones can ring at the theater, in the coffee shop, in the classroom, in the car, in the bedroom.

1. Do you think it's a good idea that a person can be reached at any time? Why or why not?

2. Where and when do you think that sending or receiving calls should not be allowed? In restaurants? At the movies? At a concert? In the classroom? Explain your point of view.

3. What kind of restrictions should be put on phone calls while a person is driving?

4. Look at the cartoon. What do you think the artist is trying to say?

"I was addicted to my cell phone, but now I have a patch for it."

1 Guided Academic Conversation Follow the directions below to conduct an interview and compare answers.

Step 1: Interview Interview a classmate on the following questions. Then have that classmate interview you. Take notes on what your classmate says and use those notes in Step 2.

1. How often do you use social media (email, Facebook, Twitter, Skype)? Explain how often and why to your classmate.

   a. more than five times a day

   b. one to four times a day

   c. every few days

   d. once a week or less

2. Do you prefer communicating with your friends on social media or by telephone? Explain which you prefer and why?

3. In your opinion, does social media make life easier or harder for people? Explain.

4. What do you use the Internet for? Explain your answer to your classmate. Some possible answers:

   a. I don't ever or almost never use it.

   b. I use it for research for my work or studies.

   c. I use it for socializing or personal interest research.

   d. I use it for work, personal interest, and just about everything in my life.

5. Would you use the Internet for romance? Explain. Some possible answers:

   a. No. This is dangerous or foolish.

   b. Yes. This is a safer way of meeting an appropriate friend or potential life partner with similar interests and beliefs.

   c. Only under certain circumstances.

6. Have you ever read or written a blog? If so, what kind of blog?

7. Write your own interview question that you want to ask people:

Step 2: Comparing Answers After you have finished with the interviews, create a Venn diagram similar to the one below to compare your answers. Put the name of your classmate above one circle and your own name above the other circle. Then write the items you agreed on in the space where the two circles cross over and items you had different answers for in each of the two separate circles. What is your conclusion? Is yours and your classmate's usage of the Internet similar or different?

Culture Note

A blog is an informal journal that a person writes on the Web. It tells the story of a trip (a travel blog), news (recent elections), personal or family updates for friends (a baby's development), or it can be on a particular topic like studying abroad. Often blogs include references and links to other websites, making them more interactive and interesting.

Example   **My classmate:** Kim   Me

social media 1–4 times/day   prefer talking on the telephone   social medial once a week or less

2 **Making Connections** Choose one of the following three topics to do extra research on, using the Internet or other sources, and report back to the class. Be sure to copy down the websites that give you the information.

1. **Hybrid Cars** Play detective and bring to class the answer to one of these three questions: (1) Which car in the world today uses the least amount of gasoline per kilometer (or mile)? How much does it use? (2) What manufacturer sells the most popular cars? How many does it sell each year? (3) What manufacturer sells the highest number of electric or hybrid cars? How many is that? Then find an interesting current fact or statistic related to hybrid or electric cars and write it down to share with the class.

2. **Jordan Education Initiative** One important example of a program enabling countries to become connected with information and communication technologies is the Jordan Education Initiative (JEI), launched in 2003 by the company Cisco in conjunction with His Majesty King Abdullah II of Jordan and a couple dozen other World Economic Forum members. The idea is that Jordan will serve as a model and that other countries, like Bahrain, Oman, and the United Arab Emirates, will follow with similar initiatives. Search on the web and find out how this initiative is progressing and bring some facts or stories about it to share with the class. You can access the latest information about the Jordan Education Initiative on its web site http://www.jei.org.jo/.

3. **Kyoto Protocol** What is happening with the Kyoto Protocol? (See page 107.) Which countries have complied with the guidelines? Which ones haven't? When was the most recent meeting about this? Where was it held and who attended it? On the basis of what you find, make your own personal prediction regarding this plan and present it to your classmates, along with your reasons for believing as you do.

Responding in Writing

FOCUS

Writing Tip: Selecting Strong Examples to Support Your Point of View

To express your point of view on a subject, start by examining how you feel about this topic and why. If you have decided that you are in favor of it, choose examples that illustrate its good effects. If you have decided that you are against it, choose examples that show the bad effects it causes. Review your list and if there are too many examples, cut out the ones that seem the weakest. Choose only the examples that are convincing and develop them with details.

3 Writing About Technology Think about your own life and the society you live in. Do you think modern technology has had a more positive impact or a more negative one? Are you basically a high-tech or a low-tech kind of person? Choose one piece of technology that has made a big impact on your society or on your life for better or for worse. Then write a paragraph about what it would be like if it would suddenly be taken away and could no longer be used. Follow the steps on below.

Step 1: Decide if you want to discuss this in the general context of society or on a personal level, referring to your own life. Choose one of the following topics, filling in the blank with the piece of technology you're writing about, and choosing one of the adjectives (either *Sad* or *Happy*).

Our (Sad / Happy) Society Without _____

My (Sad / Happy) Life Without _____

Step 2: Look back over this chapter at the ideas and vocabulary presented. Select items that can be used to develop your theme and write them down.

Step 3: Imagine what things would be like without the technology you have chosen. Make a list of examples to show how society or your life would be either worse or better without it.

Step 4: Write a good beginning sentence that expresses your feelings about this technology and its impact.

Step 5: Select three to five examples from the list you made in Step 3 and express each one in a good sentence or two.

Step 6: Write a final sentence to conclude. Two common ways of concluding are (1) to repeat the main idea (given in the first sentence) in different words, or (2) to express a personal reaction, such as a wish or a rhetorical question (one that is asked in a general way with no expectation of an answer).

Step 7: Write a title for your paragraph. Use either the theme you chose and adapted from Step 1 or another original title.

FOCUS ON TESTING

TOEFL® iBT

Using a Computer on Tests

The TOEFL® Internet-Based Test (iBT) is given by means of a computer. None of the test is on paper. In the reading section, you will see each reading passage on the computer screen for up to 20 minutes. You select most of your answers by clicking on them with a mouse. After each reading passage, one question will require you to drag items with a mouse and drop them into a summary box or a table.

An earlier version of the test, the "Computer-based TOEFL® test " (CBT), also used computers. The CBT was "adaptive," meaning that the computer chose which questions you should get, depending on your performance. The TOEFL® iBT, however, is not adaptive but "linear." Everyone taking the test at any one time will get the same questions.

During the 20 minutes for each reading, you can go back and forth between the reading and any of its questions. You can skip hard questions and answer the easy ones first. If you need to change any of your reading answers, you can. The computer provides a table of all the questions for a given reading and shows which questions you have already answered. Finally, the computer gives you a limited glossary during the test. For a few vocabulary items, shown in blue on the screen, a short definition is available if you click on the blue item.

Here are some helpful tips to remember when taking the iBT.

1. Read the directions for each question. Is it multiple choice? Should you select only one answer or two? Are you supposed to click with your mouse on an answer or drag and drop an answer?

2. A small timer appears in a corner of the screen and shows you how much time you have left. Use this on-screen timer to pace yourself.

3. You may take notes on a sheet of notepaper provided by the test supervisor. You may not take notes on the computer.

4. Make sure you understand how to use the mouse. Practice taking computerized tests in your school's language lab or library.

5. If you have any questions, don't be afraid to ask before the test starts. The supervisor is there to make sure everyone understands what to do before beginning the test.

Practice

Based on the information above, write a correct word or phrase in each blank. A correct answer can replace the word in italics. Review the information above as often as necessary. The first one is done for you as an example.

1. Test questions appear on the screen, and the test-taker clicks on the correct answer with a *pointing device*. _____ mouse _____

2. The CBT is *programmed to select questions depending on the test-taker's performance*. _____

3. The iBT is *programmed to give the same questions to all test-takers at a given time*. _____

4. The iBT reading section provides a *kind of chart* listing all the questions and showing whether you have answered them or not. _____

5. Always carefully read the *set of instructions that tell you how to answer each question*. _____

6. In addition to clicking on multiple-choice items, you may have to *move some answers with your mouse and put them in the correct place*. _____

7. The iBT reading section provides a *definition feature* which can help you understand certain words that are printed in blue. _____

8. A small *clock-like display* on the iBT screen shows you how much time you have left. _____

9. Although you cannot takes notes on the computer, you can take them *on sheets of paper* that the supervisor gives you. _____

Read the lists below. Check (✓) the strategies and vocabulary that you learned in this chapter. Look through the chapter or ask your instructor about the strategies and words that you do not understand.

Reading and Vocabulary-Building Strategies

- ☐ Skimming for the general idea
- ☐ Scanning for definitions of key terms
- ☐ Inferring the meaning of expressions from context and vocabulary
- ☐ Inferring the meaning of specialized terms
- ☐ Using a graphic organizer for comparison
- ☐ Identifying the pattern of organization in a reading
- ☐ Analyzing the main point (thesis) of an article
- ☐ Understanding compound words
- ☐ Creating a study outline
- ☐ Understanding compound adjectives

Target Vocabulary

Nouns
- benefits*
- best-case scenario
- braking
- carbon footprint
- combustion engine
- components*
- computers*
- craftsmen
- data*
- economy*
- electric motor
- emissions
- four-cylinder engine
- fuel tank
- generator
- hybrid car
- landmarks
- leapfroggers
- marketplace
- network*

- parallel hybrid
- performance
- portion
- propulsion power
- recharging (batteries)
- rpm (revolutions per minute)
- scenario*
- speeds
- series hybrid
- telecenters (also spelled telecentres)
- transmission*
- vehicle*

Verbs
- download
- upload

Preposition
- via*

Adjectives
- efficient
- English-speaking
- global*
- grassroots
- handmade
- ignited
- Internet-enabled
- Internet-linked
- knowledge-based
- large-scale
- medical*
- service-based
- tech-savvy
- well-educated
- widespread*

Expression
- do our bit
- do their own thing
- on the block

*These words are from the Academic Word List. For more information on this list, see www.victoria.ac.nz/lals/resources/academicwordlist/

6 Money Matters

> "One coin in an
> empty moneybox
> makes more noise
> than when it is full."
>
> Arabic proverb

"Money makes the world go 'round," according to an old English saying, and being able to talk about money matters is important in all cultures. The first selection describes the success story of a business that started in Spain with a small idea and grew to make money and create jobs across many borders. The second selection, written by one of the greatest short story writers of the English language, William Somerset Maugham, focuses on a more personal aspect of the financial question: the embarrassment and difficulties that a lack of money can cause in a social situation.

Connecting to the Topic

1. Look at the photo. How would you describe this woman? Do you think she is careful with money? Why or why not?

2. What things do you consider to be a waste of money? What things do you like to splurge (spend a lot of money) on, i.e., nice clothes, eating in fancy restaurants, travel, the latest technology?

3. What difficulties can money cause among friends?

Executive Takes Chance on Pizza, Transforms Spain

Strategy

Previewing a Reading

Try to get a general idea of what an article is about before fully reading it. Often, the title presents key points that can help your comprehension.

1 Scanning for Specific Information Look at the title of the article on page 132. Then read the questions below about the title and take one minute to scan the article for the information needed to answer the questions. Compare your answers with those of your classmates.

1. Who is the *executive (business manager)* mentioned in the title?

2. What does it mean to say he "takes a chance on pizza"?

3. To *transform* something means to change it, and not just in a small way. How does this man "transform Spain"? Do you think this title uses exaggeration?

Strategy

Recognizing Word Families

A good way to expand vocabulary is through recognizing word families—groups of words related in form and meaning, such as *combine, combined,* and *combination.*

2 Recognizing Word Families Scan the reading selection for words related to the words given in the first column and write them in the second column. Read the meaning in the third column. The words are in the order of their appearance in the article.

	Related Word in Reading	Meaning of Related Word
1. global	globalization	a noun meaning *the growth of something worldwide*
2. pizza		a noun meaning *a place that produces or sells pizza*
3. convenient		a noun meaning *quality of being convenient, easy, or suitable*
4. modern		a verb meaning *becoming modern*
5. manage		a noun meaning *the act or manner of managing*
6. prosperous		a verb meaning *did well or became prosperous (wealthy)*
7. special		a noun meaning *types of food, or other products, that are special*
8. afford		an adjective meaning *can be afforded by a person's financial means, not too expensive*
9. mental		a noun meaning *mental outlook, way of thinking*
10. mature		a present participle (*-ing* word) meaning *growing older and wiser, becoming more mature*

Read

Introduction

The following article gives us some examples of ***globalization:*** a term used to describe how business, travel, communications, and other institutions spread quickly throughout the globe, without being stopped by borders, distance, language, and regulations the way they were in the past. Leopoldo Fernandez was born in one country, grew up in another, and then went to work in a third country. The article discusses how he starts a business that has an impact on many other countries.

- Why do people move from one country to another? Is this always their choice?
- Have you ever lived in a different country? Would you like to do that some day?

Executive Takes Chance on Pizza, Transforms Spain

A   MADRID, Spain—Leopoldo Fernandez was earning $150,000 a year as an executive in Spain with Johnson & Johnson when he decided to open a pizzeria on the side.

B   "Keep in mind, I knew nothing about pizza. My job was about selling heart valves, heart monitors, surgical instruments," said the 47-year-old Cuban American, a former marketing director for the U.S. medical supply company.

C   Six years later, Fernandez is the president of TelePizza, a multinational company with projected sales of $120 million this year. By year's end, the Madrid-based pizza businessman's name will adorn more than 200 outlets in ten countries. The company, one of the first to answer a need for convenience goods in modernizing Spain, may even be the world's fastest growing pizza chain, according to a recent issue of the trade magazine *Pizza Today* and research by TelePizza.

D   "I thought I'd just open five little stores and keep my job at Johnson & Johnson," recalled Fernandez in an interview as he puffed a $5 Cuban cigar. Two small Cuban flags are placed on his desk top.

E   Success came "so quickly my biggest problem has been keeping on top of the growth-money management, people management, training. Most new businesses grow at 10–20 percent yearly. We've grown at 10 percent a month since we opened," Fernandez said.

F   After his first shop prospered in Madrid, Fernandez left his job, sold his house and stocks, and cobbled together $300,000 to put into the business. From then on, new pizzerias opened rapidly, first in Spain and then abroad.

G   At the time TelePizza began in the late 1980s, pizzas were available in Spain only in Italian restaurants, and home delivery of any food was rare. But with more women in the workplace and Spain still modernizing, there was a growing need for convenience foods. TelePizza's success is widely credited with setting off a boom in home-delivered fast food in Spain.

H   Hundreds of motorbikes now ply Madrid's streets delivering everything from pizza to traditional specialties like Spanish tortillas (egg and potato omelettes) and paella.

I   Like the Domino's chain of U.S. fame, TelePizza's pies come fast—the company guarantees that pizzas will arrive in under 30 minutes, depending on where customers live. They are fairly affordable, with a pie for up to four people costing $13, compared with $6 for a McDonald's quarter pounder, fries, and Coke, undelivered.

J   Some say Spain's growing appetite for fast food is undermining the country's healthy Mediterranean diet. "There's a saying, when we were poor we made better eating choices than we do now," said Consuelo Lopez Nomdedeu, a nutritionist with the government-run National College of

Health. But Fernandez dismissed such complaints. "The key is variety in the diet," he said. "I wouldn't eat pizza daily or hamburgers; nor would I eat Spanish dishes like lentils or garbanzos."

K   Along with crediting the untapped Spanish market for his success, Fernandez noted that growing up as an immigrant in the United States

▲ Making a delivery on two wheels

probably also helped. Like many other refugees fleeing the Castro revolution, Fernandez moved to Florida from Cuba in 1960 with his parents.

L   "An immigrant has to find ways to succeed because he's on the bottom," said Fernandez, who also has worked for Procter & Gamble Co., the leading U.S. consumer products company.

M   "Here, my advantage is that I understand Spanish mentality better than Americans do, and I understand Americans better than Spaniards do," Fernandez said.

N   So far, his recipe for success is working. Fernandez said TelePizza outsells its three biggest rivals in Spain—Domino's, Pizza Hut, and Pizza World—combined. The company has a fleet of more than 2,000 motorbikes in Spain and sells 25,000 pizzas daily in the Spanish market.

O   About two-thirds of TelePizza outlets in Spain are franchises while 90 percent of the 40 stores abroad are company-owned. In addition to Spain, there are TelePizza outlets located in Colombia, Chile, Portugal, Belgium, Greece, and Poland—with stores in Brazil set to open before year's end.

P   "We plan to go into the U.S. in due time," Fernandez said. "For now we are maturing and learning from growth markets."

Source: "Executive Takes Chance on Pizza, Transforms Spain" *Wisconsin State Journal* (Stephen Wade)

CLOSE TO HOME   JOHN McPHERSON

"Didn't that pizza delivery kid used to be our paperboy?"

3 Getting Meaning from Context Use the context and the clues to explain the following business terms.

1. *marketing* (line 6) A market is a place where products are bought and sold.

   So, *marketing* is _promoting the buying and selling of products_ .

2. *multinational* (line 8) Break the word apart to find its meaning.

   _____

3. *projected sales* (line 9) Think about projecting something such as fireworks into the sky. Then think about the time frame it refers to.

   _____

4. *outlets* (line 11) Break the word apart and remember we are talking about

   a product that is being marketed. _____

5. *chain* (line 13) Imagine a picture of a chain, made up of separate parts called

   links. _____

6. *boom* (line 29) The meaning can be inferred partly from the sound of this word (which is used to describe the sound of an explosion).

   _____

7. *untapped market* (line 45) To tap something means "to open or start," as in tapping an oil well. Then consider how the prefix *un-* affects the meaning.

   _____

8. *franchises* (line 66) Notice these stores are contrasted with others that are

   company-owned. _____

9. *growth markets* (line 78) Take a guess from the words themselves.

   _____

4 Checking Your Comprehension Fill in the bubble of the most appropriate answer related to the reading.

1. Before starting a pizza business, Fernandez worked for a company that

   sold _____.
   - (A) Cuban cigars
   - (B) surgical instruments
   - (C) restaurant supplies

2. TelePizza grew very fast in the 1980s because at that time in Spain

   _____ was very rare.

   (A) Italian food

   (B) good restaurants

   (C) home delivery

3. Another factor that helped the business is that there were more in

   _____ the workplace than before.

   (A) women

   (B) engineers

   (C) young people

4. According to Consuelo Lopez Nomdedeu, fast food like pizza is not good for

   Spain because it is _____.

   (A) very expensive

   (B) too foreign

   (C) not healthy

5. Fernandez feels that being an immigrant in the U.S. _____.

   (A) caused many problems for him and his family

   (B) was an advantage to him in business

   (C) did not affect him in any way

6. TelePizza has many outlets in Spain and in different countries and these are

   _____.

   (A) franchises

   (B) company-owned

   (C) both franchises and company-owned

5 **Guided Academic Conversation: Globalization and How It Affects Us** In small groups, discuss the following issues. Then compare your answers with those of another group. After Leopoldo Fernandez opened his first TelePizza, the company quickly expanded to hundreds of outlets in many countries, including Spain, Greece, Poland, Portugal, Belgium, and Colombia. Obviously, globalization was good for Mr. Fernandez, but is it good for everyone?

1. **Chain Stores** Make a list of the chain stores, restaurants, or businesses that are popular where you live. Note if they are nationally owned or foreign. Do you know the difference? What is more important: the product or the ownership, or both? Do foreign-owned businesses hurt or help the local economy? What is your group's favorite chain? Why?

2. **Owning Your Own Business** Would you like to have your own business some day, or do you prefer to work for someone else? Explain your choice. What chain stores, restaurants, or businesses from your country have outlets in other countries? Would you consider working for one of them? Would you work for a chain from a different nation? Why or why not?

3. **Fast Food: a Curse or a Blessing?** Does fast food mean bad food? What are its advantages? There must be a reason that it is so much in demand. Pretend that your group has been given money to set up a new international fast-food chain in foreign markets. What foods would you choose to export from your culture? How would you set up the atmosphere of the outlets? What name would you give to your business?

6 **Making Connections** Look up TelePizza on the Internet or in a library and look for information on one of the following topics to share with the class. (You may find that much of the information is in languages other than English. If you can't find enough, look for information on home delivery of pizza in general to find out what other businesses exist that are similar and how they are doing.)

1. What has happened to the business ownership after so many years? Is it still in the hands of the original owner or his family? Or have there been new owners?

2. What conflicts have occurred between management and employees? Have these been resolved? Does the business still exist in many countries or has it succeeded more in some than in others?

3. How successful is this business now? Has it gone up or down since its early amazing period of fast growth?

FOCUS ON TESTING

TOEFL iBT

Reading Between the Lines

In many reading comprehension tests, you are asked to read a passage and choose the best answer to some questions about it. Often these questions ask you to make an inference about the reading. Remember that an inference is a true idea that is not stated directly but can be inferred (concluded or deduced) from what is stated. In English, this is often called "reading between the lines." In order to choose the correct inference, you must decide why three of the answers are not correct. Tests can fool you, so be careful! In many tests, as in the practice test below, one of the choices is false. Another is probably true, but we don't have enough information to decide for sure. Another of the choices may be true but is already directly stated in the passage in different words; therefore, it is not an inference. Now, through the process of elimination, we have cut out three choices and are left with the one correct answer. So, choose that answer.

Practice

Following are three passages from the article on pages 132–133, "Executive Takes Chance on Pizza, Transforms Spain." Each passage is followed by a question about it. Fill in the bubble of the best answer to each question.

Passage 1

Leopoldo Fernandez was earning $150,000 a year as an executive in Spain with Johnson & Johnson when he decided to open a pizzeria on the side. "Keep in mind, I knew nothing about pizza. My job was about selling heart valves, heart monitors, surgical instruments," said the 47-year-old Cuban American, a former marketing director for the U.S. medical supply company.

What can be inferred from the passage about Leopoldo Fernandez?

A. He is middle-aged.

B. He was born in Cuba.

C. He is a risk taker.

D. He was poor before starting a business.

Passage 2

At the time TelePizza began in the late 1980s, pizzas were available in Spain only in Italian restaurants, and home delivery of any food was rare. But with more women in the workplace and Spain still modernizing, there was a growing need for convenience foods. TelePizza's success is widely credited with setting off a boom in home-delivered fast food in Spain.

What can be inferred from the passage about TelePizza's customers?

A. They like to buy on credit.

B. They do not like Italian restaurants.

C. Many are very traditional.

D. Many are working women.

Passage 3

Along with crediting the untapped Spanish market for his success, Fernandez noted that growing up as an immigrant in the United States probably also helped. Like many other refugees fleeing the Castro revolution, Fernandez moved to Florida from Cuba in 1960 with his parents.

"An immigrant has to find ways to succeed because he's on the bottom," said Fernandez, who also has worked for Procter & Gamble Co., the leading U.S. consumer products company.

What can be inferred from the passage about Fernandez's opinion of immigrants?

A. Immigrants usually don't work as hard as others.

B. Immigrants usually work harder than others.

C. Immigrants are employed by big companies.

D. Immigrants receive support from their families.

---

7 **What Do You Think?** Read the paragraph below and discuss the questions on page 138.

Buying on the Internet

People love to shop, and more and more of them are shopping on the Internet. Some are pleased with the variety of goods offered and the ease of shopping in the comfort of their own homes. Yet some are worried about the quality of goods they'll receive or the safety of their credit card numbers.

Do you like to shop on the Internet? ▶

1. Have you ever shopped on the Internet? If so, what products have you bought?

2. Do you prefer to shop online, use a catalog, or go to a store in person? Why?

3. Some consumers think it's not safe to shop on the Internet. Do you agree or not? What precautions would you take before completing a transaction on the Internet?

4. Have you ever heard of "identity theft"? What is it? Do you think it could happen if you buy products on the Internet? Explain.

PART **2** Main Ideas and Details

The Luncheon

Before You Read

Strategy

Identifying the Setting, Characters, and Conflict in a Narrative

Reading a story is easier if you first identify the key elements that every story must have. These are called the *narrative elements*.

- **setting:** the time and place
- **characters:** the main people who are in the story
- **plot:** the action that starts with a **conflict**, develops into a complication, and ends with a resolution (a solution of the conflict)

1 Identifying the Setting, Characters, and Conflict Find the setting by looking at the illustration and skimming the first few paragraphs.

1. When does the story take place (more or less)? _____

   Where? _____

2. Who are the main characters? There is of course the *narrator* (the one speaking) since the story is written in the first person (using *I* and *me*). The other character is a woman whose name we are never told. What do we know about this woman?

   Characters: _____

   About the woman: _____

3. We cannot identify in advance the whole plot, but we can find out how it begins. The action always starts with a conflict (a problem or difficulty) because if everything were fine, there would be no story. Read quickly up to line 24 and find the conflict. Explain it here.

_____

_____

You will have to read the story to see how this conflict gets complicated, rises to a climax (the most difficult and intense moment of the action), and then ends in the resolution.

2 Getting the Meaning of Words from Context The author uses exact adjectives and adverbs to describe the feelings of the characters and the appearance of their surroundings. Look for clues in the context and fill in the bubble of the word or phrase closest to the meaning of the word in italics.

1. But I was *flattered* and I was too young to have learned to say no to a woman. (lines 19–20)

- Ⓐ worried about the future
- Ⓑ pleased by the praise
- Ⓒ confused about what to do

Notice the clue in line 19.

2. She was not so young as I expected and in appearance *imposing* rather than attractive. (lines 26–27)

- Ⓐ notable
- Ⓑ good-looking
- Ⓒ unattractive

3. I was *startled* when the bill of fare was brought, for the prices were a great deal higher than I had anticipated. (lines 33–34)

- Ⓐ depressed by sad memories
- Ⓑ scared by a sudden surprise
- Ⓒ filled with hope

4. "What would you like?" I asked, hospitable still, but not exactly *effusive*. (line 56)

- Ⓐ enthusiastic
- Ⓑ silent
- Ⓒ timid

5. She gave me a bright and *amicable* flash of her white teeth. (line 57)

- Ⓐ angry
- Ⓑ false
- Ⓒ friendly

6. It would be *mortifying* to find myself ten francs short and be obliged to borrow from my guest. (lines 91–92)

- Ⓐ embarrassing
- Ⓑ boring
- Ⓒ tiring

7. The asparagus appeared. They were enormous, *succulent*, and appetizing. (line 99)

- Ⓐ too ripe
- Ⓑ dry
- Ⓒ juicy

8. I knew too—a little later, for my guest, going on with her conversation, *absentmindedly* took one. (lines 121–122)

- Ⓐ with a cruel intention
- Ⓑ without thinking
- Ⓒ in a careful way

9. The bill came and when I paid it I found that I had only enough for a quite *inadequate* tip. (lines 126–127)

- Ⓐ generous
- Ⓑ small
- Ⓒ exact

10. But I have had my revenge at last. I do not believe that I am a *vindictive* man, but... (lines 135–136)

- Ⓐ forgiving and peaceful
- Ⓑ filled with contentment
- Ⓒ set on getting revenge

Read

Strategy

Predicting Events in a Narrative
It is helpful while reading a narrative to think ahead of the action. You don't have to understand every word, just try to follow the action, understand what is happening, and think about what might happen next.

③ **Predicting Events in a Narrative** As you read the next selection, try to predict what is going to happen next. The story will be interrupted at a few points and you will be asked some questions to guide you. Do not worry about understanding every word. Just try to follow the action and understand what is happening.

The Luncheon

I caught sight of her at the play and in answer to her beckoning I went
over during the interval and sat down beside her. It was long since I had last
seen her and if someone had not mentioned her name I hardly think I would
have recognized her. She addressed me brightly.

"Well, it's many years since we first met. How time does fly! We're none   5
of us getting any younger. Do you remember the first time I saw you? You
asked me to luncheon."

Did I remember?

It was twenty years ago and I was living in Paris. I had a tiny apartment
in the Latin Quarter overlooking a cemetery and I was earning barely   10
enough money to keep body and soul together. She had read a book of mine
and had written to me about it. I answered, thanking her, and presently I
received from her another letter saying that she was passing through Paris
and would like to have a chat with me; but her time was limited and the
only free moment she had was on the following Thursday: she was spending   15
the morning at the Luxembourg and would I give her a little luncheon at
Foyot's afterwards? Foyot's is a restaurant at which the French senators eat
and it was so far beyond my means that I had never even thought of going

there. But I was flattered and I was too young to have learned to say no to a woman. (Few men, I may add, learn this until they are too old to make it of any consequence to a woman what they say.) I had eighty francs (gold francs) to last me the rest of the month and a modest luncheon should not cost more than fifteen. If I cut out coffee for the next two weeks I could manage well enough.

What do you think of the request that the woman has made of the main character? Why do you think that he accepted it? Do you think he is going to get into trouble? Why or why not?

I answered that I would meet my friend-by-correspondence at Foyot's on Thursday at half past twelve. She was not so young as I expected and in appearance imposing rather than attractive. She was in fact a woman of forty (a charming age, but not one that excites a sudden and devastating passion at first sight), and she gave me the impression of having more teeth, white and large and even, than were necessary for any practical purpose. She was talkative, but since she seemed inclined to talk about me I was prepared to be an attentive listener.

I was startled when the bill of fare was brought, for the prices were a great deal higher than I had anticipated. But she reassured me.

"I never eat anything for luncheon," she said.

"Oh, don't say that!" I answered generously.

"I never eat more than one thing. I think people eat far too much nowadays. A little fish, perhaps. I wonder if they have any salmon."

Well, it was early in the year for salmon and it was not on the bill of fare, but I asked the waiter if there was any. Yes, a beautiful salmon had just come in—it was the first they had had. I ordered it for my guest. The waiter asked her if she would have something while it was being cooked.

What did the man notice about the woman's appearance? Does it perhaps give a clue to her character? From what she has said so far, do you expect her to order any more food? Why?

"No," she answered. "I never eat more than one thing. Unless you had a little caviar. I never mind caviar."

My heart sank a little. I knew I could not afford caviar, but I could not very well tell her that. I told the waiter by all means to bring caviar. For myself I chose the cheapest dish on the menu and that was a mutton chop.

"I think you're unwise to eat meat," she said. "I don't know how you can expect to work after eating heavy things like chops. I don't believe in overloading my stomach."

Then came the question of drink.

What do you think the woman is going to say about the question of drink? What do you think she is going to do? And the man? Why?

"I never drink anything for luncheon," she said.

"Neither do I," I answered promptly.

"Except white wine," she proceeded as though I had not spoken. "These French white wines are so light. They're wonderful for the digestion."

"What would you like?" I asked, hospitable still, but not exactly effusive.

She gave me a bright and amicable flash of her white teeth.

"My doctor won't let me drink anything but champagne."

I fancy I turned a trifle pale. I ordered half a bottle. I mentioned casually that my doctor had absolutely forbidden me to drink champagne.

"What are you going to drink, then?"

"Water."

She ate the caviar and she ate the salmon. She talked gaily of art and literature and music. But I wondered what the bill would come to. When my mutton chop arrived she took me quite seriously to task.

"I see that you're in the habit of eating a heavy luncheon. I'm sure it's a mistake. Why don't you follow my example and eat just one thing? I'm sure you'd feel ever so much better for it."

"I *am* only going to eat one thing," I said, as the waiter came again with the bill of fare.

The waiter has come once again. What will happen next?

She waved him aside with an airy gesture.

"No, no, I never eat anything for luncheon. Just a bite, I never want more than that, and I eat that more as an excuse for conversation than anything else. I couldn't possibly eat anything more—unless they had some of those giant asparagus. I should be sorry to leave Paris without having some of them."

"Madame wants to know if you have any of those giant asparagus," I asked the waiter.

I tried with all my might to will him to say no. A happy smile spread over his broad, priest-like face, and he assured me that they had some so large, so splendid, so tender, that it was a marvel.

"I'm not in the least hungry," my guest sighed, "but if you insist, I don't mind having some asparagus."

I ordered them.

"Aren't you going to have any?"

"No, I never eat asparagus."

"I know there are people who don't like them. The fact is, you ruin your palate by all the meat you eat."

Something is ironic when it is the opposite of what is true or expected. What is ironic about what the woman keeps saying? How do you think the man feels about this? Do you think the man or the woman will order more food?

We waited for the asparagus to be cooked. Panic seized me. It was not a question now of how much money I should have left over for the rest of the month, but whether I had enough to pay the bill. It would be mortifying to find myself ten francs short and be obliged to borrow from my guest. I could not bring myself to do that. I knew exactly how much I had and if the bill came to more I had made up my mind that I would put my hand in my pocket and with a dramatic cry start up and say it had been picked. Of course it would be awkward if she had not money enough either to pay the bill. Then the only thing would be to leave my watch and say I would come back and pay later.

The asparagus appeared. They were enormous, succulent, and appetizing. The smell of the melted butter tickled my nostrils as the nostrils of Jehovah were tickled by the burned offerings of the virtuous Semites. I watched the abandoned woman thrust them down her throat in large voluptuous

▼ A fancy restaurant in Paris in the 1930s.

mouthfuls and in my polite way I discoursed on the condition of the drama in the Balkans. At last, she finished.

"Coffee?" I asked.

105

"Yes, just an ice cream and coffee," she answered.

I was past caring now, so I ordered coffee for myself and an ice cream and coffee for her.

"You know, there's one thing I thoroughly believe in," she said, as she ate the ice cream. "One should always get up from a meal feeling one could eat a little more."

"Are you still hungry?" I asked faintly.

"Oh, no. I'm not hungry; you see, I don't eat luncheon. I have a cup of coffee in the morning and then dinner, but I never eat more than one thing for luncheon. I was speaking for you."

"Oh, I see!"

Then a terrible thing happened. While we were waiting for the coffee, the head waiter, with an ingratiating smile on his false face, came up to us bearing a large basket full of peaches. They had the blush of an innocent girl; they had the rich tone of an Italian landscape. But surely peaches were not in season then? Lord knew what they cost. I knew too—a little later, for my guest, going on with her conversation, absentmindedly took one.

"You see, you've filled your stomach with a lot of meat"—my one miserable little chop—"and you can't eat any more. But I've just had a snack and I shall enjoy a peach."

The bill came and when I paid it I found that I had only enough for a quite inadequate tip. Her eyes rested for an instant on the three francs I left for the waiter and I knew that she thought me mean. But when I walked out of the restaurant I had the whole month before me and not a penny in my pocket.

So far the luncheon has gone badly for the man. Somerset Maugham is known for his irony and surprise endings. Can you think of some way he might turn the situation around? Will the man somehow get his revenge?

"Follow my example," she said as we shook hands, "and never eat more than one thing for luncheon."

"I'll do better than that," I retorted. "I'll eat nothing for dinner tonight."

"Humorist!" she cried gaily, jumping into a cab. "You're quite a humorist!"

But I have had my revenge at last. I do not believe that I am a vindictive man, but when the immortal gods take a hand in the matter it is pardonable to observe the result with complacency. Today she weighs twenty-one stone.*

Source: "The Luncheon" *Cosmopolitans* (W. Somerset Maugham).

*The stone is a British unit of measurement. One stone equals fourteen pounds, or 6.35 kilos

Understanding the Plot: Recalling the Series of Events

Besides setting, character, and conflict, another narrative element is the plot. The *plot* is the series of events as they occur in a narrative; they make up the action of the story.

This story, like many others, is a *framework* tale. That means that it contains "a story within a story." The narrator begins by telling us about himself in the present time as a kind of framework to a shorter story, or memory from the past, that he then tells us. (When this technique is used in a movie, it is called a *flashback*, because the picture *flashes* back to an earlier time.)

Reading Tip

Recall that you can use a chain of events diagram to take notes on a series of events.

4 **Understanding the Plot: Recalling the Series of Events** Read through the events labeled A through H that are listed below the chain of events diagram. Decide in which order they occurred as told by the narrator in the story. Then write the letter of each statement in the correct box of the diagram to represent the order of occurrence.

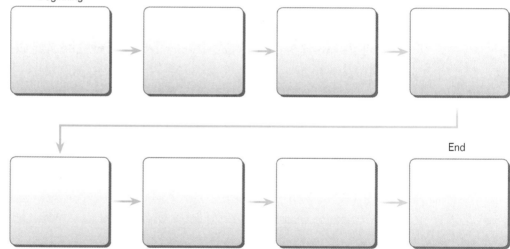

Beginning

End

A. The man remembers that he had no money for expenses for one month.

B. The man remembers that the woman ate a lot of expensive food for lunch.

C. The man mentions that the woman is very much overweight.

D. The man remembers the woman writing him a letter about his book.

E. The man meets the woman at a play, after not seeing her for many years.

F. The man remembers that he is barely able to pay the bill.

G. The man remembers the woman asking him to take her to lunch.

H. The man remembers that the woman insists she doesn't eat lunch.

Focusing on Words from the Academic Word List Use the most appropriate word from the box to fill in each of the blanks below in the section taken from the reading. Do NOT look back at the reading right away; instead, first see if you can remember the vocabulary. Check your answers on pages 142–145.

anticipated	found	inadequate
drama	imposing	inclined
enormous		

She was not so young as I expected and in appearance _____ 1 rather than attractive… She was talkative, but since she seemed _____ 2 to talk about me I was prepared to be an attentive listener.

I was startled when the bill of fare was brought, for the prices were a great deal higher than I had _____ 3 …   5

The asparagus appeared. They were _____ 4 , succulent, and appetizing… I watched the abandoned woman thrust them down her throat in large voluptuous mouthfuls and in my polite way I discoursed on the condition of the _____ 5 in the Balkans. At last, she finished…   10

The bill came and when I paid it I _____ 6 that I had only enough for a quite _____ 7 tip.

6 **Creating a Skit** With a partner, discuss the question below. Then make up a short skit (where one person is the man and one is the woman) to illustrate what the man might have done to get out of the situation. Present this skit to another pair of students and see if they agree with your solution to the man's problem. Then watch their skit and see if you agree with their solution.

Question: What should the young man have done to get out of this difficult situation? Do you think that he was trapped by the rules of courtesy and good manners? What would you have done in similar circumstances?

7 **Solving Problems** Discuss the following questions in a group of four.

1. Why do you think the woman behaved as she did? Did she want to take advantage of the young man, or was she simply ignorant of his money problems? Or didn't she care if he had problems?

2. How has the author used irony in this story to create humor?

3. Have you ever been in an embarrassing situation because of money? If so, how did you get out of it?

4. Why do you think some people continually have money problems? Is it the fault of credit cards? Is it the lack of experience or training?

5. Working with your whole group, write out what you all think is the best rule for

   managing your money: _____

   _____

Be prepared to read this to the class. Then take a vote to see which group came up with the best rule.

PART 3 Tying It All Together

1 **Making Connections** Use the Internet or library to find information about one of the following items and present it to the class.

1. The Venezuelan currency is named after a revolutionary hero who led wars of independence in what is now five other countries beside Venezuela. Which countries were these? Who was this hero? What was his name and what is the name of the unit of money in Venezuela today? What dream did he have for Latin America that was never fulfilled?

2. In Peru, the name of the currency reflects the ancient Inca culture's worship of the sun. What was the currency called until 1985? What new name was given to it then? Then, how and when was that name changed? How do you explain these changes?

3. In Canada, the one-dollar coin is named after a water bird. What is it called and why? Why is this term also somewhat of a Canadian joke? What does the dollar coin look like? What color is it and how many sides does it have? What is the two-dollar coin called and what does it look like?

4. Go to a currency exchange website and look up the names of the currencies of some other countries. Try searching some of these names and come up with an interesting fact or history of the name of a currency from some country that interests you. You could also try to find information by going to an international chat room and chatting with people from other countries about what they know about their currency's name. Be prepared to share your findings with the class.

Responding in Writing

FOCUS

Writing Tip: Making a Cluster Diagram

Using a cluster (see page 151) diagram is a good way to get your ideas flowing and to organize your ideas. When you brainstorm, put the main idea in the center circle of the diagram. Write other ideas related to the main idea around the main idea. Circle your ideas and connect them to the main idea. Then write more ideas related to your first ideas in circles and connect them to your primary ideas.

2 Using a Cluster Diagram to Organize Ideas and Write a Paragraph Successful entrepreneurs (people who start new businesses) from around the world offer advice about how to succeed in business in the following quotes. Write a paragraph about one of the quotes telling what you think it means and why you like it or dislike it. Read the quotes; then follow the steps outlined below.

1. "Lead, follow, or get out of the way."
   —Thomas Paine

2. "Never get discouraged and quit. Because if you never quit, you're never broken."
   —Ted Turner, founder of CNN and TNT

3. "Develop a product where there is no market, then create one."
   —Akio Morita, Sony Electronic

4. "Success is the one percent of your work that results from the 99 percent that is called failure."
   —Soichiro Honda, Honda cars and motorcycles

5. "Build 'em strong and sell 'em cheap." "Concentrate on one product used by everyone, every day."
   —Baron Marcel Bich, Bic pens, razors

6. "A computer on every desk and in every home."
—Bill Gates, Microsoft Corporation

▲ Bill Gates, former CEO of Microsoft, is a successful international businessman and philanthropist.

Step 1: Choose the quotation that is most interesting to you and write it down, with the name of its author, at the beginning of your composition.

Step 2: Brainstorm your ideas (by yourself, or with someone who has chosen the same quotation) on what this quotation means and why you like or dislike it by using a cluster diagram like the example on page 151. In a circle in the center of your paper, put the quotation you chose, then write any ideas that come to you that relate to the quotation, circle them, and connect them to the quotation. Then write ideas related to the first ideas in circles and connect them to the primary ideas. (A cluster diagram is a good way to get your ideas flowing and to begin to organize them.)

Step 3: Considering just the points you want to make from your cluster diagram, make up a good beginning sentence to introduce the main point of your paragraph.

Step 4: Write each of the points you want to use from the cluster diagram into sentences to support your main point.

Step 5: Write a final sentence to conclude. Remember, two common ways of concluding are: (1) to repeat the main idea (given in the first sentence) in different words; or (2) to express a personal reaction, such as a wish or a rhetorical question (one that is asked in a general way with no expectation of an answer).

Step 6: Check over your paragraph for spelling and punctuation. Read it through to make sure that it makes sense.

Step 7: Write a title for your paragraph that describes it. The title should not be too broad ("Computers," for the example above), but should describe exactly what your main point is ("Gates's Philosophy of Marketing"). You could even try to make it creative with alliteration (using words that begin with a similar letter) or by saying something funny. Most important is for your title to make sense and relate to your main point. Hand in your cluster diagram along with your paragraph.

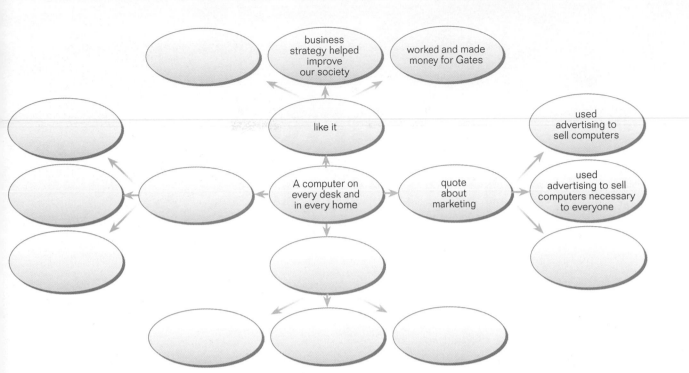

7 Remarkable Individuals

"A good reputation sits
still; a bad one runs about."

Russian proverb

In this CHAPTER

People can be remarkable in many ways. The first reading in this chapter is about a man who has had a profound influence on society through the greatness of his intellect for over 2,500 years. The second is about five present-day heroes of extraordinary courage who fought ardently on four different continents for the rights and dignity of the oppressed.

Connecting to the Topic

1. Look at the photo? What are the man and girl doing? What do you think their relationship is to each other?

2. This chapter is about remarkable people. What makes a person remarkable? Does someone need to be famous in order to be remarkable? Why or why not?

3. What three people past or present do you consider to be remarkable? What makes them remarkable in your opinion?

Confucius, 551 B.C.E. – 479 B.C.E.*

Before You Read

1 Skimming for the General Idea Who was Confucius? Skim the article on pages 156–157 for the answer to this question. (Remember that skimming means moving your eyes quickly over the whole selection while taking note of the key words and ideas.) After you skim, fill in the bubble of the statement that best expresses the overall idea of the reading. Why is it better than the other two?

   Ⓐ Confucius is a historical figure famous for his brilliant invention of a new philosophy that transformed the society of his times and has remained popular in China continuously until the present day.

   Ⓑ Confucius was a powerful leader of ancient China whose ideas about mathematics, science, and human behavior formed the basis for traditional values and later inspired the communist government.

   Ⓒ Confucius was the learned teacher responsible for a book of ethical and moral principles that has influenced Chinese society for many centuries, surviving attacks by different groups opposed to these principles.

Strategy

Figuring Out Words from Structure Clues
Structure, as well as context, can help you figure out the meaning of words. Deconstruct (break apart) a word into its smaller parts, such as prefixes, suffixes, or smaller words to help figure it out.

Compound Words: Some words in English are compound words, which are made up of two or more smaller words.
supermarket: The smaller words, *super* and *market*, indicate a big market.
taxpayer: The smaller words, *tax* and *payer*, indicate someone who pays taxes.

Prefixes and Suffixes: Some words contain a smaller word and a prefix or a suffix. An example is *adulthood*: The suffix *-hood* shows a shared quality or condition, so *adulthood* is the shared condition of being adults (people who have grown older and are not children).

2 Figuring Out Words from Structure Clues Separate the following words into smaller words, prefixes, or suffixes. Then use the clues (and your creativity) to make up a working definition.

*B.C.E. means "Before the Common Era," which begins with the year 1, assumed to be approximately the year of the birth of Jesus Christ.

Word	Clue and Definition
1. childhood	The suffix -*hood* shows a shared quality or condition. So *neighborhood* is the shared condition of neighbors (who all live in the same place), and *childhood* is _____.
2. background	The *ground* is the place where things are done, and *back* can refer to going back in space or time, so a person's *background* refers to _____ .
3. principality	A *kingdom* is a territory ruled by a king, and a *principality* is a _____ .
4. cornerstones	The stones in the corners give the main support for a building. So the *cornerstones* of a philosophy are _____ .
5. benevolent	The root *bene-* means "good" (as in *benefit*, a good thing), and the root *vol* means "wishing" or "willing" (as in *volunteer*, one willing to do something), so *benevolent* means _____ .
6. defender	The suffix -*er* means "one who...," so a *defender* is _____ .
7. outlook	Breaking the word into two smaller words, your *outlook* is the way you _____ .
8. innovator	To *innovate* means "to start something new" and the suffix -*or* means the same as -*er*, so an *innovator* is _____ .
9. commoners	*Commoners* are people who _____ .

Introduction

The following selection describes the background and philosophy of the great ancient Chinese philosopher Confucius, whose ideas continue to impact people all over the world right up to the present day.

- Have you heard about Confucius before? If so, what ideas do you associate with this name?
- Can you think of any other great men or women whose ideas have lasted for hundreds or thousands of years?

Confucius, 551 B.C.E. – 479 B.C.E.

A   No other philosopher in the world has had more enduring influence than Confucius. For over two thousand years his concept of government,

▲ Confucius

and his ideas about personal conduct and morality, permeated Chinese life and culture. Even today, his thoughts remain influential.

B   There was little in his childhood background that predicted the remarkable prestige that Confucius eventually achieved. He was born in a small principality in northeastern China, was reared in poverty, and had no formal education. Through diligent study, however, he educated himself and became a learned man. For a while he held a minor government post; but he soon resigned that position and spent most of his life as a teacher. Eventually, his most important teachings were gathered together into a book, the *Analects*, which was compiled by his disciples.

C   The two cornerstones of his system of personal conduct were *jen* and *li*. *Jen* might be defined as "benevolent concern for one's fellow men." *Li* is a term less easily translated: it combines the notions of etiquette, good manners, and due concern for rituals and customs. Confucius believed that a man should strive after truth and virtue rather than wealth (and in his personal life he seems to have acted on that principle). In addition, he was the first major philosopher to state the Golden Rule, which he phrased as "Do not do unto others that which you would not have them do unto you."

D   Confucius believed that respect and obedience are owed by children to their parents, by wives to their husbands, and by subjects to their rulers. But he was never a defender of tyranny. On the contrary, the starting point of his political outlook is that the state exists for the benefit of the people, not the rulers. Another of his key political ideas is that a leader should govern primarily by moral example, rather than by force.

E   Confucius did not claim to be an innovator, but always said that he was merely urging a return to the moral standards of former times. In fact, however, the reforms which he urged represented a change from—and a great improvement over—the governmental practices of earlier days.

F   At the time of his death, Confucius was a respected, but not yet greatly influential, teacher and philosopher. Gradually, though, his ideas became widely accepted throughout China. Then in the third century B.C.E., Shih Huang Ti united all of China under his rule and decided to reform the country entirely and make a complete break with the past. Shih Huang

Ti therefore decided to suppress Confucian teachings, and he ordered the burning of all copies of Confucius' works. (He also ordered the destruction of most other philosophical works.)

G   Most Confucian books were indeed destroyed; but some copies survived the holocaust, and a few years later, after the dynasty founded by the "First Emperor" had fallen, Confucianism re-emerged. Under the next dynasty, the Han, Confucianism became the official state philosophy, a position it maintained throughout most of the next two millennia.

H   Indeed, for much of that period, the civil service examinations in China were based primarily on knowledge of Confucian classics. Since those examinations were the main route by which commoners could enter the administration and achieve political power, the governing class of the largest nation on Earth was largely composed of men who had carefully studied the works of Confucius and absorbed his principles.

I   This enormous influence persisted until the 19th century, when the impact of the West created revolutionary changes in China. Then in the 20th century, the Communist party seized power in China. It was their belief that, in order to both modernize China and to eliminate economic injustice, it was necessary to make radical changes in society. As the ideas of Confucius were highly conservative, the communists made a major effort to eradicate his influence, the first such effort since Shih Huang Ti, 22 centuries earlier.

Source: "Confucius" *The 100: A Ranking of the Most Influential Persons In History* (Michael H. Hart)

After You Read

3 **Identifying Key Terms** The terms in the column on the left are from the reading. Choose the best explanation for each of them from the column on the right. One item on the right will be left over.

1. _____ *The Analects*

2. _____ a Confucian teaching

3. _____ the Golden Rule

4. _____ *jen*

5. _____ *li*

6. _____ Shi Huang Ti

a. A leader must sometimes use tyranny to achieve benefits for the state.

b. benevolent concern for other people

c. collection of the teachings of Confucius, made by his disciples

d. Don't do to others what you don't want them to do to you.

e. emperor of China in the third century who suppressed Confucianism

f. etiquette, good manners, and concern for rituals and customs

g. The state exists for the people, and leaders should govern by example, not force.

4 Forming New Words from the Same Word Family Fill in each blank with the word from the reading that is related to the word in italics (from the same word family).

1. the adjective related to *endure*   more ____enduring____ influence

2. the adjective related to *influence*   his thoughts remain _____

3. the adverb related to *easy*   a term less _____ translated

4. the adjective related to *politics*   his key _____ ideas

5. the adverb related to *primary*   _____ by moral example

6. the adjective related to *government*   the _____ practices

7. the adjective related to *Confucius*   to suppress _____ teachings

8. the adjective related to *philosophy*   other _____ works

9. the verb related to *modern*   to _____ China

5 Matching Words to Their Definitions Match each word on the left with the correct synonym or definition on the right. For a word you are not sure about, scan the reading for it, and use the context to infer its meaning.

1. _____ enduring   a. fame, good reputation

2. _____ permeated   b. the attempt to completely erase or do away with a group of people or an idea

3. _____ reared
                           c. try hard, make an effort, attempt
4. _____ prestige
                           d. get rid of completely, erase, do away with
5. _____ diligent
                           e. filled, were present in all parts of
6. _____ resigned
                           f. abuse of power, cruel treatment of people under you
7. _____ notions
                           g. rule, government
8. _____ etiquette
                           h. hardworking, industrious, persistent, reliable
9 _____ strive
                           i. took control of, grabbed
10. _____ tyranny
                           j. lasting, continuing
11. _____ suppress
                           k. ideas, concepts
12. _____ holocaust
                           l. gave up, quit
13. _____ dynasty
                           m. push down, stop something from having an influence
14. _____ seized
                           n raised, brought up
15. _____ eradicate
                           o. good manners, correct way of acting

Finding Facts to Support or Disprove General Statements

Look for specific facts in your reading to support or disprove general statements about a subject. This will help give you a clearer idea about that subject.

6 Finding Facts to Support or Disprove General Statements Working with a small group, read the following four statements about Confucius aloud and decide whether they are true or false. Then find specific facts in the reading to support or disprove them. Compare your ideas with those of another group.

1. Confucius was a commoner, from a humble background.

2. He was a brilliant man who achieved greatness through the help of rich and influential friends.

3. The philosophy of Confucius has always been admired and respected in China.

4. A society that follows Confucian teachings would be orderly and peaceful.

7 Guided Academic Conversation In small groups, discuss the following questions.

1. In your opinion, why has Confucianism had such an enduring influence?

2. How do you think that governments should exert control over their citizens? Should some ideas be prohibited? Can ideas really be prohibited? Explain.

3. What do you think of the Golden Rule? Is it a universal rule for human behavior? Why or why not?

4. Some people believe that even in the world of today, *jen* and *li* are still the two most important principles for human social behavior. On two large pieces of paper, work in your group to draw representations of what *jen* and *li* mean to you, *jen* on one paper and *li* on the other. These can be elaborate drawings, stick figures, simple objects representing the concept, or even words that represent it well. (**Hint:** for *li* you might think particularly of etiquette or rituals particular to a culture or society that your group thinks are good.) Then each group in turn explains their drawing in front of the class.

8 What Do You Think? Rating Leaders Remarkable leaders—history makers—can be either good or bad. Brainstorm some examples of those leaders who most people would consider good and those who most people would consider bad. Do a search on the Internet to identify a leader you think of as particularly good or bad, and bring in some information on this leader to share with the class. Each student should write the name of the leader he or she chose on the board, and tell what is good or bad about that leader.

9 Rating Leaders Using a Continuum Graph In groups, try to place all the leaders chosen by the class on a continuum graph to show which ones you think did the most harm and the most good for their communities and the world. Then discuss the questions below.

The Most Harm   The Most Good

1. What makes the difference between a good leader and a bad leader?
2. Do both types have some of the same characteristics? What are they?
3. Can a leader be both good and bad? Give some examples.

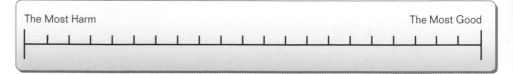

PART 2 Main Ideas and Details

Courage Begins with One Voice

Before You Read

Reading Tip

You can see from the title and illustrations that the following article is about people who show great courage in working for human rights. An article like this usually includes a general description of the subject and specific examples, but these can be organized in various ways.

1 Previewing to Determine Organization Look at the following three patterns of organization. Then skim the article and decide which pattern is used. Circle the number of the pattern used in the article.

1. Two or more specific examples / General description
2. General description / Two or more specific examples
3. One lively specific example / General description / Other specific examples

2 Using Expressive Synonyms Find synonyms (words or phrases) from the reading to replace the common words and phrases in italics.

1. There is a common _____ (*complaint*) that there are no more heroes…

2. … these women and men spoke to me with compelling _____ (*speaking ability*)…

3. Their determination, _____ (*bravery*), and commitment…

4. … in the face of _____ (*very great*) danger…

5 … challenge each of us to _____ (*work*) for a more decent society. (Look for a four-word expression.)

6. The crisis of authority is one of the causes for all the _____ (*cruel acts*)...

7. ... and a writer of _____ (*strong*) essays on repression and dissent.

8. ... they are still ready to _____ (*give up*) their lives...

9. Today, she _____ (*keeps track of*) rights violations...

10. ... the two greatest _____ (*barriers*) to human progress...

11. The decisions we make about how to _____ (*lead*) our lives...

12. ... to _____ (*pay*) for the alleged crimes of their relatives.

Read

Introduction
Kerry Kennedy has interviewed impressive people who are doing great things for their fellow human beings in countries as diverse as India, the Czech Republic, Cambodia, Costa Rica, and Ghana. Read the following selection to learn more about courage and five heroes who possess this quality.

- Can you guess what kinds of humanitarian work these "heroes" are doing?
- If you were to choose one person to add to a list of courageous individuals who help society, whom would you choose?

"Courage Begins with One Voice"

A   There is a common lament that there are no more heroes... That perception is wrong. I have spent the last two years interviewing 51 people from 40 countries about the nature of courage. Imprisoned, tortured, threatened with death, these women and men spoke to me with compelling eloquence on the subjects to which they have devoted their lives and for which they are willing to sacrifice them—from free expression to women's rights, from environmental defense to eradicating slavery.

B   Among them are the internationally celebrated, including Nobel Prize laureates. But most of them are unknown and (as yet) unsung beyond their national boundaries... Their determination, valor, and commitment in the face of overwhelming danger challenge each of us to take up the torch for a more decent society.

Kailash Satyarthi, India
C   "Small children of six, seven years and older are forced to work 14 hours a day without a break or a day for rest," says Kailash Satyarthi of the more than six million children in India who work in bonded labor—a form of slavery

▲ Kailash Satyarthi, India (58)

where a desperate family is forced to hand over a child as guaranty for a debt. "If they cry for their parents, they are beaten and tortured. They are often kept half-fed and are not permitted to talk or laugh out loud." Since 1990, Satyarthi has helped to free more than 40,000 people, including 28,000 children, from overcrowded, filthy, and isolated factories, particularly in the massive carpet industry. "I have faced threats, and two of my colleagues have been killed," says Satyarthi, who heads the South Asian Coalition on Child Servitude. "But I think of it all as a test. If you decide to stand up against such social evils, you have to be fully prepared— physically, mentally, and spiritually."

Vaclav Havel, Czech Republic

D   "The crisis of authority is one of the causes for all the atrocities we are seeing in the world today," says Vaclav Havel, 63, Czechoslovakia's leading playwright and a writer of compelling essays on repression and dissent. "The postcommunist world presented a chance for new moral leaders. But gradually people were repressed, and much of that opportunity was lost." In 1989, he was elected president of the newly formed Czech Republic, the first non-communist leader in more than 40 years. Havel remains one of democracy's most principled voices. "There are certain leaders one can respect, like the Dalai Lama," he says. "Although often they have no hope, they are still ready to sacrifice their lives and their freedom.

▲ Vaclav Havel, Czech Republic (1936–2011)

They are ready to assume responsibility for the world—or the part of the world they live in. Courage means going against majority opinion in the name of the truth."

Kek Galabru, Cambodia

E   There are around 600 to 900 people tortured by the police in custody every year to whom we give medical assistance," says Kek Galabru, 58. "Without us they would die." A medical doctor, Galabru played a key role in

▲ Dr. Kek Galabru, Cambodia (70)

opening negotiations that led to the 1991 peace accords ending the Cambodian civil war, which left more than a million people dead.

F   Today, she monitors rights violations through the Cambodian League for the Promotion and Defense of Human Rights, which she founded. "Many times with our work, we are so depressed," she says. "It could be so easy for us to take our suitcases, take an airplane, and not look back. But then we say, 'Impossible, they trust us.' When a victim comes to see us and says, 'I know I would have died if you were not here,' that gives us more energy. If we only save one person, it's a victory."

Oscar Arias Sanchez, Costa Rica

G   "War, and the preparation for war, are the two greatest obstacles to human progress, fostering a vicious cycle of arms buildups, violence, and poverty," says Oscar Arias Sanchez, 60, the former president of Costa Rica.* Arias was awarded the Nobel Peace Prize in 1987 for his role in ending conflict in Central America. He continues to campaign for democracy and demilitarization worldwide. "Three billion people live in tragic poverty," he says, "and 40,000 children die each day from diseases that could be prevented. War is a missed opportunity for humanitarian investment. It is a crime against every child who calls out for food rather than for guns. The decisions we make about how to conduct our lives, about the kind of people we want to be, have important consequences. It is clear that one must stand on the side of life."

Juliana Dogbadzi, Ghana

H   "When I was seven, my parents sent me to a shrine where I was a slave to a fetish priest for 17 years," says Juliana Dogbadzi, 26, referring to the

▲ Oscar Arias Sanchez, Costa Rica (72)

*After this article was written, former president Oscar Arias Sanchez was reelected president of Costa Rica in 2006. He completed his term in 2010.

▲ *Trokosi* women

religious and cultural practice known as *Trokosi*, in which young girls, mostly virgins, are sent into servitude to atone for the alleged crimes of their relatives. "Each day, we woke up at 5:00 A.M., cleaned the compound, prepared a meal for the priest, worked until 6:00 P.M. and returned to sleep without food," she says. Sexual services also were required, resulting in unwanted pregnancies. 100

"Unlike most of the others," says Dogbadzi, "I got over the fear instilled by the *Trokosi* system. This was my weapon." Today, after a daring escape, she travels the country speaking out against *Trokosi* and trying to win freedom for other slaves. "What I do is dangerous," she says, "but I am prepared to die for a good cause." 105

Source: "Courage Begins With One Voice" *Parade Magazine* (Kerry Kennedy) from *Speak Truth to Power* (Kerry Kennedy)

After You Read

FOCUS

Identifying The Voices In a Reading

An author sometimes presents different voices in an article by quoting (repeating) the exact words of other people. This adds interest and variety to the reading. It is important to notice when the author speaks and when it is someone else.

3 Identifying the Voices In this reading, all five of the human rights heroes are quoted. Read the quotations from the reading and match the letter of the correct speaker to each quotation.

1. _____ "War, and the preparation for war, are the two greatest obstacles to human progress,…"

2. _____ "I have faced threats, and two of my colleagues have been killed… But I think of it all as a test."

3. _____ "The post-communist world presented a chance for new moral leaders. But gradually people were repressed, and much of that opportunity was lost."

4. _____ "Each day, we woke up at 5:00 A.M., cleaned the compound, prepared a meal for the priest, worked until 6:00 P.M. and returned to sleep without food,…"

5. _____ "Many times with our work, we are so depressed. It could be so easy for us to take our suitcases, take an airplane, and not look back."

a. Kailash Satyarthi, India

b. Vaclav Havel, Czech Republic

c. Kek Galabru, Cambodia

d. Oscar Arias Sanchez, Costa Rica

e. Juliana Dogbadzi, Ghana

FOCUS

Using Noun Suffixes to Create New Words

Various suffixes (*-ance, -ence, -itude, -ity, -ment, -tion, -sion*) are commonly added to verbs or adjectives to turn them into nouns. Some examples include: *performance, gratitude, clarity, commitment, examination, confusion*. Sometimes small spelling changes are also necessary, as when we change *accountable* to *accountability*.

4 **Using Noun Suffixes to Create New Words** Read the sentences below. In each blank write the correct noun that is described in parentheses, using the italicized word plus a suffix. The nouns are from the reading.

1. That (way to *perceive*) _____perception_____ is wrong.

2. From free (action to *express*) _____ to women's rights,…

3. Their determination, valor, and (choice to *commit*) _____

   in the face of overwhelming danger…

4. … and a writer of compelling essays on (act to *repress*)

   _____ and dissent.

5. They are ready to assume (the attitude of being *responsible*)

   _____ for the world…

6. … we give medical (action to *assist*) _____,…

7. A medical doctor, Galabru played a key role in opening (actions to *negotiate*)

   _____ …

8. War, and the (action to *prepare*) _____ for war, ...

9. He continues to campaign for democracy and (the act to *demilitarize*) _____ worldwide.

10. War is a missed opportunity for humanitarian (action to *invest*) _____.

11. The (choices to *decide*) _____ we make...

12. ... young girls, mostly virgins, are sent into (obligation to *serve*) _____...

5 **Focusing on Words from the Academic Word List** Use the most appropriate word from the box to fill in each of the blanks below in the paragraphs taken from Part 2. Do NOT look back at the reading right away; instead, first see if you can remember the vocabulary. Check your answers on pages 162–163.

assistance	depressed	founded	monitors	role
civil	energy	medical	promotion	violations

E   "There are around 600 to 900 people tortured by the police in custody every year to whom we give medical _____," says Kek Galabru, 58. "Without us they would die." A _____ doctor, Galabru played a key _____ in opening negotiations that led to the 1991 peace accords ending the Cambodian _____ war, which left more than a million people dead.

F   Today, she _____ rights _____ through the Cambodian League for the _____ and Defense of Human Rights, which she _____. "Many times with our work, we are so _____," she says. "It could be so easy for us to take our suitcases, take an airplane, and not look back. But then we say, 'Impossible, they trust us.' When a victim comes to see us and says, 'I know I would have died if you were not here,' that gives us more _____. If we only save one person, it's a victory."

6 **Guided Academic Conversation: How Do You Measure Courage?** Not all questions have correct answers; some answers are a matter of opinion. It is often interesting to exchange opinions with others. Discuss the following questions with two or more classmates. Use specific points and examples from the reading to support your point of view. Then compare your opinions with those of other groups.

1. Judging from what you have read in the article, which of the five people mentioned has faced the most danger? Why? Who are the enemies of that person and why do they want to do harm to him or her?

2. Which of these people has the most difficult life? Do you think that his/her life will improve in the future or not? Explain.

3. Most people want to be happy. Are these people happy or not? What motivates them to keep on doing the work they are doing? Would you want this kind of life for yourself? Why or why not?

4. In your opinion, which of these people is the most courageous? Why?

PART 3 **Tying It All Together**

1 **Making Connections** Work by yourself or with a partner on one of the following research tasks. Look on the Internet or in the library for specific examples to answer the questions and find interesting facts to report back to the class.

1. **Confucius in the World Today** How do modern Chinese people view the teachings of Confucius? Are his books still selling? Does he influence movies or popular culture? Does his influence extend to other countries besides China? What other Chinese philosophers are popular now?

2. **Update on Courage** Look up any one of the people presented in the article, "Courage Begins with One Voice" and find more information on what they are doing. What are their most recent activities? If that person has died, are there other people continuing their work? What is the popular opinion about them and their work? Are there any people who speak against them? Explain.

3. **A Hero (or Heroine) from My Own Culture** Find a hero or heroine from your own culture who is alive today or whose influence continues on, even if he or she has died. You may choose a philosopher, writer, politician, entertainer, sports star— anyone you admire. Explain why this person is remarkable and how he or she has influenced others.

Writing Tip: Using a Venn Diagram to Compare and Contrast

To write a paper that compares and/or contrasts two things or people, start by making three lists: one about the qualities unique to one thing or person, one about the qualities unique to the other, and one about the things they have in common. Using a Venn diagram will help you to better visualize the comparison and the contrast. (Put the similarities in circle C and the different traits of one individual in circle A and of the other individual in circle B.) Hand this in with your finished essay so your teacher can see the process you used to prepare for writing.

2 **Comparing and Contrasting Two Leaders** Choose any two of the leaders you have learned about in this chapter and that you think would be interesting to compare and contrast. You can choose them from the readings or from the research you did on the Internet.

Step 1. List the most important similarities and differences between these two remarkable people. For this purpose, use a Venn diagram, like the one below, to set out your thoughts clearly on the similarities and differences.

Person 1: _____   Person 2: _____

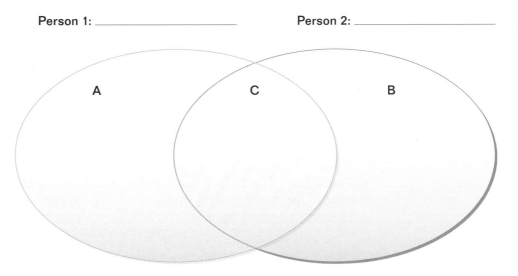

Step 2: Write an introductory paragraph describing each person and his or her importance and influence. Try to write a sentence to end this paragraph that expresses your view or the main overall point that you will want to make after considering the points you made in your diagram or list in Step 1.

Step 3: Write paragraph 2 describing similarities between the two. (You can include words such as: *similarly, like, in the same way*.)

Step 4: Write paragraph 3 describing the differences between the two. (You can include words such as: on the other hand, but, unlike, in contrast to.)

Step 5: Write a concluding paragraph summarizing your main point about these two leaders.

Step 6: After you have finished your paper, read and revise what you have written. Make sure that a sentence in the introduction does indeed express the direction you have taken in your conclusion. Be sure to think of a good title and write it at the top of your essay. Your teacher may also want to see your Venn diagram and preparatory notes.

FOCUS ON TESTING

TOEFL® iBT

Sentence-Insertion Questions on Tests

For each reading on the TOEFL® Internet-Based Test (iBT), a one sentence-insertion question is asked. In the reading you will see four dark squares. Your job is to find the square that marks the best place to add the new sentence. Here is an example of this type of question.

Example

Notice the four squares [■] that indicate where the following sentence could be added to the passage.

Most deep-vein coal mining is now done by machine, not by human workers.

Where would the sentence best fit?

Click on a square [■] to add the sentence to the passage.

Notice that you must click on a square within the reading passage, not within a list of options. This lets you actually see how the sentence fits into each of four contexts. After you have looked at all four possibilities, you should choose the place where it fits most smoothly and accurately.

Practice

Read the following short passage about dangerous jobs. Answer the sentence-insertion question that follows.

The Most Dangerous Jobs in the U.S.

A   What is the most dangerous work you can do? In other words, which jobs give you the greatest chance of being harmed while at work? The Bureau of Labor Statistics (part of the U.S. Department of Labor) has issued reports that try to answer this question. It has drawn up a list of the top ten most dangerous jobs, based on the number of persons killed in various types of work.

B   One clear pattern in the statistics is that weather makes a big difference. No occupation in the top ten is an office-based or factory-based job. Instead, all of the most hazardous jobs involve working outside or in motor vehicles. Fishing is the most dangerous, more than 20 times as hazardous as the average job in the United States. Logging (cutting down trees) is almost equally dangerous. Workers in both of these jobs face tough weather conditions, including storms that can overturn boats, topple trees, or unleash deadly lightning bolts. Loggers also worry about trees that fall in an uncontrolled way after being cut. Getting struck by a heavy object is the leading cause of death among timber-cutters. ■

C   Crashes are the biggest threats to airplane pilots (3rd on the top ten list) and truck drivers (9th). ■ Both problems could be reduced by performing better maintenance on vehicles and by reducing tiredness or stress in the pilots and drivers. ■ Icy, wet, or foggy conditions often contribute to the worst crashes. Other kinds of vehicle-related accidents—tractors falling over, construction machinery striking someone, etc.—are not actually crashes but can be deadly. They are the leading cause of death among construction workers (6th on the list) and farmers (10th). ■

D   Working in high places is very hazardous as well. Metalworkers on buildings (4th on the list), roofers (5th), and construction workers (6th) all need safer harnesses and other equipment to reduce the rate of falls. They also need to be more cautious when bad weather approaches, because they are often exposed to lightning strikes.

E   Finally, there are occupations that work with inherently dangerous things or people. Electricity has profound power, and it is no surprise that people who install electrical systems are on the list (8th). Taxi-cab drivers don't have to fear accidents as much as their own customers. Drivers who work at night are often the targets of violent criminals who hope to steal a driver's money. They are 7th on the list because so many of them are attacked by customers trying to rob them.

Question:

Notice the four squares [■] that indicate where the following sentence could be added to the passage.

Working in the air or on the road involves exposure to weather hazards as well.

Where would the sentence best fit?

Click on a square [■] to add the sentence to the passage.

NOTE: Because this is not a computer-based test, circle a square to add it to the passage.

Self-Assessment Log

Read the lists below. Check (✓) the strategies and vocabulary that you learned in this chapter. Look through the chapter or ask your instructor about the strategies and words that you do not understand.

Reading and Vocabulary-Building Strategies

- ☐ Skimming for the general idea
- ☐ Figuring out words from structure clues
- ☐ Forming new words from the same word family
- ☐ Finding facts to support or disprove general statements
- ☐ Previewing to determine organization
- ☐ Using expressive synonyms
- ☐ Identifying the voices in a reading
- ☐ Using noun suffixes to create new words

Target Vocabulary

Nouns

- assistance*
- atrocities
- background
- childhood
- commitment*
- commoners
- cornerstones
- decisions
- defender
- demilitarization
- dynasty
- eloquence
- energy*
- etiquette
- expression
- (the) Golden Rule
- holocaust
- innovator*
- investment*
- lament
- negotiations
- notions*
- obstacles
- outlook

- perception*
- preparation
- prestige
- principality
- promotion*
- repression
- responsibility
- role*
- servitude
- tyranny
- valor
- violations*

Verbs

- atone
- conduct*
- eradicate
- founded*
- modernize
- monitors*
- permeated
- reared
- resigned
- sacrifice

- seized
- strive
- suppress

Adjectives

- benevolent
- civil*
- compelling
- Confucian
- depressed*
- diligent
- enduring
- governmental
- influential
- medical*
- overwhelming
- philosophical*
- political

Adverbs

- easily
- primarily*

Expression

- take up the torch

*These words are from the Academic Word List. For more information on this list, see www.victoria.ac.nz/lals/resources/academicwordlist/

8 Creativity

> "Creativity comes from looking for the unexpected and stepping outside of your own experience."
>
> Masaru Ibuka
> Co-founder of Sony

Why are some people more creative than others? Are we born with the ability to create or is it something that we can learn? In this chapter, we explore the creative process of a man from the early 20th century, Thomas Edison, who had 1,093 patents for inventions. Then we take a look at two 21st century creative geniuses, architect Zaha Hadid and technology geek, Steve Jobs.

Connecting to the Topic

1. Look at the photo of the statue on page 172. It is one of the most revered works of sculpture in the world. Do you know the name of this famous statue? Why do you think it is so famous? What is the name of the artist who created it?

2. The quote on page 172 is by a businessman who, with a partner, developed a well-known company. What do you think the quote means?

3. What are the many fields of creativity? What are some of the most famous works of art or inventions of all time?

Pure Genius

Before You Read

1 **Scanning for Compound Words** The article "Pure Genius" on page 177 about the famous inventor Thomas Edison contains many compound words. Scan the article for the compound words described below and write them in the blanks provided. (If necessary, look back at the Strategy *Understanding Compound Words* in Chapter 1, page 10, and review it.) The items are listed in the order of their appearance in the reading.

▲ Portrait of Thomas Alva Edison, taken in 1921

Example

an invention, beginning with *t*, useful for writers and journalists

typewriter

1. a hyphenated adjective starting with *c*, describing the material used in the mold for a concrete house

_____

2. the 3,500 things that Edison recorded his notes in

_____

3. a hyphenated adjective describing the vaults (storage chambers) where these notes are kept

_____

4. a noun starting with *b*, expressing the turbulent (excited) action of Edison's mind at work

_____

5. an adjective beginning with *e*, and referring to ordinary life

_____

6. a hyphenated adjective describing a contraption (gadget, machine) that was pulled by horses

_____

7. a hyphenated adjective beginning with *l*, and describing a type of filament (thread)

_____

8. a noun starting with *s*, referring to flexible boards used by gymnasts for jumping in the air

_____

9. a hyphenated adjective starting with *h*, describing people who don't hear well

_____

10. a hyphenated adjective beginning with *s*, meaning "doubtful"

_____

11. an adjective beginning with *d*, describing something fundamental or essential to a person

_____

12. a three-word hyphenated adjective describing the nature of many of Edison's works

_____

Strategy

Recognizing Nouns and Verbs by Definition and Context

In English, as in many other languages, the same word can often function as either a noun or a verb. Two examples are the words *address* and *buy*. Consider the following sentences as examples. In which sentences does the underlined word function as a noun? In which does it function as a verb? How do you know?

- The new president will <u>address</u> the meeting tonight.
- The <u>address</u> of the hotel is printed on the card.
- We are sure that this is the best <u>buy</u>.
- They will <u>buy</u> the building next year in the spring.

The meaning of the words are often (but not always) similar, whether they function as verbs or nouns, but their pronunciation will sometimes be different with the stress coming on a different syllable.* Is this the case in the examples above? Explain. Notice that the way to determine the meaning and function of words is by their context.

*A good dictionary will show you the different stress patterns.

Choose the correct words from the list to fill in the blanks by examining their context and the definitions given in parenthesis. (Can you find the three words in the list that can function as either noun or verb depending on context?)

assumptions	dud	patents	quotas
conduct	generate	persist	research
deficiencies	inspiration	quantity	rethink

1. Thomas Edison was granted 1,093 (*licenses for use*) _____ for his inventions…

2. He did not hire people who had too many (*beliefs accepted without proof*) _____ built into their everyday life.

3. Edison tried to continually (*produce*) _____ many ideas.

4. He felt that out of (*a large amount*) _____ would come quality.

5. He set idea (*number requirements*) _____ for all his workers.

6. He once said that genius is 99% perspiration (sweat) and 1% (*emotional or intellectual stimulation*) _____.

7. For every brilliant idea Edison had there was a (*thing that failed*) _____ like the horse-drawn contraption that would collect snow…

8. He would (*perform, carry out*) _____ experiments on will power again and again to see if he could move an object with his mind alone.

9. He continued to (*keep on trying*) _____ even after failing thousands of times.

10. At times Edison would review his notebooks to (*consider again*) _____ ideas and inventions he'd abandoned in the past.

11. He would (*investigate carefully*) _____ failed ideas of other inventors to see if he could adapt them to new inventions.

12. He believed strongly that we can often turn (*defects, weaknesses*) _____ to our advantage.

Introduction

There are many kinds of creative people. Some seem to be mad geniuses, creating works that shock the public and only later come to be accepted as brilliant. This was not the case of the great American inventor Thomas Edison who, with precision, care, and hard work, invented many devices and came up with new ideas that would change human life forever. The following reading describes both the man and his methods.

Pure Genius

A Thomas Edison was granted 1,093 patents for inventions that ranged from the light bulb, typewriter, electric pen, phonograph, motion picture camera, and alkaline storage battery—to the talking doll and a concrete house that could be built in one day from a cast-iron mold. When he died in 1931, he left 3,500 notebooks which are preserved today in the temperature-controlled ⁵ vaults of the West Orange Laboratory Archives at the Edison National Historic Site in New Jersey. The pages read like a turbulent brainstorm and present a verbal and visual biography of Edison's mind at work.

B Here are a few creativity lessons that emerge from a review of the way he worked: ¹⁰

1. Challenge All Assumptions.

C Before hiring an assistant, Edison would invite the candidate over for soup. If the person salted the soup before tasting it, Edison would not hire him for the job. He did not hire people who had too many assumptions built into their everyday life. He wanted people who consistently challenged assumptions.

2. Quantity.

D He believed to discover a good idea you had to generate many ideas. Out ¹⁵ of quantity comes quality. He set idea quotas for all his workers. His own quota was one minor invention every 10 days and a major invention every six months. It took over 50,000 experiments to invent the alkaline storage cell battery and 9,000 to perfect the light bulb. Edison looked at creativity as simply good, honest, hard work. Genius, he once said, is 99% perspiration ²⁰ and 1% inspiration. For every brilliant idea he had there was a dud like the horse-drawn contraption that would collect snow and ice in the winter and compress it into blocks that families could use in the summer as a refrigerant.

3. Nothing is Wasted.

E When an experiment failed, he would always ask what the failure revealed and would enthusiastically record what he had learned. His notebooks contain ²⁵ pages of material on what he learned from his abortive ideas, including his many experiments on will power. He conducted countless experiments with rubber tubes extended from his forehead trying to will the physical movement of a pendulum. Once when an assistant asked why he continued to persist trying to discover a long-lasting filament for the light bulb after failing thousands of times, Edison explained that he didn't understand the question. In his mind he hadn't failed once. Instead, he said he discovered thousands of things that didn't work. Finally, he completed Patent 251,539 for the light bulb that ensured his fame and fortune. Whenever he succeeded with a new idea, he would review his notebooks to rethink ideas and inventions he'd abandoned in the past in the light of what he'd recently learned.

4. Constantly Improve Your Ideas and Products and the Ideas and Products of Others.

▲ Edison did not invent the light bulb; he perfected it for consumer use.

F   Contrary to popular belief, Edison did not invent the light bulb: his genius, rather, was to perfect the bulb as a consumer item. Edison also studied all his inventions and ideas as springboards for other inventions and ideas in their own right. To Edison, the telephone (sounds transmitted) suggested the phonograph (sounds recorded), which suggested motion pictures (images recorded). Simple, in retrospect, isn't it? Genius usually is.

G   Edison would often jot down titles of books, failed patents, and research papers written by other inventors. He would research them and try to figure out where those inventors quit or left off, so his own patentable work could begin. He advised his assistants to adapt the ideas of others. He told them to make it a habit to keep on the lookout for novel and interesting ideas that others have used successfully. To Edison, your idea needs to be original only in its adaptation to the problem you are working on.

5. Turn Deficiencies to Your Advantage.

H   No one knows for sure what caused Edison's hearing problems, but after the age of twelve he could no longer hear birds singing. As a teenager working in a telegraph office jammed with clattering telegraph machines, he viewed his poor hearing as a distinct advantage because he could focus on his instrument on his desk and not be distracted. As a renowned inventor, he received pleas from hearing-impaired people all over the world to invent a hearing aid, but he declined believing this so-called disability gave him valuable mental space in which to think.

6. Record Your Ideas and Thoughts.

I   Edison had a deep-seated need to articulate his ideas on paper, to see for himself the relentlessly cause-and-effect nature of many of his works. Leonardo da Vinci was Edison's spiritual mentor, and his notebooks illustrate the depth of their kinship. An obsessive draftsman, hoarder of ideas, supreme egoist, engineer, and botanist—a conceptual inventor, scientist, and mathematician, Edison recorded and illustrated every step on his voyage to discovery.

Source: "Pure Genius" from *Psychology Today* (Michael Michalko)

3 **Matching Set Phrases or Expressions to their Context** Set phrases or expressions are groups of words that have a special meaning when used together. Read the following sentences taken from the article about Thomas Edison and match each set phrase from the list to the description of its meaning that is given in parentheses.

Example

The pages read like a turbulent brainstorm and present a verbal and visual biography of Edison's mind (*while it is in operation*) _____*at work*_____.

as springboards	for sure	in the light of
at work	in his mind	on the lookout
contrary to popular belief	in retrospect	

1. Once when an assistant asked why he persisted… after failing thousands of times, Edison explained that he didn't understand the question. (*The way he thought about it*) _____ he hadn't failed once.

2. Whenever he succeeded with a new idea, he would review his notebooks to rethink ideas… he'd abandoned… (*by considering them in the context of*) _____ what he'd recently learned.

3. (*In contrast to what most people imagine*) _____, Edison did not invent the light bulb…

4. Edison also studied all his inventions and ideas (*to use as a means of inspiration*) _____ for other inventions and ideas…

5. To Edison, the telephone (sounds transmitted) suggested the phonograph (sounds recorded), which suggested motion pictures (images recorded). Simple, (*when you think back on it*) _____, isn't it?

6. He told them (his assistants)… to keep (*being observant and watchful*) _____ for novel… ideas that others have used successfully.

7. No one knows (*with certainty*) _____ what caused Edison's hearing problems…

Strategy

Inferring Character from Actions

Sometimes a reading does not describe directly the character (personality) of an historical figure; instead it tells about that person's life and actions. From what that person did or did not do, we can then infer (draw conclusions about) what he or she was like. For example, someone who spent a great deal of time alone and did not enjoy talking with other people was probably shy (timid) or introverted.

4 Inferring Character from Actions: True or False Based on what you have read about Edison's life and actions, which of the following inferences about his character are true? Place *T* in front of those and *F* in front of the inferences that do not apply to Edison. Support your choices with facts from the reading.

Thomas Edison was…

1. _____ a confirmed pessimist

2. _____ a strict and demanding boss

3. _____ a well-rounded individual with many hobbies and interests

4. _____ a workaholic

5. _____ an easy-going man who had many brilliant ideas

6. _____ an original thinker with no need to study the works of others

7. _____ an outgoing family man with lots of friends.

8. _____ generous and compassionate

9. _____ patient, careful, and disciplined

10. _____ sloppy and badly organized

5 Guided Academic Conversation In small groups, discuss the following questions. Afterwards, compare your answers with those of another group.

1. In the light of all that has happened since Thomas Edison's death in 1931, which of his inventions do you consider the most important? Why? Which ones mentioned in the article are not very important in retrospect? Explain.

2. How did Edison test people who applied to work as his assistant? Which ones did he hire, and why? What do you think of this test? What kinds of tests do people have to pass nowadays when applying for a job?

3. Thomas Edison believed that "out of quantity comes quality." What did he mean by that? Do you agree with him or not? Why? Is this a fact or an opinion?

4. The article states, "For every brilliant idea he had there was a dud …" Do you think that is true of all creative people or not? Explain.

5. Why did Edison refuse, when hearing-impaired people from all over the world begged him to invent a hearing aid? What do you think of this decision?

6 **What Do You Think?** Read the paragraph below and in small groups discuss the questions that follow.

On Being Creative

Do you sometimes think that you would like to be a creative genius? Maybe you go to an art museum and see a painting by Monet or Rembrandt, or a mural by Diego Rivera, and think, "I wish I could paint that." Or you go to a concert hall where the orchestra is playing a Beethoven symphony or a piano sonata by Chopin, and you sit stunned at the beauty of the music. Maybe you go to a jazz club and listen to an improvised riff by a piano player or jazz trombonist, and you wonder, "How could he do that?" Whatever the discipline, you have to admire the creative process that produces a work of art or a technological invention.

1. What is your best description of a creative genius?
2. If you were to create something, what would it be? Which creative field do you think is the most difficult?
3. Who are your favorite composers, either classical, modern, or someone from your culture? Who are your favorite artists?
4. If you were a technological genius, what would you like to invent?

"I Don't Do Nice"

Before You Read

1 **Previewing an Interview for Organization and Key Ideas** Previewing before you read almost always aids comprehension. Working by yourself or with a partner, use these questions to preview the interview that follows.

1. **Photos.** By looking at the photos, what can you infer about the person being interviewed? Look also at the brief introduction given at the very beginning of the interview. What information does it give us?

2. **Title.** Scan the interview to find an explanation for the title, which appears to be the exact words of this person. What does it mean? What can you infer about her from these words?

3. **Organization of questions and answers.** An interview is based on questions asked by an interviewer and answers given by the person being interviewed (sometimes called the *interviewee*). There are two basic types of organization of an interview: (a) listing the exact questions asked by the interviewer, each one followed by the exact answer given to it by the interviewee, or (b) a detailed description of the characteristics, work and life of the person being interviewed, along with direct quotes by that person to show examples. Which of these two types of organization is used in this interview? In your opinion, what advantages or disadvantages does it have?

2 **Guessing the Meaning of Words from Structure and Context** Use structure clues (such as finding a smaller word inside a larger one) or the context to guess the meaning of each italicized word in the phrases taken from the interview. Fill in the bubble of the correct synonym or definition for each one.

1. Zaha Hadid is talking me through her latest *commissions*. (The article then mentions a bridge, a terminal, a skyscraper, a museum, an opera house...)

   (A) books written about her projects

   (B) people who assist in designing

   (C) prizes won in competitions

   (D) works ordered by her clients

2. Magazines fight for *"exclusives"* on our latest buildings.

   (A) agreements to publish the only article

   (B) descriptions of the mistakes and problems

   (C) invitations to the opening celebrations

   (D) new details to share with others

3. Then we went by boat, and then on a smaller one made of reeds, to visit villages in the *marshes*.

   (A) cities

   (B) deserts

   (C) mountains

   (D) wetlands

4. (After talking about the very old architecture of Iraq, Hadid explains:) "I'm trying to discover... forms of urban planning, that do something of the same thing in a *contemporary* way."

   (A) exciting

   (B) old-fashioned

   (C) pleasant

   (D) up-to-date

5. What's more, she says, architecture requires 100% *dedication*. "If it doesn't kill you, then you're no good. I mean, really—you have to go at it full time."

   (A) education

   (B) hard work and effort

   (C) health

   (D) intelligence

6. … Hadid was brought up in an intellectual family, for whom education and the understanding of other cultures… were an absolute *priority*.

   (A) doubt

   (B) mystery

   (C) main concern

   (D) problem

7. "… when women do succeed, the *press*, even the industry *press*, spend far too much time talking about how we dress, what shoes we're wearing…"

   (A) friends, relatives, and coworkers

   (B) government employees

   (C) magazines and newspapers

   (D) male business associates

8. "Of course, I believe *imaginative* architecture can make a difference to people's lives…"

   (A) complex

   (B) creative

   (C) decorated

   (D) expensive

9. "… but I wish it was possible to *divert* some of the effort we put into ambitious museums and galleries into the basic architectural building blocks of society."

   (A) decrease

   (B) eliminate

   (C) increase

   (D) redirect

10. "We were without work for so long that I haven't lost the habit of saying "yes" to every job. Call this *insecurity*, if you like."

   (A) desire for fame

   (B) fear of safety

   (C) lack of confidence

   (D) love of danger

> ### Introduction
>
> Like Thomas Edison, the world-famous architect Zaha Hadid has excelled by being creative, productive, and extremely hardworking. Her creations are unique, imaginative, and beneficial to people in many parts of the world. But her genius is of a different kind. Where Edison was practical and methodical, Hadid has been varied and fanciful, finding artistic inspiration in diverse forms and unusual places. In the following interview, she ponders her situation as a singular, successful woman in a highly competitive field dominated by men.

"I Don't Do Nice"

A   In the cavernous meeting room of the former school that houses her London-based practice, Zaha Hadid is talking me through her latest

▲ Zaha Hadid at Glasgow's Riverside Museum, which she designed.

commissions. I count about 18 major designs: a bridge in Abu Dhabi; a maritime terminal in Salerno; a library for the University of Seville; a skyscraper in Marseille; a museum of modern art in Rome. There's also an opera house for Dubai that extends out from the auditorium into the sea, like some magnificent starfish.

B   "Magazines fight for "exclusives" on our latest buildings," Hadid explains. "Last year, one design magazine was so crazy to be first to publish the Phaeno Science Centre in Wolfsburg, it sent its reporter dressed in a hard hat pretending to be a construction worker, so he could get the first pictures with a little camera."

C   Architecture has been in Hadid's blood, ever since she first visited Sumer in the south of Iraq, where architecture itself began and the first cities were built. Her father, she says, was a friend of Wilfred Thesiger, the English explorer. "I knew the marshes of southern Iraq from his books and photographs before I ever went there myself. When I did, as a teenager, I was amazed. My father took us to see the Sumerian cities. Then we went by boat, and then on a smaller one made of reeds, to visit villages in the marshes. The beauty of the landscape—where sand, water, reeds, birds, buildings, and people all somehow flowed together—has never left me."

D   It's a landscape that continues to inspire her. "I'm trying to discover— invent, I suppose—an architecture, and forms of urban planning, that do something of the same thing in a contemporary way. I started out trying to create buildings that would sparkle like isolated jewels; now I want them to connect, to form a new kind of landscape, to flow together with contemporary cities and the lives of their peoples."

E   In 2006, Hadid is still the world's only major woman architect, by which I mean an architect who will go down in the history books. "There have been some well-known women architects in the U.S.," she says. "But they have always been part of husband-and-wife teams, like Bob Venturi and Denise Scott Brown (who designed the National Gallery's Sainsbury Wing). There have been very intelligent women architects working in local authorities and government offices worldwide, too. But for a woman to go out alone into architecture is still very, very hard. It's still a man's world."

F   What's more, she says, architecture requires 100% dedication. "If it doesn't kill you, then you're no good. I mean, really—you have to go at it full-time. You can't afford to dip in and out. When women break off to have babies, it's hard for them to reconnect on the big scale. And when women do succeed, the press, even the industry press, spend far too much time talking about how we dress, what shoes we're wearing, who we're meant to be seeing. That's pretty sad for women, especially when it's written by women who really should know better.

G   "In another way, I can be my own worst enemy. As a woman, I'm expected to want everything to be nice, and to be nice myself. A very English thing. I don't design nice buildings—I don't like them. I like architecture to have some raw, vital, earthy quality. You don't need to make concrete perfectly smooth or paint it or polish it. If you consider changes in the play of light on a building before it's built, you can vary the color and feel of concrete by daylight alone. Some winters ago, I flew from New York to Chicago in the snow; at sunset, the landscape and cityscapes became no colors other than

▼ Hadid's Zaragoza Bridge Pavilion in Spain

starkly contrasted black and white, while the rivers and lakes were blood red. Amazing. You wouldn't call that a nice landscape, but it had the quality of light and life I would love to get into our buildings."

H Hadid is a Muslim, but she was educated by Catholic nuns in Baghdad, and then at a school in Switzerland. At home, Hadid was brought up in an intellectual family, for whom education and the understanding of other cultures—there are many in Iraq—were an absolute priority. After the 1958 *coup d'etat* that brought down Feisal, the British-sponsored Iraqi monarch, and before the Ba'ath party seized power 10 years later, education was top of the Iraqi political agenda.

I "When I went to the marsh villages," Hadid says, "there were new schools among the reeds. Girls were being educated for the first time. It was a wonderful, if brief, moment in Iraqi history. Today, there is nothing but destruction.

J Much as Hadid would like to build in Baghdad as well as Beirut, this is hardly the right time. Her efforts are necessarily concentrated elsewhere, in the cultural arena. "What I would really love to build are schools, hospitals, social housing. Of course I believe imaginative architecture can make a difference to people's lives, but I wish it was possible to divert some of the effort we put into ambitious museums and galleries into the basic architectural building blocks of society."

K Meanwhile, she is being asked to design more and more daring buildings: skyscrapers, concert halls, and the Aquatic Centre, or swimming pool, for the 2012 London Olympics. How can she take on so many projects without diluting the inventiveness of her designs? "We were without work for so long that I haven't lost the habit of saying yes to every job. Call this insecurity if you like. I mean, look around you here at the practice: you'll find 150 architects clinging from the rafters. I'm aware that we could slip into a slick mass-production mode, but I don't think we will. Maybe, though, I'll have to start saying no."

Source: "I Don't Do Nice" from *The Guardian* (Jonathan Glancey)

▼ Hadid designed the Aquatics Centre for London's 2012 Olympics.

Strategy

Understanding the Power of Pictorial Language

Using language that presents pictures can be a creative and effective way to express ideas. Pictorial language is vivid and helps a reader to visualize the person, place, or thing being described by comparing it to something well-known or familiar.

Sometimes the picture comes in the form of a *simile*, a comparison that usually starts with *like* or *as*. For example, *Love came into her life suddenly, like a lightning bolt.* Other times, a *metaphor* is used, an implied comparison without the words *like* or *as*. For example, *The moon was a silver ribbon floating on the dark water.*

3 Understanding the Power of Pictorial Language Both the interviewer, Jonathan Glancey, and the interviewee, Zaha Hadid, use pictorial language in the reading selection. Read the following excerpts from the interview and explain what two things are being compared and what effect this has. The first item is done as an example.

1. In the *cavernous* meeting room…

   The room is being compared to a cave. This makes it seem big and set apart from normal life.

2. There's also an opera house for Dubai that extends out… into the sea, *like some magnificent starfish.*

   _____

   _____

3. I started out trying to create buildings that *would sparkle like isolated jewels.*

   _____

   _____

4. … now I want them (the buildings I design) to connect, *to form a new kind of landscape, to flow together with contemporary cities* and the lives of their peoples."

   _____

   _____

5. I like architecture to have some *raw, vital, earthy quality.*

   _____

6. I mean, look around you here at the practice: you'll find 150 architects *clinging from the rafters.*

   _____

4 Focusing on Words from the Academic Word List Use the most appropriate word from the box to fill in each of the blanks in the following paragraph, taken from the reading in Part 2. Do NOT look back at the reading right away; instead, first see if you can remember the vocabulary. Check your answers on pages 184–185.

authorities	create	intelligent	publish
construction	design	isolated	teams
contemporary	designed	major	

B   "Magazines fight for 'exclusives' on our latest buildings," Hadid explains. "Last year, one _____ magazine was so crazy to be first to
_____ the Phaeno Science Centre in Wolfsburg, it sent its
reporter dressed in a hard hat pretending to be a _____ worker,
so he could get the first pictures with a little camera."

D   ... I started out trying to _____ buildings that would
sparkle like _____ jewels; now I want them to connect, to form
a new kind of landscape, to flow together with _____ cities
and the lives of their peoples."

E   ... Hadid is still the world's only _____ woman architect... 10
"There have been some well-known women architects in the US," she says.
"But they have always been part of husband-and-wife _____, like
Bob Venturi and Denise Scott Brown (who _____ the National
Gallery's Sainsbury Wing). There have been very _____
women architects working in local _____ and government 15
offices worldwide, too. But for a woman to go out alone into architecture is
still very, very hard..."

5 **Guided Academic Conversation** In small groups, discuss the following questions. Afterwards, compare your answers with those of another group.

1. What was it about the villages in the marshes that Hadid visited as a young girl that she liked so much? How does it affect what she wants to do now as an architect? What kinds of designs could bring more nature into the cities?

2. Why are there so few women architects? Do you think perhaps that it is not a good job for a woman? Why or why not? Why do you think that Hadid works so hard? Is it really because she has to or because she wants to?

3. According to Zaha Hadid, how does the press treat her because she is a woman? In general, do you think that the press presents men and women politicians or celebrities differently? Or are they treated pretty much the same? Explain.

4. Honestly, what do you think of Hadid's designs? Are there other architects that you admire? What buildings or other constructions make you feel really good? What ones do you consider beautiful?

FOCUS ON TESTING

Thinking Twice about Tricky Questions

The multiple-choice exercise is a common format for testing reading comprehension. Usually it requires you to look back at the reading and scan for information. The items generally follow the order of appearance in the reading, so when you take the test, try looking for the answer to the first question at the beginning of the reading. Continue through the other items from that point on.

Sometimes a multiple-choice question is *tricky* because the answer is not given directly in the reading. Instead, it is necessary to *infer* the correct answer from other facts given in the reading.

The following multiple-choice test is based on the interview of Zaha Hadid. Look at question 1 below for an example of a tricky question. Why is it tricky? What is the right answer? What facts from the interview did you use as a basis for your inference?

1. The famous architect Zaha Hadid can best be described as _____.

   (A) a shy person who tries very hard to be liked by others

   (B) a well-rounded individual with many interests and activities

   (C) a hard worker who doesn't care what other people think

   (D) an emotional, feminine woman devoted to her family

Practice

Complete the rest of the items in the test. Which ones are straight memory questions with answers given directly in the reading? Which ones are tricky and require inferences? Fill in the bubble of the phrase that best completes each sentence.

2. Hadid has designed and built _____.

   (A) a museum of modern art in Italy

   (B) an opera house in Dubai

   (C) a library for a university in Spain

   (D) all of the above and more

3. Her first inspiration to become an architect came to her as a teenager on a trip to villages in the marshes of southern _____.

- (A) Abu Dhabi
- (B) England
- (C) Iraq
- (D) states in the U.S.

4. When Hadid designs, she wants to _____.

- (A) build structures that please everyone
- (B) create a strong emotional response
- (C) make the most money possible
- (D) produce buildings with smooth, polished lines

5. What she would really love to build is _____.

- (A) hospitals, schools, and social housing
- (B) imaginative museums and galleries
- (C) more and more daring buildings
- (D) Olympic swimming pools and aquatic centers

6. In regards to her personal and social life, Hadid _____.

- (A) constantly attends parties and social events
- (B) devotes most of her time to her husband and children
- (C) is probably single and does not socialize much
- (D) likes to be seen and photographed with celebrities

PART **3**   Tying It All Together

 1 **Making Connections** Research one of the following topics using the Internet. Share your findings with the class in the form of an oral report accompanied by notes, photos, and illustrations.

1. Research the life and works of another renowned (well-known) inventor who had different methods from those of Thomas Edison. What are his (or her) most outstanding inventions and how and where are (or were) they used?

2. Research the life and works of another famous architect who has (or had) a very different style from that of Zaha Hadid. What and where has he (or she) built and why have these structures won fame?

3. In Part 1, the author of the reading "Pure Genius" compares Thomas Edison to the well-known Italian artist and inventor Leonardo da Vinci, who lived from 1452 to 1519. Some people would not agree with this comparison. In what ways were these two men similar? In what ways were they different?

4. Camille Claudel, the renowned French sculptress, who lived from 1864 to 1943, was, like Zaha Hadid, a talented artist in a profession dominated by men. However, in many ways, the two women and the societies they lived in were not similar. How are the lives and works of these two famous women different? What reasons can you give to explain some of these differences?

Writing Tip: Make a Plan before Beginning to Describe an Object or Invention

To describe an invention or an object, first figure out a logical sequence (order) for the details or ideas you plan to include. Looking at these details, decide how you want to structure the description. Will you follow a spatial plan, starting at the top and move down, or moving from right to left? Will you start outside (a building) and then move inside? Will you begin with colors and then move to patterns and images? Or will you explain first the appearance and then the uses?

Decide on a plan and make an outline before you begin. Then, feel free to change if you need to do so to make the description clear.

2 **Describing an Architectural Marvel or a Marvelous Machine** Think of a piece of architecture (a building, bridge, tower, stadium, etc.) or a machine (car, airplane, computer, power station) that you consider beautiful and inspiring. Bring a picture (or other illustration) of it to class, but do not show it to anyone. Then write a one- or two-paragraph description of it, following these steps:

Step 1: Make a list of the details that you want to include to show the beauty and importance of this object or machine.

Step 2: Decide on the order that you want to use to present these details and make an outline to show which you will present first, which in the middle, and which ones at the end.

Step 3: Write a strong introductory sentence at the beginning to catch the interest of your reader. For example, you can mention an unusual or striking detail, or you can ask a question to stimulate curiosity.

Step 4: Try to add a sentence at the end that sums up (expresses briefly) your outlook on the art object or invention and shows why it is amazing. Read and revise your sentence, then the whole description to make it as clear and interesting as possible.

Step 5: If there is time, work in a group of five students. Put the pictures (or illustrations) in the middle so everyone can see them but without showing who put each one there. Then take turns reading the descriptions aloud. It should be obvious after each one which picture corresponds to it. Discuss how well the description matches the picture. Does it give a good idea of what the object or invention looks like? Who presented the most accurate description? The most interesting one? Explain.

3 Around the Globe: Steve Jobs, Another Creative Genius for the 21st Century
Read about how Steve Jobs changed the way many of us work, enjoy ourselves, and create things. Before you read, look at the pictures of the devices that this man created. Have you used any of these things? What do you think or know about them? Share your thoughts with a partner. Then read the article and take notes on three or four things from it that you thought were important or interesting. Share these with your partner or the class.

Steve Jobs
1955-2011

Steve Jobs,
Another Creative Genius for the 21st Century

A   Creativity in the 21st century has taken a marked turn toward technology. In the world of instant communication, names like Bill Gates, Mark Zuckerberg, and Steve Wozniak bring to mind creative technological geniuses. But the name most often mentioned in the cyber world as a creative genius is Steve Jobs, co-founder of Apple Inc., one of the most successful companies in history.

B   Paul and Clara Jobs adopted Steve Jobs right after his birth in 1955. Paul Jobs, a machinist, taught his son rudimentary electronics and how to work with his hands. Clara Jobs taught her son to read even before he ever went to school. Young Steve liked to tinker in the family garage with his father, taking apart radios and televisions and rebuilding them.

C   A precocious child, yet a prankster, Steve was often in trouble at school. However, if something interested him, he spent hours working on it, inventing and improving it.

D   In high school, he and his other "technological geek" friends— Bill Fernandez and Steve Wozniak— built their own computer board, which they called

◄ iPad

"The Cream City Computer." The friends spent hours and hours in the garage, listening to music and inventing new technology.

E   Jobs started college in Portland, Oregon, but realizing that college would cost his parents most of their savings and not finding the required courses stimulating, he dropped out after six months. However, Jobs hung around the campus for another 18 months sitting in on courses that interested him—comparing and contrasting different disciplines, combining arts and sciences. One of his favorite courses was calligraphy, a discipline that was to have much impact later in the design of fonts for Apple computers.

▲ iPod

F   After his short stay in college, Jobs traveled to India, searching for spiritual enlightenment. Experimenting in different practices and lifestyles, Jobs eventually found Zen Buddhism, a practice he was to follow all of his life. Jobs said that those who couldn't relate to his counter-culture experience would not ever be able to fully relate to his thinking.

G   Upon returning from India, Jobs went to work for the Atari Company in Los Gatos, California. The computer revolution was burgeoning in this area called Silicon Valley, a place that is known as the core of computer innovation. In 1976, Jobs and his high school friend, Steve Wozniak, started their own enterprise called "Apple Computer Company." They initially made computer boards, but then moved into making their own computers.

H   In 1984, Apple introduced the innovative Macintosh computer to compete with Bill Gates' Microsoft computers. Sales were not as good as expected, however, and the company needed reorganization. Differences among management caused multiple problems. Jobs had hired John Scully away from Microsoft as Apple's CEO, but Scully and Jobs didn't get along and the two of them were often at odds.

I   In May 1985, Jobs called a meeting to depose Scully from his managerial position, but the board, noting Jobs'

◀ MacBook

erratic and temperamental managerial style, sided with Scully. Jobs was fired from Apple, the company he had co-founded. Later, Jobs was to say that being fired from Apple was the best thing that could have happened to him. "The heaviness of being successful was replaced by the lightness of being a beginner again, less sure about everything. It freed me to enter one of the creative periods of my life."

J   Jobs' creative ventures included buying Pixar films, an animated film company, where he produced such popular films as *Toy Story* and *Finding Nemo*.

K   In 1996, Jobs returned to Apple as CEO of the company. Apple went on to create a computer revolution with such products and the MacBook, iTunes, the iPod, the iPhone, and the iPad. Jobs had the technical expertise to see his products through and the demanding personality of a perfectionist. He never released his products before he was sure that they were 99.99 percent perfect.

▲ iPhone

L   But it was his vision that he felt was most important to the company. In the famous graduation speech he gave at Stanford University in 2005, he stated:

M   *Your time is limited, so don't waste it living someone else's life. Don't let the noise of others' opinions drown out your own inner voice.*

N   *This approach has never let me down, and it has made all the difference in my life. The only way to do great work is to love what you do. If you haven't found it yet, keep looking. Don't settle.*

1. Steve Jobs didn't complete his college education. Do you think this was a good idea in his case? Do you think it's generally a good idea for people who are creative?

2. Jobs was fired from Apple in 1985. Why do you think he was fired? Why do you think he was hired back?

3. In the commencement address he gave in 2005 at the Stanford University graduation ceremony, Jobs said "the only way to do great work is to love what you do." Do you think this is necessarily true? Why or why not?

Self-Assessment Log

Read the lists below. Check (✓) the strategies and vocabulary that you learned in this chapter. Look through the chapter or ask your instructor about the strategies and words that you do not understand.

Reading and Vocabulary-Building Strategies

☐ Scanning for compound words
☐ Recognizing nouns and verbs by definition and context
☐ Inferring character from actions
☐ Previewing an interview for organization and key ideas
☐ Understanding the power of pictorial language
☐ Making a plan before beginning to describe an object or invention

Target Vocabulary

Nouns

▨ architect	▨ invention	▨ generate*
▨ architecture	▨ marshes	▨ persist*
▨ assumptions*	▨ mentor	▨ publish*
▨ authorities*	▨ patents	▨ research*
▨ commissions*	▨ priority*	▨ rethink
▨ construction*	▨ quantity	▨ transmitted*
▨ contraption	▨ quotas	
▨ dedication	▨ teams*	**Adjectives**
▨ deficiencies	▨ typewriter	▨ cavernous
▨ design*		▨ conceptual*
▨ draftsman	**Verbs**	▨ contemporary*
▨ dud	▨ articulate	▨ intelligent*
▨ exclusives*	▨ compress	▨ isolated*
▨ experiment	▨ conduct*	▨ major*
▨ genius	▨ create*	▨ imaginative
▨ insecurity	▨ diluting	▨ preserved
▨ inspiration	▨ divert	▨ turbulent

Idioms and Expressions

▨ as springboards
▨ contrary to popular belief
▨ for sure
▨ in the light of
▨ in retrospect
▨ on the lookout

*These words are from the Academic Word List. For more information on this list, see www.victoria.ac.nz/lals/resources/academicwordlist/

9 Human Behavior

"Let a person so act by day that he or she may rest happily by night."

Japanese proverb

In this
CHAPTER

Human behavior can be viewed in many ways.
Anthropologists, psychologists, and sociologists study
human behavior. It has also been observed and recorded
for centuries in literature. In this chapter, we start with a
selection from an anthropology textbook that examines
the way people evaluate their own culture and other
cultures. Next comes a short story that focuses on how
people are influenced by their environment.

Connecting to the Topic

1. Look at the photo. Where are these people? What do you think their
   relationship is to each other?

2. This chapter discusses how people evaluate their own culture and other
   cultures. What difficulties can arise when people do not understand and/
   or value other cultures?

3. In what ways are people influenced by culture?

Ethnocentrism

Before You Read

1 **Skimming for the Main Idea** Skim the first two paragraphs of the article to find the author's explanation of *ethnocentrism* and write it here.

_____

_____

2 **Scanning for the Development of the Main Idea** Scan the article to answer the following questions.

1. Like most readings taken from textbooks, this one is written in rather long paragraphs. How many of the seven paragraphs begin with a sentence containing the word *ethnocentrism*? _____

2. The main idea is the meaning and importance of ethnocentrism. It is developed through examples. Put a check in front of the aspects of human culture that are discussed in the reading as examples of ethnocentrism.

   _____ choice of clothing

   _____ food preferences

   _____ language

   _____ marriage ceremonies

   _____ myths and folktales

3 **Using Prefixes to Build New Words**
   Select the correct prefix to form the new word described in each sentence and based on the word in italics. All these new words are used in the article. Two of the prefixes are used twice. (See page 11 to review what prefixes are.)

   > **Prefixes:** *dis-, in-, ir-, non-, sub-, un-*

   1. Certain groups of people live in both the *arctic* and the

      _subarctic_____.

   2. To some Westerners, it is not *conceivable* that many adults in Asia don't drink

      milk; it is simply _____.

   3. Anthropologists study large *groups* of people which are divided into smaller

      _____

4. People have a tendency to think of those from their own culture as *human* and to view people from other cultures as _____.

5. Customs from our own culture seem *natural*, but customs from other cultures appear _____.

6. The way of thinking of our own ethnic group appears *rational*, but the way of thinking of another ethnic group appears _____.

7. The clothing and food of our own country seems *tasteful*, but the clothing and food of other countries seems _____.

8. It is often hard for someone from a *Western* society to learn the correct manners and customs of a _____ society.

Read

> ### Introduction
> The following reading about ethnocentrism is taken from an anthropology textbook used in classes for English-speaking students at the university level.
>
> - What do you think people learn by studying anthropology?
> - Have you ever taken a course in it? Would you like to? Why or why not?

Ethnocentrism

A   Culture shock can be an excellent lesson in relative values and in understanding human differences. The reason culture shock occurs is that we are not prepared for these differences. Because of the way we are taught in our culture, we are all *ethnocentric*. This term comes from the Greek root *ethnos*, meaning a people or group. Thus, it refers to the fact that our outlook 5 or world view is centered on our own way of life. Ethnocentrism is the belief that one's own patterns of behavior are the best: the most natural, beautiful, right, or important. Therefore, other people, to the extent that they live differently, live by standards that are inhuman, irrational, unnatural, or wrong. 10

B   Ethnocentrism is the view that one's own culture is better than all others; it is the way all people feel about themselves as compared to outsiders. There is no one in our society who is not ethnocentric to some degree, no matter how liberal and open-minded he or she might claim to be. People will always find some aspect of another culture distasteful, be it sexual 15 practices, a way of treating friends or relatives, or simply a food that they cannot manage to get down with a smile. This is not something we should be ashamed of, because it is a natural outcome of growing up in any society.

However, as anthropologists who study other cultures, it is something we should constantly be aware of, so that when we are tempted to make value judgments about another way of life, we can look at the situation objectively and take our bias into account.

C   Ethnocentrism can be seen in many aspects of culture—myths, folktales, proverbs, and even language. For example, in many languages, especially those of non-Western societies, the word used to refer to one's own tribe or ethnic group literally means "mankind" or "human." This implies that members of other groups are less than human. For example, the term *Eskimo*, used to refer to groups that inhabit the arctic and subarctic regions, is an Indian word used by neighbors of the Inuit people who observed their strange way of life but did not share it. The term means "eaters of raw flesh," and as such is an ethnocentric observation about cultural practices that were normal to one group and repulsive to another. On the other hand, if we look at one subgroup among the Alaskan natives, we find them calling themselves *Inuit*, which means "real people" (they obviously did not think eating raw flesh was anything out of the ordinary). Here, then, is a contrast between one's own group, which is real, and the rest of the world, which is not so "real." Both terms, *Eskimo* and *Inuit*, are equally ethnocentric—one as an observation about differences, the other as a self-evaluation. However, *Inuit* is now seen as a more appropriate term because of its origin.

D   Another example of ethnocentrism in language can be found in the origin of the English term *barbarian*. Originally a Greek word, the term was used to refer to tribes that lived around the edge of ancient Greek society. The Greeks referred to these people as barbars because they could not understand their speech. *Bar-bar* was the Greek word for the sound a dog makes, like our word *bow-wow*. The Greeks, in a classic example of ethnocentrism, considered those whose speech they could not understand to be on the same level as dogs, which also could not be understood. They did not grant such people the status of human being, much as the word *Eskimo* gives those people subhuman status.

E   Shifting from language to myths and folktales, we find a good example of ethnocentrism in the creation myth of the Cherokee Indians. According to this story, the Creator made three clay images of a man and baked them in an oven. In his haste to admire his handiwork, he took the first image out of the oven before it was fully baked and found that it was too pale. He waited a while and then removed the second image; it was just right, a full reddish-brown hue. He was so pleased with his work that he sat there and admired it, completely forgetting about the third image. Finally he smelled it burning, but by the time he could rescue it from the oven it had already been burnt, and it came out completely black!

F   Food preferences are perhaps the most familiar aspect of ethnocentrism. Every culture has developed preferences for certain kinds of food and drink, and equally strong negative attitudes toward others. It is interesting to note that much of this ethnocentrism is in our heads and not in our tongues, for

▲ In many Western countries, meat from cows (beef) is a favorite food.

something can taste delicious until we are told what it is. We have all heard stories about people being fed a meal of snake or horse meat or something equally repugnant in American culture and commenting on how tasty it was—until they were told what they had just eaten, upon which they turned green and hurriedly asked to be excused from the table.

G   Certain food preferences seem natural to us. We usually do not recognize that they are natural only because we have grown up with them; they are quite likely to be unnatural to someone from a different culture. In southeast Asia, for example, the majority of adults do not drink milk. To many Americans, it is inconceivable that people in other parts of the world do not drink milk, since to us it is a "natural" food. In China, dog meat is a delicacy; but the thought of eating a dog is enough to make most Americans feel sick. Yet we can see how this is a part of a cultural pattern. Americans keep dogs as pets and tend to think of dogs as almost human. Therefore, we* would not dream of eating dog meat. Horses, too, sometimes become pets, and horse meat is also rejected by most Americans, although not because of its taste...
On the other hand, we generally do not feel affection for cows or pigs, and we eat their meat without any feeling of regret. In India, a cow receives the kind of care that a horse or even a dog receives in our country, and the attitude of Indians toward eating beef is similar to our

▲ In India, cows are considered sacred and not are eaten.

feeling about eating dog meat. On the other hand, in China, dogs are not treated as kindly as they are in the United States. Since they are not pets, the attitude of Chinese people toward dogs is similar to our attitude toward cows.

Source: "Ethnocentrism" *The Human Portrait: Introduction Of Cultural Anthropology, Second Edition* (John Freidl)

*The use of the pronoun *we* shows us that this excerpt is from a textbook used primarily in U.S. universities. The American author discusses the ethnocentrism of his own people.

4 **Scanning for Words with Clues** Working alone or with a partner, scan the reading selection for the words that correspond to the following clues.

1   two synonyms that mean *the way one looks at the world*

   outlook _____

2. two antonyms for *narrow-minded*, one beginning with *l* and one with *o*

   _____

3. a short word beginning with *b* that means *subjective viewpoint or slanted opinion*

   _____

4. a hyphenated term that means *an estimate about the worth or goodness of oneself*

   _____

5. two adjectives beginning with *r* and meaning the opposite of *pleasing*

   _____

6. a noun that means a *crude, ignorant person* and has its origin in the sound made by a dog

   _____

7. another word for *shade* in reference to colors

   _____

8. an adjective meaning *impossible to believe*

   _____

5 **The Support Game: Finding Support for Main Ideas** How fast are you at finding information? Divide the class into teams of three to five players. Each team makes three lists of examples from the reading selection, one for each of the following main ideas. At a certain point the teacher calls "time" and each team reports on their findings. Which team is the winner? Who are the class experts on ethnocentrism?

1. Ethnocentrism is present in language.
2. Ethnocentrism is present in myths.
3. Ethnocentrism is present in food preferences.

6 **Focusing on Words from the Academic Word List** Use the most appropriate word from the box to fill in each of the blanks on page 203 in the section taken from the reading on pages 199–201. Do NOT look back at the reading right away; instead, try first to see if you can remember the vocabulary. The word *culture* will be used twice.

aspect	constantly	objectively
aware	culture	outcome
bias	liberal	sexual

B   Ethnocentrism is the view that one's own _____ is better

than all others; it is the way all people feel about themselves as compared

to outsiders. There is no one in our society who is not ethnocentric to some

degree, no matter how _____ and open-minded he or she might

claim to be. People will always find some _____ of another

_____ distasteful, be it _____ practices, a way of

treating friends or relatives, or simply a food that they cannot manage to get

down with a smile. This is not something we should be ashamed of, because

it is a natural _____ of growing up in any society. However,

as anthropologists who study other cultures, it is something we should

_____ be _____ of, so that when we are tempted

to make value judgments about another way of life, we can look at the

situation _____ and take our _____ into account.

 7 Guided Academic Conversation In small groups, discuss the following
topics. Then compare your opinions with those of another group.

1. **Culture Shock** What do you think is the meaning of this term (used in the
first sentence of the selection)? When does culture shock occur? Have you ever
experienced this? Is it a good or a bad experience for a person to go through? Or
can it be both? Explain.

2. **Examining Your Own Culture** What examples are there of ethnocentrism in the
food preferences of your culture? What foods from other cultures are considered
disgusting or repugnant? How do you feel about eating different types of
food? Are there any words or phrases in your language that suggest a feeling
of superiority with reference to other cultures? Tell the story of a popular myth
from your culture. Is there anything ethnocentric about it?

3. **Purpose and Evaluation** In simple words, write what you think is the main purpose
of the article. Do you feel that the author achieved his purpose or not? Why?

Questions About an Author's Purposes or Attitudes

The TOEFL® iBT includes "reading-to-learn" questions. These test your overall understanding of the reading, including implications, the author's purposes in writing, the author's feelings about a topic, how sure an author is about a certain point, or the interrelationships among several ideas. Here we will look at reading-to-learn questions about the author's purposes, implications, and attitudes.

Here are some questions like the "reading-to-learn" items on the TOEFL® iBT. These are based on the reading "Ethnocentrism" on pages 199–201.

1. The author's attitude toward ethnocentrism is best expressed by which of the following?

2. What does the author mean by the phrase, "it is a natural outcome of growing up in any society"?

3. Which of the following does the third paragraph most strongly imply?

4. Why does the author mention dogs in the fourth paragraph?

To answer such questions, you have to consider the reading as a whole. Very often, the key sentence or phrase given in the question could, by itself, have many meanings. You must use other information from the reading to decide which possible meaning the author intends.

Practice

Read the following passage about gestures and ethnocentrism. Then answer the reading-to-learn questions that follow it.

Gestural Ethnocentrism

A   Gestures are so naturally a part of any culture that they are almost automatic, used with little conscious thought about their meaning. Nonetheless, they are vital to communication. Even someone who learns the language of another culture communicates only poorly if the words are paired with the wrong gestures. A person who clings to his or her own system of non-verbal communication and fails to adapt to that of a host culture demonstrates a sort of "gestural ethnocentrism." When I wave my hand in a certain way, I expect the gesture to mean the same no matter where I go. That is pure narrowness on my part—and a big mistake.

B   To illustrate possible trouble arising from gestural ethnocentricity, we will look at what may happen when an American visits Malaysia. We will focus on the non-verbal messages of Malaysians who are ethnically Malay. Malaysians who are ethnically Indian, Chinese, Iban, European, and so forth have their own characteristic gestures but have probably also learned the dominant Malay set.

C   Malaysian handshakes communicate a tenderness and respect that seems absent from the typical European handshake. One holds out the right hand, just as in the Western version, but the palms touch only very gently. After a short contact period, Malaysians then disengage their right hands, which they bring up to the left side of the chest. There, the right hand is laid palm-down over the heart, much as an American might do while reciting the Pledge of Allegiance. The elegance, even nobility, of this gesture is impressive. Nonetheless, because it is far removed from the hearty, almost competitive, handshake that American visitors ethnocentrically expect, this beautiful gesture may be mistaken for something weak or unenthusiastic.

D   Malaysians, especially Malays, frequently hold hands with members of the same sex. It is not at all unusual to see two schoolboys walking down the street holding hands, or two men standing in line at a government office holding hands as they talk. The same would be true of two schoolgirls or two grown women. The gesture simply means friendship. Gesturally ethnocentric Westerners, especially men, often find the hand-holding disturbing because its meaning in their home societies is very different.

E   Westerners wrapped up in gestural ethnocentrism may do certain things that mean little to them but are very offensive to many Malaysians. Among these are standing with one's hands on the hips. To a Malaysian, it is likely to mean anger, and anger means insult. In Malaysian company, one should never hold up an index finger to say, "Come here." Such a gesture is reserved for animals or extremely naughty little children. Directed at an adult, it is a very harsh insult. Nor should one point at things with an index finger—a completely neutral gesture in the U.S. or Canada but a social mistake in Malaysia. To point things out, one should use the thumb or the entire hand, all fingers together. And never, never pound the fist of one hand into the palm of the other to emphasize a point. That is the equivalent of flashing a middle finger at another driver on the American roads.

1. Why does the author mention ethnic groups in Paragraph B?
   - (A) to say which group of Malaysians use the best gestures
   - (B) to show that Malaysian society discriminates against some ethnic groups
   - (C) to emphasize that only Malays use and understand these gestures
   - (D) to limit the discussion to one ethnic group's gestures

2. What is the author's attitude toward Malay handshakes?
   - (A) They are too unenthusiastic.
   - (B) They are too competitive.
   - (C) They communicate warmth and respect.
   - (D) They are used in reciting the Pledge of Allegiance.

3. What does the author imply about Western men in Paragraph D?

  (A) They see romantic love in a gesture that is meant to show friendship.

  (B) They have a hard time making male friends.

  (C) They never hold hands with anyone else.

  (D) They offend Malaysians by holding hands with members of the opposite sex.

4. What does Paragraph E imply about the gesture of pounding a fist into the palm of the other hand?

  (A) It is illegal.

  (B) It is exceptionally rude.

  (C) It is elegant.

  (D) It means "come here."

5. Throughout the passage, what is the author's attitude toward Malay gestures?

  (A) They are pleasant.

  (B) They are harsh.

  (C) They are meaningless.

  (D) They are not used anymore.

8 **Around the Globe** On pages 207 is a selection of ancient love poems from three different parts of the world. They allow us to examine some of the common themes about love that have come down to us through the centuries. In groups of three to five, read the three poems out loud and then answer the questions that come after the poems and compare your opinions of them.

▼ Love changes people's behavior.

He drifts on blue water
under the clear moon
picking lilies on South Lake.
Every lotus blossom
Speaks of love,
Until his heart will break.

Li Po, 8th century, Chinese poet (male)

I wake, my passion blazing
my breast a fire raging, exploding flame,
while within me, my heart chars

Ono No Komachi, 9th century, Japanese (female)

The Sun Never Says
Even
After
All this time
The sun never says to the earth
"You Owe Me"
Look
What happens
With a love like that
It lights the
Whole
Sky.

Hafiz, 14th century, Persian Sufi poet (male)

1. For each poem, list briefly in your own words what you think is the main point or feeling expressed. Then compare and discuss your answers with your group.

2. Which of these three poems do you like best and why?

3. What emotions and themes are present in love poems (or songs about love) nowadays? Are they very different from these ancient poems or do they express the same eternal themes related to love? Can you give some examples?

A Clean, Well-Lighted Place

Before You Read

> The next story takes place in a café in Paris. It was written by the American writer Ernest Hemingway (1899–1961), who lived in Paris for many years. Hemingway is not the sort of writer who describes his characters in great detail. Therefore, the reader must infer a lot about the characters from what they say and do.

1 Previewing for Characters and Plot Skim the story to answer these questions.

1. How many characters are there in the story?

2. Which predominates (has a bigger place): dialogue (speaking) or action?

3. Do you feel the general tone of the story is happy or sad? Why?

2 Getting the Meaning of Words from Context Read the following excerpts from the story and decide from context which meaning corresponds best to each italicized word. Even though some of the words are Spanish, the meaning should still be clear from the context. Mark the correct answer.

1. "Last week he tried to commit suicide," one waiter said.
   "Why?"
   "He was in *despair*."
   "What about?"
   "Nothing."
   "How do you know that it was nothing?"
   "He has plenty of money."

   (A) poor health   (B) a sad state of mind   (C) financial trouble

(In this case, you are told the man has money, so C is not correct. Also, if the man were in poor health, the waiter would not have said he was in despair about "nothing," so A is not correct. That leaves letter B, the right answer.)

2. The waiter took the bottle back inside the café. He sat down at the table with his *colleague* again.

   (A) client
   (B) boss
   (C) co-worker

3. "Finished," he said, speaking with that *omission of syntax* stupid people employ when talking to drunken people or foreigners. "No more tonight. Close now."

   (A) shortening of phrases
   (B) strange accent
   (C) blurred speech

4. "Are you trying to insult me?" (younger waiter speaking)
   "No, *hombre*, only to make a joke."...
   "Each night I am reluctant to close up because there may be someone who needs the café." (older waiter speaking)
   "*Hombre*, there are bodegas open all night long." (Note: *hombre* is a Spanish word.)

   (A) a funny insult
   (B) a word you say to a friend
   (C) the name of one of the waiters

5. "A little cup," said the waiter.
   The barman poured it for him. ...
   "You want another *copita*?" the barman asked. ... (Note: *copita* is a Spanish word.)

   (A) a small alcoholic drink
   (B) a tiny saucer
   (C) a spicy Spanish food

6. Now, without thinking further, he would go home to his room. He would lie in the bed and finally, with daylight, he would go to sleep. After all, he said to himself, it is probably only *insomnia*. Many must have it.

   (A) a serious illness
   (B) severe nervous depression
   (C) the inability to sleep

Introduction

Ernest Hemingway (1899–1961) is one of the most widely read of all modern American authors. His books have been translated into many languages. He always writes in a very simple, clear style, usually with a lot of dialogue, and with a deep and complex meaning hidden underneath. The following story, which traces the conversations between a customer and some waiters at a café near closing time, deals with loneliness, aging, and compassion.

- Do you think people have a responsibility to be compassionate towards strangers, even if it puts them at an inconvenience?
- Why do some people become so lonely as they grow older? Is this a factor in some cultures and not much in others?

▼ Ernest Hemingway

It was late and everyone had left the café except an old man who sat in the shadow the leaves of the tree made against the electric light. In the daytime the street was dusty, but at night the dew settled the dust and the old man liked to sit late because he was deaf and now at night it was quiet and he felt the difference. The two waiters inside the café knew that the old man was a little drunk, and while he was a good client they knew that if he became too drunk he would leave without paying, so they kept watch on him.

"Last week he tried to commit suicide," one waiter said.

"Why?"

"He was in despair."

"What about?"

"Nothing."

"How do you know it was nothing?"

"He has plenty of money."

They sat together at a table that was close against the wall near the door of the café and looked at the terrace where the tables were all empty except where the old man sat in the shadow of the leaves of the tree that moved slightly in the wind. A girl and a soldier went by in the street. The street light shone on the brass number on his collar. The girl wore no head covering and hurried beside him.

"The guard will pick him up," one waiter said.

"What does it matter if he gets what he's after?"

"He had better get off the street now. The guard will get him. They went by five minutes ago."

The old man sitting in the shadow rapped on his saucer with his glass. The younger waiter went over to him.

"What do you want?"

The old man looked at him. "Another brandy," he said.

"You'll be drunk," the waiter said. The old man looked at him. The waiter went away.

"He'll stay all night," he said to his colleague. "I'm sleepy now. I never get into bed before three o'clock. He should have killed himself last week."

The waiter took the brandy bottle and another saucer from the counter inside the café and marched out to the old man's table. He put down the saucer and poured the glass full of brandy.

"You should have killed yourself last week," he said to the deaf man. The old man motioned with his finger. "A little more," he said. The waiter poured on into the glass so that the brandy slopped over and ran down the stem into the top saucer of the pile. "Thank you," the old man said. The waiter took the bottle back inside the café. He sat down at the table with his colleague again.

"He's drunk now," he said.

"He's drunk every night."

"What did he want to kill himself for?"

"How should I know."

"How did he do it?"

"He hung himself with a rope."

"Who cut him down?"

"His niece."

"Why did they do it?"

"Fear for his soul."

"How much money has he got?"

"He's got plenty."

"He must be 80 years old."

"Anyway I should say he was 80."

"I wish he would go home. I never get to bed before three o'clock. What kind of hour is that to go to bed?"

"He stays up because he likes it."

"He's lonely. I'm not lonely. I have a wife waiting in bed for me."

"He had a wife once too."

"A wife would be no good to him now."

"You can't tell. He might be better with a wife."

"His niece looks after him."

"I know. You said she cut him down."

"I wouldn't want to be that old. An old man is a nasty thing."

"Not always. This old man is clean. He drinks without spilling. Even now, drunk. Look at him."

"I don't want to look at him. I wish he would go home. He has no regard for those who must work."

The old man looked from his glass across the square, then over at the waiters.

"Another brandy," he said, pointing to his glass. The waiter who was in a hurry came over.

"Finished," he said, speaking with that omission of syntax stupid people employ when talking to drunken people or foreigners. "No more tonight. Close now."

"Another," said the old man.

"No. Finished." The waiter wiped the edge of the table with a towel and shook his head.

The old man stood up, slowly counted the saucers, took a leather coin purse from his pocket and paid for the drinks, leaving half a peseta tip.

The waiter watched him go down the street, a very old man walking unsteadily but with dignity.

"Why didn't you let him stay and drink?" the unhurried waiter asked. 85 They were putting up the shutters. "It's not half-past two."

"I want to go home to bed."

"What is an hour?"

"More to me than to him."

"An hour is the same." 90

"You talk like an old man yourself. He can buy a bottle and drink at home."

"It's not the same."

"No, it's not," agreed the waiter with a wife. He did not wish to be unjust. He was only in a hurry. 95

"And you? You have no fear of going home before your usual hour?"

"Are you trying to insult me?"

"No, *hombre*, only to make a joke."

"No," the waiter who was in a hurry said, rising from pulling down the metal shutters. "I have confidence. I am all confidence." 100

"You have health, confidence, and a job," the old waiter said. "You have everything."

"And what do you lack?"

"Everything but work."

"You have everything I have." 105

"No. I have never had confidence and I am not young."

"Come on. Stop talking nonsense and lock up."

"I am of those who like to stay late at the café," the older waiter said. "With all those who do not want to go to bed. With all those who need a light for the night." 110

"I want to go home and into bed."

"We are of two different kinds," the older waiter said. He was now dressed to go home. "It is not only a question of youth and confidence although those things are very beautiful. Each night I am reluctant to close up because there may be someone who needs the café." 115

"*Hombre*, there are *bodegas* open all night long."

"You do not understand. This is a clean and pleasant café. It is well lighted. The light is very good and also, now, there are shadows of the leaves."

"Good night," said the younger waiter. 120

"Good night," the other said. Turning off the electric light he continued the conversation with himself. It is the light of course but it is necessary that the place be clean and pleasant. You do not want music. Certainly you do not want music. Nor can you stand before a bar with dignity although that is all that is provided for these hours. What did he fear? It was not fear or 125 dread. It was nothing that he knew too well. It was all a nothing and a man was nothing too. It was only that and light was all it needed and a certain cleanness and order. Some lived in it and never felt it but he knew it all was *nada y pues nada y nada y pues nada.** Our *nada* who are in *nada*, *nada* be thy name thy kingdom *nada* thy will be *nada* in *nada* as it is in *nada*. Give us this *nada* our daily *nada* and *nada* us our *nada* as we *nada* our *nada* and *nada* us not into *nada* but deliver us from *nada*; *pues nada*. Hail nothing full of nothing, nothing is with thee. He smiled and stood before a bar with a shining steam pressure coffee machine.

"What's yours?" asked the barman.

"*Nada*."

"*Otro loco mâs*[†]," said the barman and turned away.

"A little cup," said the waiter.

The barman poured it for him.

"The light is very bright and pleasant but the bar is unpolished," the waiter said.

The barman looked at him but did not answer. It was too late at night for conversation.

"You want another *copita*?" the barman asked.

"No, thank you," said the waiter and went out. He disliked bars and *bodegas*. A clean, well-lighted café was a very different thing. Now, without thinking further, he would go home to his room. He would lie in the bed and finally, with daylight, he would go to sleep. After all, he said to himself, it is probably only insomnia. Many must have it.

Source: "A Clean, Well-Lighted Place" *The Short Stories of Ernest Hemingway* (Ernest Hemingway)

---

*Nada is the Spanish word for "nothing." *Y pues nada means* "and then nothing." The older waiter then recites the most famous of all Christian prayers, the "Lord's Prayer," which begins "Our Father which art in Heaven, hallowed be Thy name…" However, instead of saying the correct words, he replaces many of them with the word *nada*. Afterward, he does the same with a small part of another prayer.

[†]Another crazy one

3 **Making Inferences About Characters** Working alone or with others, make inferences about the characters in the story from the following words and actions. To express your inferences about the characters, you can use words like *maybe, perhaps, probably, must.*

1. We are told that the old man who is drinking tried to commit suicide the week before. (line 8) Finish the inference below.

   The old man:

   The old man must be very sad about something. He has problems. He

   is probably...

2. When asked what the old man was in despair about, this conversation follows:
   "Nothing."
   "How do you know it was nothing?"
   "He has plenty of money." (lines 12–14)
   The waiter who spoke last:

   _____

   _____

   _____

   _____

3. The younger waiter says, "He'll stay all night... I'm sleepy now. I never get into bed before three o'clock. He should have killed himself last week." (lines 32–33)

   The younger waiter:

   _____

   _____

   _____

   _____

4. After the younger waiter has told the old man that the café is closed, the older waiter says, "Why didn't you let him stay and drink?... It's not half-past two." (lines 85–86)

   The older waiter:

   _____

   _____

   _____

   _____

5. After the man and the younger waiter leave, the older waiter stays for a while and thinks. He recites a prayer in his mind but substitutes the word nada for many of the important words. (lines 130–133)

The older waiter:

_____

_____

_____

_____

Strategy

Expressing the Theme

A story presents specific characters with their problems, feelings, and interactions. From these specifics, you can make a generalization about human behavior or human nature; this is the theme of the story.

4 **Expressing the Theme** Here are three possible expressions of the theme of "A Clean, Well-Lighted Place." With a partner or a small group, decide which of the three you think is the best theme statement for the story, and why. If you do not like any of them, write your own theme statement.

1. Those who are sad and alone depend on the kindness of others to keep going.

2. Some people have understanding and compassion for others and some don't.

3. Very small details can sometimes make the difference between life and death.

5 **Guided Academic Conversation** In small groups, discuss the following topics. Afterwards, compare your opinions with those of your classmates.

1. **Your Own Interpretation** At one point, the older waiter says to the younger one, "We are of two different kinds." What does he mean by this? Which one of them do you identify with more: the older waiter or the younger one? Why? Do you believe there are two different kinds of people? Explain.

2. **The Hemingway Style** Even today, many years after his death, Hemingway is a popular author whose books are read by people all over the world. It is said that his style is simple and clear and that his stories have universal meaning. In your opinion, what element is the most important in this story: the characters, the plot, or the setting? Explain. Why do you think that Hemingway included some Spanish words? Did you like the story? Why or why not?

What Do You Think? Read the paragraph below and discuss the questions that follow.

Manners

Manners apply to a distinctive way of acting or a social attitude towards others. A person can have good manners or bad manners. Some experts say that in the 21st century, we have lost our good manners and don't know how to act in certain social situations. We don't have respect for others, we don't eat properly, we don't dress properly, we don't behave properly.

1. Do you think that overall we have lost our good manners? Give some examples.

2. Do you think that manners from past generations were too strict and that nowadays we don't need those types of restrictions? Explain.

3. What manners would you change in your society? What manners would you change of foreigners you meet, or of those that visit your country?

▼ A person with bad manners is considered rude.

1 **Making Connections** Choose one of the two topics below. Research the topic on the Internet and prepare some information to present to the class.

1. **Different Attitudes Toward Clothing and Styles** This may include head coverings, jewelry, ceremonial clothing, traditional costumes for different occasions (such as weddings or other ceremonies), or even hairstyles. Find examples of ethnocentrism in styles, where in some places certain items are used only by women but in others only by men, or where one culture would not permit the items used in another.

2. **The Importance of Hemingway** Look up some biographical and literary information about Ernest Hemingway. What other famous works has he written and what are they about? What are the main features of his style (in more detail than above)? Include some interesting facts about his life in your presentation. Or, as another alternative, read a different story by this famous author and describe its plot, setting, and characters.

Responding in Writing

FOCUS

Writing Tip: Creating a Dialogue

To write a dialogue, carefully select your speakers, make sure they stay in character, include their words in quotation marks, and follow a model for correct punctuation and formatting.

2 **Writing a Dialogue** In pairs, write a dialogue (a conversation) between two people about manners. Use the selection "A Clean, Well-Lighted Place" as a model for how to format the speakers' words in quotation marks and how to use punctuation around quotation marks. Follow these steps:

Step 1: Carefully choose your two speakers. What different view on manners will each one represent? (i.e., Does one feel the younger generation is ruder than in the past and the other disagree? Does one feel that a certain way of behaving is appropriate and another feel that it is not? Be creative in making up their opinions.) List these two speakers' names along with their important characteristics, which might include such factors as age, gender, cultural background, appearance, etc.

Step 2: Decide on how the conversation should progress. Make a list of the main points that will be argued and of the examples that support each argument (or side). Decide what the outcome will be. (Will one speaker win, will they continue to disagree in the end, or will they find common ground in their views?)

Step 3: Write the dialogue following the list of points you made in Step 2 and following the model for dialogue in the selection, "A Clean, Well-Lighted Place."

Step 4: Read and revise the dialogue to make sure that each speaker stays "in character" (that is to say, that they say things that seem appropriate for their character as described in Step 1).

Step 5: Read your dialogues to another pair of classmates. Does the other pair have any critiques or comments about your dialogue that may help you revise a little more before handing in the assignment?

Step 6: Make final revisions and hand in your dialogue to the teacher.

Self-Assessment Log

Read the lists below. Check (✓) the strategies and vocabulary that you learned in this chapter. Look through the chapter or ask your instructor about the strategies and words that you do not understand.

Reading and Vocabulary-Building Strategies

☐ Skimming for the main idea
☐ Scanning for the development of the main idea
☐ Using prefixes to build new words
☐ Scanning for words with clues
☐ Finding support for main ideas
☐ Previewing for characters and plot
☐ Getting the meaning of words from context
☐ Making inferences about characters
☐ Expressing the them

Target Vocabulary

Nouns

■ aspect*
■ barbarian
■ bias*
■ colleague*
■ culture*
■ despair
■ ethnocentrism
■ hue
■ insomnia
■ omission of syntax

■ outcome*
■ outlook
■ self-evaluation
■ subgroup
■ world view

Adjectives

■ aware*
■ distasteful
■ inconceivable*

■ inhuman
■ irrational*
■ liberal*
■ non-Western
■ open-minded
■ repugnant
■ repulsive
■ sexual*
■ subarctic
■ unnatural

Adverbs

■ constantly*
■ objectively*

* These words are from the Academic Word List. For more information on this list,
  see www.victoria.ac.nz/lals/resources/academicwordlist/

10
Crime and Punishment

"The way of justice is mysterious."

Sanskrit proverb

In this
CHAPTER

What causes people to commit crimes? How should criminals be punished? To study the answers to these questions, we begin with a magazine article looking at some criminals who try to overcome what they see as their "crime addiction" through meetings and a spiritual program. This is followed by a fictional selection, a mystery story with a murder to be solved and a surprise ending.

Connecting to the Topic

1. Look at the photos. What do you think is happening in each frame? What do you think happened after the last frame?

2. Have you ever been the victim of a crime? What happened?

3. Do you think that criminals can be reformed? Why or why not?

Hooked on Crime

Strategy

Identifying the Interviewees in an Article

Articles in a magazine or newspaper will often use interviews of key people and experts to get the story across. In this way, these people are similar to the "main characters" in a narrative. Sorting out who these "interviewees" are can help you understand better the overall story and its purpose.

1 Scanning: Identifying the Interviewees In this story, criminals are meeting around a table to talk about their "addiction to crime." Some of the people interviewed for the story are attending this meeting; others are "experts" in certain areas relating to crime.

Scan the article for the names below, and write a very short description of each person. (The first one is done for you as an example. You do not have to write everything, just enough to help you identify the person.)

1. Stan Mingo: _a man with a "crime addiction" who is starting the meeting_

2. Gary Johnson: _____

3. Rick A: _____

4. Benedikt Fischer: _____

5. George: _____

6 Rick B: _____

2 Getting the Meaning of Specialized Terms from Context Readings and discussions relating to crime include their own specialized vocabulary. Learning some crime-related terms will help you to read the selection and to discuss issues of crime and punishment.

Guess the meaning of each term or phrase in italics by breaking words into smaller parts or finding clues in the words that are nearby. Then match it with the correct definition in the column on the right.

Terms	Definitions
1. __g__ He has a *dependency* on alcohol. He drinks every day.	a. thefts, stealing things
	b. relapse, go back to old ways
2. _____ It's in the city's *hard-luck* Downtown Eastside. You shouldn't go there alone.	c. fixing the wrong that was done
3. _____ Her mind is *addled* by crack cocaine. She talks in a crazy way.	d. scaring people into paying money
4. _____ They have been ground down by *homelessness*. At night they have nowhere to go.	e. buying and selling drugs
	f. before, when there was money
5. _____ He was in jail for *robberies*. He took many things that didn't belong to him.	g. condition of needing (and being controlled by)
6. _____ He was in jail for *extortion*. He intimidated people.	h. tricks to cheat people
7. _____ He was in jail for *assault*. He liked to hit people.	i. without drugs or alcohol
8. _____ He was in jail for *trafficking*. Many addicts made deals with him.	j. confused, mixed up mentally
9. _____ He was in jail for small-time *cons*. He knew how to fool others.	k. fulfilled my sentence in prison
10. _____ *Back when things were flush*, they bought many things.	l. attacking or beating up someone
11. _____ If a person takes *heroin* just a few times, it is very hard to leave it alone.	m. a place of misfortune, with people in tough situations
12. _____ He's been *clean* for four months and a day. Maybe he can get a job.	n. an addictive drug
13. _____ I *did my time*, but that's not making amends.	o. living on the streets
14. _____ I did my time, but that's not *making amends*. There's still more I have to do.	
15. _____ He knows some members will *backslide*. It's hard to learn good habits.	

Introduction

The following article from *Macleans Magazine* introduces some criminals from Vancouver (a city in western Canada) who believe that they have an "addiction" (powerful physical and/or psychological urge) to crime. They meet regularly in the dining hall at the Salvation Army (a charity organization) to discuss this "addiction" and how to get over it and lead a life without crime.

- Do you think that crime can be an addiction? Why or why not?
- What do you think these people will do to try to prevent themselves from committing crimes?

Hooked on Crime

Vancouver Crooks Meeting to Talk About Their Compulsion to be Lawless

A   It's Tuesday evening, 7 P.M., and the last of the stragglers takes his seat. The lights in the Salvation Army dining hall are extinguished; candles are lit. A dozen men and one woman sit around a rectangle of tables waiting for Stan Mingo to start tonight's meeting. It's doubtful anywhere in Vancouver tonight there is a larger gathering of career criminals, at least outside the prison system. The men range from their 20s to their 50s, and from clean-cut to jailhouse hard. The woman, in her 50s, has a son up for robbery. "They've got no proof," she says. The men nod politely, like they've never heard that one before. The air smells of strong coffee. People drop coins into a cup making the rounds. "My name is Stan," says the burly guy at the head of the table. "I have a crime addiction."

B   With that, Mingo begins another weekly meeting of the founding chapter of Crime Addiction Anonymous— dedicated to the contentious

▲ A group therapy session

premise that crime can be an illness as tenacious as dependency on alcohol or drugs. The program was founded by Mingo, who washed up almost a year ago at the Salvation Army's Harbour Light Detox and Recovery Centre in the city's hard-luck Downtown Eastside. He was addled by crack cocaine, and ground down by homelessness and doubts about his abilities as a master criminal. He's spent more than half his 50 years in jail, for robberies, extortion, attempted murder, assault, trafficking, and small-time cons. Prison tattoos cover his upper torso like an illustrated criminal curriculum vitae*. The problem, he concedes, is crime can be thrilling. "It's fun to go in and rob a bank. It's a trip, man. It's a power trip to rob anybody, even with a knife in a back alley." There were few limits. He wouldn't harm old people, he says, "and most women, unless she acted and fought like a man."

C   Back when things were flush, he owned a home, a motorcycle, even a Vancouver restaurant, where the daily special was the heroin behind the counter. He called it *The Alibi*. Say what you want about Mingo, he has a sense of humour.

D   He credits Harbour Light with saving his life, and for providing the inspiration and wherewithal to draft the plan for CAA. The first meeting was held in May. A second chapter has since opened, also in the neighbourhood. The program's strength is that it was created by the members, not imposed on them, says Harbour Light associate executive director Gary Johnson. Asked if crime can be addictive, Johnson responds without hesitation: "Absolutely." There is some irony in the fact that the group steals heavily from the 12-step, spiritually based Alcoholics Anonymous program, started in 1935 and now used in more than 150 countries. A spokesman for AA's general service office in New York City, however, says other groups are welcome to share its traditions. "They are spiritual principles we don't claim a right to if somebody wants to adopt them for themselves," notes Rick A.[†] who, in the AA tradition, asked his surname not be used. AA's principles have been applied to addictions from narcotics and nicotine to gambling and sex. As for crime, Rick concedes, "This is the first time I've heard of that."

E   Whether crime is, well, a legitimate addiction is an open question. "I'm very cautious in labeling anything with this very appealing and sexy label of addiction," says Benedikt Fischer, associate professor of criminology and public health at the University of Toronto, and research scientist with the Toronto-based Centre for Addiction and Mental Health. The term addiction is rather imprecise and often not "terribly helpful," he says. Crimes are committed for many reasons—economic need, compulsiveness, even an attraction to "the rush."

Curriculum vitae is a Latin expression that is used a lot in English and sometimes is abbreviated as CV. It means a document which lists information about a person's education, work experience, and qualifications. People applying for a job are usually asked to send in their CV.

[†]Since there were two participants named Rick at this meeting, they have been designated as Rick A. and Rick B. to help the reader to tell the difference between them.

F Many of the men tonight are also fighting drugs or alcohol. They find crime similarly irresistible. Jason, in his 20s, says he's been clean for four months and a day. Money is tight. When he sees crack dealers, "I just want to take them out. Smash their heads and take their money. The scary part is I like hurting people, too, you know." He pauses. "I'm hugely grateful for this meeting."

G George, his dark hair streaked with grey, figures he's stolen or conned $80,000 from family members. "If you've ever seen the look in your family's eyes after you break their hearts," he says, "it's tough."

H Tonight's topic is Step Nine: making amends. It's no easy task, they agree. Where do you find all the people you've hurt? How do you pay all that money back? Rick B. lowers his shaved head, clasps his hands on the table. "How do you make amends to a dead person?" he asks. "I did my time, but that's not making amends." Is prayer making amends? It's been 100 days, he says, "no crime, no dope." He's feeling guilt and shame for the first time in years. "It's like we're thawing out, becoming human again."

I Mingo knows the group faces skepticism. He knows some members will backslide. "For me, it's a new vision. I have strength and hope of recovery." The evening's wrenching hour of confession ends with arms linked in a group prayer. Some hurry into the night. Others help Mingo rearrange the hall's furniture. He gathers his papers and asks about the collection cup, which usually adds about $5 to the group's modest coffers. It's gone. Ripped off, apparently, in mid-meeting.

J Mingo, momentarily flummoxed, roars with laughter. What's a guy to do? He jabs a meaty finger at the writer's notebook. "That's crime addiction, man," he says. "Write that down."

Source: "Hooked on Crime" *Macleans Magazine* (Ken MacQueen)

After You Read

Strategy

Understanding the Setting

The setting of the story means where it takes place, and the same can apply to an article. If you don't understand where the action is occurring, it can be confusing to understand what is going on. When you read an article, try to identify where it takes place and who or what organizations are involved.

3 Understanding the Setting Fill in the blanks, using the context to understand the full meaning of the following names for organizations or places in the article.

1. The article mentions *Alcoholics Anonymous* (AA), a very well-known program with 12 spiritual steps that help people recover when they have been abusing _____. *Anonymous* means that people are not named or are unknown, so at meetings for these groups, the members' full names are _____ to each other.

2. *Crime Addiction Anonymous* is modeled after *Alcoholics Anonymous*, so it is a program with _____ spiritual steps that help people recover when they have a problem with _____. In this program also, the members' full names are _____ to each other.

3. The restaurant Mingo used to own was called *The Alibi*. An *alibi* is the story that an accused person tells to prove their innocence by stating that they were somewhere else when a crime was being committed. The article says that Mingo shows his "sense of humour" by this name for his restaurant because the food at this restaurant serves as an _____ to cover up the crime of also serving _____ (see line 39 in the story).

4. *Detox* is short for *detoxification*, the removal of a toxic or addictive substance (like excessive alcohol or drugs) from the body. *The Salvation Army* is a charity organization, and its *Harbour Light Detox and Recovery Centre* is a center where people can receive help getting over their _____.
A *harbour* is a protected area on the sea coast where ships come, and harbors often have a *light* to guide ships in safely, so the center is called *Harbour Light* because _____. (**Hint:** Use your imagination for this answer!) The article says Mingo "washed up" at the center because it is comparing Mingo to _____.

4 Guessing the Meaning of Adjectives from Context and Structure
Use your intuition, knowledge of word structure, and the context to select the best meanings for the words in italics in the phrases below.

1. Some of the men at the meeting are *clean-cut*.
   - Ⓐ rough looking and menacing
   - Ⓑ shaven and well groomed
   - Ⓒ old and unhealthy

2. Some of the men at the meeting are *jailhouse hard*.
   - Ⓐ rough looking and menacing
   - Ⓑ shaven and well groomed
   - Ⓒ old and unhealthy

3. Crime Addiction Anonymous is dedicated to the *contentious* premise (basic idea) that crime can be an illness as strong as dependency on alcohol or drugs.
   - Ⓐ true
   - Ⓑ debatable
   - Ⓒ ridiculous

4. The evening's *wrenching* hour of confession ends with arms linked in a group prayer.
   - Ⓐ unfair
   - Ⓑ final
   - Ⓒ difficult

5. The collection cup usually adds about $5 to the group's *modest* coffers (money boxes).
   - Ⓐ fairly small
   - Ⓑ substantial
   - Ⓒ empty

6. He jabs a *meaty* finger at the writer's notebook.
   - Ⓐ tiny
   - Ⓑ dirty
   - Ⓒ large

5 Focusing on Words From the Academic Word List.
Use the most appropriate word from the box to fill in each of the blanks below in the paragraph taken from Part 2. Do NOT look back at the reading right away; instead, first see if you can remember the vocabulary. The word *principles* will be used twice. Check your answers on page 225.

chapter	credits	imposed	responds
created	draft	principles	tradition

D   He _____ Harbour Light with saving his life, and for
1
providing the inspiration and wherewithal to _____ the plan
2
for CAA. The first meeting was held in May. A second _____
3
has since opened, also in the neighbourhood. The program's strength is that
it was _____ by the members, not _____ on   5
4   5
them, says Harbour Light associate executive director Gary Johnson. Asked
if crime can be addictive, Johnson _____ without hesitation:
6
"Absolutely." There is some irony in the fact that the group steals heavily
from the 12-step, spiritually based Alcoholics Anonymous program, started
in 1935 and now used in more than 150 countries. A spokesman for AA's   10
general service office in New York City, however, says other groups are
welcome to share its traditions. "They are spiritual _____ we
7
don't claim a right to if somebody wants to adopt them for themselves," notes
Rick A, who, in the AA _____, asked his surname not be used.
8
AA's _____ have been applied to addictions from narcotics and   15
9
nicotine to gambling and sex. As for crime, Rick concedes, "This is the first
time I've heard of that."

FOCUS

Identifying Spelling Variations

Spelling can vary in English depending on the country of origin. There are minor spelling differences between Canadian English and U.S. English. Canadians tend to spell words like *honour, cheque,* and *kilometre* in the traditional way as they do in Britain. Americans have altered these words to *honor, check,* and *kilometer,* often shortening or simplifying them.

6 Identifying Spelling Variations Change the following italicized words which are spelled in the American style to the Canadian style as they appear in *Hooked on Crime* (which came from a Canadian magazine).

1. recovery *center* _____

2. *Harbor* Light _____

3. sense of *humor* _____

4. in the *neighborhood* _____

7 Guided Academic Conversation In small groups, discuss five of the following six questions. Be prepared to report on the opinions of your group after you finish.

1. The reading says of Stan Mingo, "Prison tattoos cover his upper torso like an illustrated criminal curriculum vitae." What is a curriculum vitae? What does it normally list and for whom? Explain how Mingo's tattoos can be seen as a "criminal curriculum vitae."

2. Irony means a situation or event that is humorous because it is the opposite of what it seems it should be. So why does the article say, "There is some irony in the fact that the group steals heavily from the 12-step, spiritually based Alcoholics Anonymous program"? What is ironic about this?

3. Why does Benedikt Fischer worry that the word *addiction* is a "very appealing and sexy label" for crime? Do you agree? What problems might arise from calling crime an "addiction"?

4. What other reasons do you think there might be for committing crimes, other than the "rush" mentioned here? List as many as you can think of. What do you think is the most common reason for committing crimes in the country you're living in? Would this be different in some other countries, and if so, why?

5. After talking about feeling guilt and shame, Rick B. says, "It's like we're thawing out, becoming human again." Is crime a "spiritual" problem?

6. What is Step Nine in the Crime Addiction Anonymous program, according to the article? Do you think it is a good idea for criminals to do this, and how do you think they should do it?

8 What Do You Think? Read the paragraph below and then discuss the questions on page 231.

Using the Death Penalty

"Capital punishment" is another way of saying "the death penalty." It means that when a person commits a crime such as murder, the state then has the right, under the law, to execute that person. Some countries—for example, Iran, China, Japan, Pakistan, and the Democratic Republic of the Congo, have laws permitting this. In the United States, whether the death penalty is legal or not is decided by each state. Mexico, Canada, Australia,

and most European countries do not have the death penalty. Increasing numbers of places, like Taiwan, are considering abolishing the death penalty. Some people consider the death penalty unnecessarily cruel; others think it's fair punishment for certain crimes.

◀ A crowd protesting the death penalty

1. Do you agree with the death penalty for certain crimes? Why or why not?

2. Do you think the threat of capital punishment stops people from committing murder? Explain.

3. Do you think killers should be kept in prison for the rest of their lives? Why or why not?

4. What are the various types of punishments for different crimes in your country?

Main Ideas and Details

Eye Witness

Before You Read

1 Identifying Narrative Elements You may recall that the three elements of a narrative (story) are setting, characters, and plot (which starts out with a conflict). (See "The Luncheon" Chapter 6, Part 2.) In the detective story that follows on pages 232–236, the setting is New York City, about 65 years ago. Read the title, look at the illustration, and skim lines 1 to 25. Then answer these questions about the characters.

1. What does the title tell us about one of the main characters? What does he look like? What is his name? (You have to read carefully to find this out.) Why is he important? Whom does he want to speak to?

2. Who is telling the narrative? Is it the *omniscient narrator* (someone who knows everything), or is it one of the characters in the story? Explain. What is the narrator's name? You have to read carefully to find out this information.

3. Who is Magruder?

4. We are told at the beginning that the crime involved both a mugging (attacking someone with the intention to rob) and a murder. Who was the victim? What do we know about her?

1. The sight of the murder has caused a physical change in the face of the man who saw it. It has given him a _____tic_____ over his left cheekbone. (lines 2–3)

2. The narrator reacts to the eye witness' request to see the lieutenant and says, "None of us _____ will do, huh?" (line 12)

3. Magruder had been on the (police) force for a long time and was used to every type of *person*. But instead of saying person, the author uses police slang and says "every type of _____." (line 14)

4. Magruder uses slang to refer to the lieutenant. He asks, "You think maybe the _____ would like to see him personally?" (lines 17–18)

5. The narrator thinks at first that the witness is being stubborn. But when he looks in his eyes he doesn't see stubbornness. He sees _____. (line 32)

6. The narrator tries to scare the witness into talking to him. He uses a legal term and says that not talking about evidence can make a person an _____ *after the fact*. (line 37)

7. The author describes how the witness then thought about whether to talk with the detective or not. He uses a verb that means *considered, turned (something) over in his mind*. The witness _____ for another moment and then said… (line 61)

Read

Introduction

Murder mysteries present a murder and a number of suspects (people who may or may not be the murderers). These types of stories are also called *whodunnits* (bad grammar for "who did it?") because part of the interest is to guess which suspect is the murderer. Detective stories concentrate more on the reason for committing the crime and the process of solving it by the detectives or the police.

The following short story was written by Ewan Hunter (1926–2005) under the pen name of Ed McBain. One of the classic American detective authors, he wrote over 50 books and numerous short stories about crime. Many of his stories are based on true events that occurred years ago in the 87th precinct (police district) of New York. Read the story and follow the clues. Are you a good enough detective to discover who the murderer is?

He had seen a murder, and the sight had sunken into the brown pits that were his eyes. It had tightened the thin line of his mouth and given him a tic over his left cheekbone.

He sat now with his hat in his hand, his fingers nervously exploring the narrow brim. He was a thin man with a moustache that completely dominated the confined planes of his face.

He was dressed neatly, his trousers carefully raised in a crease protecting lift... "That him?" I asked.

"That's him," Magruder said.

"And he saw the mugging?"

"He says he saw it. He won't talk to anyone but the lieutenant."

"None of us underlings will do, huh?"

Magruder shrugged. He'd been on the force for a long time now, and he was used to just about every type of taxpayer. I looked over to where the thin man sat on the bench against the wall.

"Well," I said, "let me see what I can get out of him."

Magruder cocked an eyebrow and asked, "You think maybe the Old Man would like to see him personally?"

"Maybe. If he's got something. If not, we'd be wasting his time. And especially in this case, I don't think..."

"Yeah," Magruder agreed.

I left Magruder and walked over to the little man. He looked up when I approached him, and then blinked.

"Mr. Struthers?"

"Yes," he said warily.

▼ The scene of the crime

"I'm Detective Cappeli. My partner tells me you have some information about the…"

"You're not the lieutenant, are you?"

"No," I said, "but I'm working very closely with him on this case."

"I won't talk to anyone but the lieutenant," he said. His eyes met mine for an instant, and then turned away. He was not being stubborn, I decided. I hadn't seen stubbornness in his eyes. I'd seen fear.

"Why, Mr. Struthers?"

"Why what? Why won't I tell my story to anyone else? Because I won't, that's why."

"Mr. Struthers, withholding evidence is a serious crime. It makes you an accessory after the fact. We'd hate to have to…"

"I'm not withholding anything. Get the lieutenant, and I'll tell you everything I saw. That's all, get the lieutenant."

I waited for a moment before trying again. "Are you familiar with the case at all, sir?"

Struthers considered his answer. "Just what I read in the papers. And what I saw."

"You know that it was Lieutenant Anderson's wife who was mugged? That the mugger was after her purse and killed her without getting it?"

"Yes, I know that."

"Can you see then why we don't want to bring the lieutenant into this until it's absolutely necessary? So far, we've had ten people confessing to the crime, and eight people who claim to have seen the mugging and murder."

"I did see it," Struthers protested.

"I'm not saying you didn't, sir. But I'd like to be sure before I bring the lieutenant in on it."

"I just don't want any slip-ups," Struthers said. "I… I don't want him coming after me next."

"We'll offer you every possible protection, sir. The lieutenant, as you can well imagine, has a strong personal interest in this case. He'll certainly see that no harm comes to you."

Struthers looked around him suspiciously. "Well, do we have to talk here?"

"No, sir, you can come into my office."

He deliberated for another moment, and then said, "All right." He stood up abruptly, his fingers still roaming the hat brim. When we got to my office, I offered him a chair and a cigarette. He took the seat, but declined the smoke.

"Now then, what did you see?"

"I saw the mugger, the man who killed her." Struthers lowered his voice. "But he saw me, too. That's why I want to make absolutely certain that… that I won't get into any trouble over this."

"You won't, sir. I can assure you. Where did you see the killing?"

"On Third and Elm. Right near the old paint factory. I was on my way home from the movies."

"What did you see?"

"Well, the woman, Mrs. Anderson—I didn't know it was her at the time, of course—was standing on a corner waiting for the bus. I was walking down toward her. I walk that way often, especially coming home from the show. It was a nice night and…"

"What happened?"

"Well, it was dark, and I was walking pretty quiet, I guess. I wear gummies—gum sole shoes."

"Go on."

"The mugger came out of the shadows and grabbed Mrs. Anderson around the throat, from behind her. She threw up her arm, and her purse opened and everything inside fell on the sidewalk. Then he lifted his hand and brought it down, and she screamed, and he yelled, 'Quiet, you bitch!' He lifted his hand again and brought it down again, all the time yelling, 'Here, you bitch, here, here,' while he was stabbing her. He must have lifted the knife at least a dozen times."

"And you saw him? You saw his face?"

"Yes. She dropped to the ground, and he came running up the street toward me. I tried to get against the building, but I was too late. We stood face to face, and for a minute I thought he was going to kill me, too. But he gave a kind of moan and ran up the street." "Why didn't you come to the police at once?"

"I… I guess I was scared. Mister, I still am. You've got to promise me I won't get into any trouble. I'm a married man, and I got two kids. I can't afford to…"

"Could you pick him out of a line-up? We've already rounded up a lot of men, some with records as muggers. Could you pick the killer?"

"Yes. But not if he can see me. If he sees me, it's all off. I won't go through with it if he can see me."

"He won't see you, sir. We'll put you behind a screen."

"So long as he doesn't see me. He knows what I look like, too, and I got a family. I won't identify him if he knows I'm the one doing it."

"You've got nothing to worry about." I clicked down Magruder's toggle on the intercom, and when he answered, I said, "Looks like we've got something here, Mac. Get the boys ready for a run-through, will you?"

"Right. I'll buzz you."

We sat around and waited for Magruder to buzz.

"I won't do it unless I'm behind a screen," Struthers said.

"You'll have a one-way mirror, sir."

We'd waited for about five minutes when the door opened. A voice lined with anguish and fatigue said, "Mac tells me you've got a witness."

I turned from the window, ready to say, "Yes, sir." And Struthers turned to face the door at the same time.

His eyebrows lifted, and his eyes grew wide.

He stared at the figure in the doorway, and I watched both men as their eyes met and locked for an instant.

"No!" Struthers said suddenly. "I… I've changed my mind. I… I can't do it. I have to go. I have to go."

He slammed his hat onto his head and ran out quickly, almost before I'd gotten to my feet.

"Now what the hell got into him all of a sudden?" I asked.

Lieutenant Anderson shrugged wearily. "I don't know," he said. "I don't know."

Source: "Eye Witness," *The McBain Brief* (Ed McBain)

▲ A police offficer

3 Finding Descriptive Adverbs Good writers use adverbs to precisely describe the actions of their characters. Read the sentences below and note the clues in parentheses. Choose one of the adverbs from the box below to complete each phrase taken from the story.

abruptly	nervously	quickly	warily
carefully	personally	suspiciously	wearily

1. He sat now with his hat in his hand, his fingers (with tension) _nervously_ exploring the narrow brim.

2. He was dressed neatly, his trousers (with care) _____ raised…

3. "You think maybe the Old Man would like to see him (in person) _____?"

4. "Yes," he said (with caution) _____.

5. Struthers looked around him (with doubt and mistrust) _____.

6. He stood up (in a sudden, rough manner) _____, his fingers still roaming the hat brim.

7. He slammed his hat onto his head and ran out (with a fast movement) _____…

8. Lieutenant Anderson shrugged (in a tired way) _____.

Strategy

Understanding the Plot

The plot is the main sequence of events in a story. It is important to follow the main events and the order in which they occur to understand the story well. Begin with the *conflict*, then follow the *complications* that develop it to the *climax* (the point of highest tension), and then take special note of the *ending* that resolves the conflict, for good or for bad.

One way to understand the plot is to imagine the storyboard. A *storyboard* is a series of pictures that illustrates each part of a story's plot—like a sort of cartoon. It is used by directors who are making movies and it is shown to the actors to guide them. Storyboards may also include written descriptions along with the pictures that illustrate them.

4 **Making a Storyboard of "Eye Witness" for TV** Work with a partner. Pretend that you are making a TV show based on the story "Eye Witness." First you have to create a storyboard illustrating your story. Follow the steps below to help you complete the storyboard.

Descriptions:	Illustrations
1.	1.
2.	2.
3.	3.
4.	4.

1. Draw a storyboard like the one above on a piece of paper. Be sure to make the boxes big enough for your descriptions and illustrations. Start by numbering the boxes on the left from 1–4. (You can add more boxes later if you need them.)

2. Next, decide what you think are the *main events* (or main scenes) in the plot that you want to illustrate; make a list of them on a separate piece of paper. Write a description of what is happening in each event in the column on the left (for example, "Detective Cappeli talks to Mr. Struthers"). You should have at least four events, but you may include more if you want.

3. Look over your list. A plot usually starts with a *conflict* or problem. Do you have a scene that shows this? Then come the *complications*, extra difficulties that make the tension grow. Then comes the *climax*, the moment of greatest tension, the moment that will decide how the story ends! When does that occur in the story? How can you show it? Finally comes the *ending* that resolves the conflict (one way or the other).

4. Now illustrate each event in the box to the right of the description. (These may be stick figures or more elegant illustrations—you are the artists, so you decide.)

5. Exchange and compare storyboards with other classmates.

   - Did you all choose the same main events
   - Were your scenes similar or different? How and why?

5 You Are on TV! If time permits, work with a group and present the scenes from one of the storyboards to the class. One student should be the director and assign the parts. Remember, actors, to put your faces into the proper expression and use any props you can find (objects used in shows to make the story seem real). Your teacher will tell you how many minutes you have to prepare. Lights, camera, action!

6 Guided Academic Conversation In a small group, discuss the following topics.

1. **Solving the Murder** Who really murdered Mrs. Anderson? Do you all agree on who the killer is? Exactly how and when in the story did you know? Make a the story? Are there any false clues? Was there really a mugging? What was the motive for this crime? Compare your ideas with those of other groups.

2. **Mystery or Detective?** Do you think this story was a murder mystery or a detective story? Or was it a combination? Explain.

3. **Getting Away with Murder** There is an expression in English to refer to someone who does something wrong and doesn't get caught. People say, "That guy got away with murder!" In this story, who "got away with murder"? Why? Does this happen in real life? If so, how and why does it happen?

4. **Why So Popular?** Since murder is such a terrible thing, why do you think that stories about it are so popular? Do people like to get scared? Or do they like to play detective and try to follow the clues to solve the crime? How can you explain this incredible popularity?

FOCUS ON TESTING

TOEFL iBT

Prose Summaries on Tests

In the Focus on Testing section of Chapter 9, you learned about "reading-to-learn" questions on the TOEFL® iBT. You also practiced answering some multiple-choice questions of this type.

Another "reading-to-learn" question format is not multiple-choice. It involves piecing together a summary of a reading by dragging and dropping possible sentences for the summary. This is called a "prose summary" task.

Practice

Read the following passage, then complete the "prose summary" task that follows.

Privatized Prisons

A   Research published by King's College London shows that the total prison population in 211 countries worldwide is about ten million. Of this number, about one-half are in three countries: the United States (2.7 million), China (1.6 million), and Russia (about 0.9 million). The pressure from such huge populations of imprisoned persons has stressed the prison systems in many countries, especially in the U. S. America imprisons a larger proportion of its residents than any other nation. Not enough resources are available to deal with all those prisoners. To solve the problem, many governments have contracted with private companies to operate prisons.

B   *Privatizing* a prison means turning its operations over to a business that hopes to earn a profit because it is paid by the government for its services. Advocates of privatization say that companies are more efficient than governments. Also, the private company bears the cost of providing pay and benefits to the prison guards and administration. This takes a great burden off the government. And a private company can move faster to establish a prison than the government can. In some cases, when the prison population in a state has suddenly jumped, private companies have been able to start up new prisons in just two or three weeks.

C   Critics of privatization say that quality in prisons drops when a private company takes over. Seeking greater profits, they say, a company is likely to cut corners. Too few guards, lack of medical care for prisoners, non-nutritious food, and many other faults may result as the company seeks greater profits. Also, critics say, private prison companies may take money from a state government or the Federal Bureau of Prisons and then spend it on something besides a prison. Executives get richer, critics contend, as prisoners suffer more. A further criticism of privatization holds that it encourages the courts to imprison criminals rather than seek their rehabilitation. Passing a drug-user to a company prison, for example, is a lot easier than treating the drug use as a sickness and helping the user recover. Privatized prisons are unlikely to spend much money on effective rehabilitation because the companies have an interest in keeping the prison population high.

D   Private prisons are not just a U.S. phenomenon. They have sprung up in Australia, Kyrgyzstan, Mexico, the United Kingdom, South Africa, and many other nations. The prison-operating companies are based overwhelmingly in the U.S. or the U.K. Prison populations are on the rise worldwide. From 1999 to 2005, they increased by 70 percent in Brazil, 40 percent in Japan, and 37 percent in Mexico. In the U.S., the increase was only 3.4 percent, but the prison population was large to begin with. With the pressures of ever more convicts to house and feed, governments are likely to provide a lot of money to these American and British contractors in the years to come.

Practice

An introductory sentence for a brief summary of the passage is provided below. Complete the summary by selecting the three answer choices that express the main ideas in the passage. Some sentences do not belong in the summary because they express ideas that are not presented in the passage or are minor ideas in the passage. Write the letter of each of your choices on one of the blanks in the Summary on p. 241.

Summary

Controversy surrounds the practice of contracting with private companies to run prisons that used to be run by national or local governments.

- _____
- _____
- _____

a. Critics of privatization argue that it results in lower-quality prisons.

b. Between 1999 and 2005, many nations experienced huge increases in their prison populations.

c. Supporters of privatization do not care about the health or safety of prisoners.

d. Privatization, its supporters say, saves governments a lot of money.

e. Privatization has been used in many countries around the world to deal with rising prison populations.

PART **3** Tying It All Together

1 Interpreting Charts Read the paragraph in the box below. Then work with a partner: look at the chart on page 242, fill in the blanks, and answer the questions that follow. After you finish, compare your answers with those of the rest of the class.

The U.S. Prison Population

Some people feel that one problem with crime in the U.S. is that the administration and maintenance of prisons has become a big business. For many small towns, having a prison nearby is a source of jobs. Police officers, detectives, prison guards, lawyers, and court psychologists make a good living when there are lots of criminals. In the 1980s, new laws came in that made the simple possession of certain drugs a serious crime, punishable by imprisonment. By the end of the year 2009, one in every 135 people in America was behind bars! It used to be different. In 1973, only one in every 1,042 people in America was behind bars. This change did not happen because the rate of violent crime went up. In fact, it was just the opposite. The rate of violent crime went down considerably since the early 1970s.*

---

*Source: The U.S. Department of Justice, Bureau of Justice Statistics, *Prisoners in 2009*

U.S. State and Federal Prison Population*					
	Dec. 31, 2000	Dec. 31, 2005	Dec. 31, 2008	Dec. 31, 2009	% change from Dec. 31, 2008– Dec. 31, 2009
State	1,245,845	1,340,311	1,408,479	1,405,622	–.2
Federal	145,416	187,618	201,280	208,118	+ 3.4
Total	1,391,261	1,527,929	1,609,759	1,613,740	+ 1.7

*Source: The U.S. Department of Justice, Bureau of Justice Statistics, *Prisoners in 2009*

1. The chart gives statistics about changes in the U.S. prison population over a period of _____ years.

2. Did the number of prisoners in the U.S. go up or down in that period of time? It went _____.

3. Which changed more: the population in the State prisons or the population in the Federal prisons? _____

With your partner, discuss the questions below.

1. Do you think it is good for a country to have many people in prison? Why or why not?

2. How do you think this situation compares with that of your own country?

3. In your opinion, what, if anything, can the U.S. government do to lower the number of people in its prisons?

2 Making Connections Choose one of the following four tasks to research. From the library or on the Internet, find information about that person or topic.

1. Give a brief description of a legendary person, political figure, or folk hero who commits crimes, such as Zorro, Jesse James, Dracula, or Robin Hood. This could be someone from any culture. Tell who he or she was and why some people feared or hated him or her. Also, describe the points of view of others who see this legendary figure in a positive light.

2. Following from the *What Do You Think?* (page 230), choose a country and research the view there on the death penalty and the reasons for this view. If the law there favors the death penalty, in which types of cases? If the law does not, what other punishment is used for serious crimes? Report on this to the class. If possible, tell about some famous case(s) in which the issue of capital punishment was important.

3. Who was the real Ed McBain? Was the name Ewan Hunter the name he was born with? How did he get started as a writer of crime stories? Give a report on his life and work.

4. Look up Sherlock Holmes or some other famous detective, real or fictitious, and describe what he looked like, how he became well known and what method he used to solve crimes.

Famous fictional detective Sherlock Holmes ▶
might warn prospective criminals by saying
"Crime does not pay."

Writing Tip: Developing Your Viewpoint

Use a summary of something you have read as a lead into your viewpoint on the reading. Remember that the summary should not express your personal opinion of the event. Then you can use your summary of the event to connect to your personal viewpoint.

3 Writing About a Real Crime Find an article (in a newspaper or on the Internet) about a real crime that has been committed. Using that story, write two paragraphs on one of the two topics below. To develop your point of view, follow the steps that come after the topics.

Topics

1. What do you imagine were the reasons for this crime being committed and why? In your imagination, what really led up to this crime occurring?

2. From the information you have on this crime, what do you think should be the best punishment for this crime and why? What effects would this punishment have on the accused, the victims, on society?

Step 1: Write a brief summary of the article to begin your composition. Remember that a summary does not include your opinions. It just repeats the main points that you have read.

Step 2: Using a cluster diagram (see page 149 and 151) or a list, outline all your main points on the topic.

Step 3: Write a sentence that sums up your main idea on the topic you have chosen. Write this sentence after the summary so that the summary leads into your opinion on the topic.

Step 4: Write the rest of the composition, using strong examples (see page 124) to support your position.

Step 5: Work with a classmate. Exchange your compositions and check them over for spelling, grammar, and punctuation. Are quotations and information listed with the source (name of the book or website)? Then read aloud to each other for the meaning. Are the ideas clear and in a good order? Give suggestions to each other. Revise your work again and sign at the bottom of your classmate's composition as *Reviewer*. Then hand in all of your work (including a copy of the original article, your cluster diagram or outline and notes) to the teacher.

Self-Assessment Log

Read the lists below. Check (✓) the strategies and vocabulary that you learned in this chapter. Look through the chapter or ask your instructor about the strategies and words that you do not understand.

Reading and Vocabulary-Building Strategies

- ☐ Identifying the interviewees in an article
- ☐ Getting the meaning of specialized terms from context
- ☐ Understanding the setting
- ☐ Guessing the meaning of adjectives from context and structure
- ☐ Identifying spelling variations
- ☐ Identifying narrative elements
- ☐ Scanning for specific terms
- ☐ Finding descriptive adverbs
- ☐ Understanding the plot
- ☐ Interpreting charts

Target Vocabulary

Nouns	Verbs	Adjectives	Adverbs
accessory	addled	burly	abruptly
assault	backslide	clean (in the sense of "free from drugs")	carefully
chapter* (of an organization)	created*		nervously
cons	credits*	clean-cut	personally
dependency	deliberated	contentious	quickly
extortion	draft*	hard-luck	suspiciously
fear	imposed*	jailhouse hard	warily
heroin	responds*	meaty	wearily
homelessness		modest	
principles*		wrenching	**Idioms and Expressions**
robberies			back when things were flush
taxpayer			I did my time (to do time)
tic			making amends (make amends)
tradition*			the Old Man
trafficking			
underlings			

*These words are from the Academic Word List. For more information on this list, see www.victoria.ac.nz/lals/resources/academicwordlist/

Outward Bound

Call Kim Ssang Su a man of the people. On a chilly night in the picturesque mountains south of Seoul, Kim, CEO of LG Electronics Inc., holds aloft a paper cup filled to the rim with *soju*, a clear, sweet potato-based Korean alcohol with a vicious bite. Surrounding him are a dozen of the 300 LG suppliers' managers whom Kim has spent the day lecturing and rallying. They have also been hiking up a snow-covered mountainside— necessary training, he says, for the grand plans he has for South Korea's second largest electronics firm. At the end of the day, he treats a group of LG Electronics employees to an outdoor barbecue of grilled pork and bowls of fiery red kimchi. "Great people! Great company!" he barks. "Great company! Great company!" they chant back, pumping their fists in perfect unison. Kim downs the *soju* in one gulp, then marches off to another table for another round of *soju* and another cheer. Then another, and another.

Eight tables and countless cups later, he is red faced, still screaming chants and bearhugging an unfortunate reporter. When dancing girls in short skirts and blond wigs start jiggling to ear-numbing Korean pop music, the tireless Kim, 59, cavorts in a mosh pit of drunken workers near a makeshift stage. Later he ascends the stage himself, microphone in hand, to croon out a popular oldie called Nui (Sister). "We love our CEO," says Kim Young Kee, an LG executive vice president. "He shows us a good time."

CEOs rarely stoop to carouse with the common man in an Asia dominated by secretive business clans and élite old-boy networks. But Kim is no ordinary Asian boss. He began his career 35 years ago as a nondescript engineer at an LG refrigerator factory, climbed the ranks, and claimed the CEO post in October. Now he aims to duplicate the same feat with LG—lifting a consumer-electronics company little known outside Asia into the stratosphere of global brands with Sony, Panasonic and Samsung. "I want to go down in LG history," says Kim. "After death, a tiger leaves its skin. A man leaves his name."

LG seems well on its way. While most of the electronics industry, including Sony, suffered sagging growth and profits in recent years, LG's market presence surged. Revenues jumped 18% last year, to $17 billion, and net profits rose 33%, to $556 million. LG has the electronics world bracketed. At the commodity end, low-cost plants in China make the firm a power in developing markets. At the big-bucks, high-tech end, LG's home in broadband-rich South Korea has fostered a focus at LG on design and function that fits perfectly into the emerging digital home. Last year LG was the world's largest seller of mobile phones operating on the CDMA standard (a type of mobile-phone technology). It makes dazzling flat-screen televisions and other leading-edge gadgets. LG.Philips LCD, a joint venture formed in 1999 with Royal Philips Electronics, became the world's biggest maker of the LCD panels used in flat-screen TVs and monitors in 2003, with 22% of the global market. The unit's operating profit soared 307% last year, to $935 million.

The growth has brought LG to the cusp of greatness but not quite into the industry's aristocracy. Still missing is the global brand name crucial for commanding high premiums and outpacing low-cost manufacturers in China. It is an accomplishment hardly any Asian corporations have managed to achieve. "We've had success at the foothills," says Woo Nam Kyun, president of LG's digital-TV operation. "Now we have to climb the mountain."

The climb LG has chosen is Mount U.S.A. This year LG is making its biggest thrust ever into the U.S. market, with a $100 million budget for advertising alone. Last year LG spent $10 million refurbishing a billboard in New York City's Times Square into a giant flat-screen TV, and it helped renovate a Los Angeles concert hall. LG is also buffing up its U.S. product line. Last July, LG began introducing its first LG-branded flat LCD and plasma TVs in the U.S., and next year it will launch its first high-definition TVs with built-in hard-disc drives that can record movies. An LG refrigerator with an LCD TV set in the door is already on the market.

LG faces plenty of competition. Its biggest rival at home and abroad, Samsung Electronics, whose revenues of $36.4 billion are two times as large as LG's, has already hit the U.S.—and scored big successes. Samsung is also ahead of LG in developing a truly global brand. LG executives hope that competition from Samsung will make their company stronger. "Their presence as a very strong competitor in our neighborhood has always kept us alert and awake," says LG's Woo. "This has helped us compete in overseas markets as well. I can be more successful with Samsung's success."

LG's first crack at the U.S. market ended in disappointment. Beginning in the 1980s, LG sold cheap TVs under the brand Goldstar, after the company's former name, Lucky-Goldstar. In 1995, LG purchased American TV maker Zenith Electronics Corp. and began using that moniker on its products. But four years later, Zenith filed for bankruptcy, a victim of cutthroat competition. To avoid a repeat of that failure, LG was content until recently to supply other companies with appliances that sell in the U.S. under their own brands. Chances are, the average American may own an LG-made product but not know it. LG says it sells 43% of all room air-conditioners in the U.S., for example, but many under brand names like GE and Kenmore.

These days, however, a monumental transition is taking place in U.S. living rooms, and LG smells opportunity. Consumers are tossing aside boxy TVs and clunky VCRs in favor of wide, flat screens, DVD players and, eventually, computer-like systems with digitized video and music recorders and Internet services. With this emerging gadgetry, LG is surprisingly well positioned. LG.Philips has been a leader in developing large, flat displays, and LG makes 70% of all set-top boxes for receiving digital satellite TV sold in the U.S.

In this new digital world, LG has a distinct advantage in its ultra-wired South Korean home base. The demanding Korean market, where an amazing 84% of households using the Internet have high-speed access, propels LG to develop more advanced products and provides a testing ground for new technologies. LG has outpaced Nokia and Motorola in cramming the hottest new features into a mobile phone. One of its latest models, the SC8000, which came out in Korea in April, combines a PDA, an MP3 player, a digital camera and a camcorder. The advantage is paying off. In May, LG launched a new mobile phone in Korea with a 2-megapixel color screen simultaneously with Samsung. In the past, LG lagged at least several months behind its competitor's phone launches, missing out on higher prices and margins. LG became the largest supplier of mobile phones last year to service provider Verizon Communications.

It may seem odd that at this crucial time LG has turned over its top job to a farm boy from a tiny village in eastern South Korea. Kim Ssang Su spent his childhood knee-deep in the family's rice paddies. Even now, Kim is a bit of a fish out of water. He took over from the debonair John Koo, a senior member of LG's prestigious founding family. Kim has never worked outside Korea or, before becoming CEO, even at LG's glitzy Seoul headquarters, known locally as the "Twin Towers." He had spent his entire career buried in LG's stuffy bureaucracy at the company's main appliance factory in the industrial city of Changwon. He admits to being more comfortable in the field visiting factory floors and design centers than in his spacious office overlooking Seoul's Han River.

It would be wrong, though, to underestimate Kim, who has become near legend in Seoul for the turnaround he engineered at LG's appliance business. When he took over in 1996, LG was making washing machines and refrigerators that seemed little more than cannon fodder for lowcost Chinese companies like Haier. Kim sliced costs by moving production of low-end products to China. He proved there is room for innovation in basic white goods, introducing, for example, appliances like air-conditioners that can be controlled from the Internet. The result: sales reached $4.7 billion last year, more than twice the number when Kim took control.

Kim is infusing LG's other businesses with the same vigor. Called a "commander in the field" by executives, he storms about LG's factories and offices poring over details, issuing commands and spurring on the staff by giving them what he terms "stretch goals," or aggressive targets. Awake at 5:30 each morning for a brisk walk, he openly prefers "morning people" and holds 7 a.m. breakfast meetings with top executives. "I don't like the expression 'nice,'" Kim says. "I don't want LG to be perceived as nice. None of the great companies in the world are nice." Kim's relentless nature has put some executives on the defensive. "He likes to be heavily involved," complains a top manager. "I would prefer that he delegate a bit more."

Kim is backing up his tough talk with a strategy

to augment the company's design and technology prowess. For instance, LG.Philips announced in March it would invest $22 billion with its suppliers in new flat-screen production facilities over the next 10 years. Kim is recruiting engineers at a furious pace, aiming to increase research-and-development teams to 60% of LG's total payroll by 2005, from 40% today. One recent afternoon at the LG Electronics Corporate Design Center in Seoul, young Koreans in jeans and hip black sweaters were packing up plastic models of computer monitors and microwaves to move to new offices. With the number of designers up 15% in the past year, to 390, the center has added an entire new floor. "As we emphasize our brand, design becomes more critical," says the center's president, Lee Hee Gook. "We're making ourselves more competitive."

Can Kim build LG into a global titan? Hurdles abound. LG still sometimes cuts prices to drive sales, softening both profit margins and its brand image. For example, LG sees 5% profit margins on its mobile phones; Samsung earns in excess of 20%. Nor does it help that LG Electronics is a member of one of South Korea's mammoth, family-controlled conglomerates, called *chaebols*, which are infamous for mysterious and convoluted business practices. In February the company broke a promise to investors by pledging $130 million to buy bonds of a nearly bankrupt affiliate, credit-card issuer LG Card. Kim says his company joined in because a failure at LG Card would have damaged LG's image. Michael Lee, an executive vice president at LG Corp., the conglomerate's holding company, says affiliates had a "moral obligation" to help out and calls the LG Card case an exception. The LG *chaebol*, he says, has reorganized its shareholding structure to allow affiliates to be managed more independently. Because of concerns relating to its being a *chaebol*, LG—like many other Korean companies—is valued more cheaply than many of its international competitors.

Still, in Asia, LG has taken on the world's best and proved it can hold its own. In China and India, LG has become a preferred brand. In China, which Kim calls the "toughest marketplace in the world," sales last year rose 40%, to $2.8 billion. In India, LG has beaten out Sony and Samsung to claim the No. 1 market share in everything from TV sets to refrigerators to CDMA phones.

And in just a few months, LG is making inroads into the U.S. Its increasingly popular mobile phones hold fourth place in market share.

Lisa Smith, general manager for appliances at U.S. retailer Best Buy Co., began carrying LG refrigerators and washers and dryers last July, and their jazzy designs, such as yellow and blue lights on dryer control panels that look like car dashboards, have made them a hit with younger shoppers. "[LG has] done a fantastic job of raising the bar in the U.S. market," Smith says. "The products are popular, and they continue to gain momentum."

In the end, Kim can take LG to the top only if he manages to solve that pesky branding problem. Its rival did it: four years ago, few in the electronics industry could have predicted the growing dominance of Samsung, despite its solid technology and financial clout. Samsung's surprise was its savvy at brand building. "In terms of the ingredients, LG has everything—the quality, the packaging, the global marketing reach," says Nam Park, an analyst at HSBC Securities in Hong Kong. "What's missing is the magic. It's missing that je ne sais quoi." If Kim finds it, he'll probably pour himself a glass of *soju* and let go a very, very loud cheer.

"Outward Bound: *Call Kim Ssang Su a Man of the People*" by Michael Schuman. *Time*, Asia, Vol. 163, No. 25, June 21, 2004. Time, Inc. Reprinted with permission. All rights reserved.

Vocabulary Index

*These words are from the Academic Word List. For more information on this list, see www.victoria.ac.nz/lals/resources/academicwordlist/

distinguish
eclectic
ecotourism
elite
enchanted
fiber
flock
found* (find)
frontiers
grain
heart disease
hence*
hippies
inappropriate*
indigenous
inexpensive
legumes
locals
monounsaturates
natural resources
peasant
physical*
prevent
prosperity
requests
stinginess
subculture
taboo
tourists
treats
up-front
virtually*

Chapter 5

benefits*
best-case scenario
braking
carbon footprint
combustion engine
components*
computers*
craftsmen
data*
do our bit
do their own thing
download
economy*
efficient
electric motor
emissions
English-speaking
four-cylinder engine
fuel consumption
generator
global*

grassroots
handmade
hybrid car
ignited
Internet-enabled
Internet-linked
knowledge-based
landmarks
large-scale
leapfroggers
marketplace
medical*
network*
on the block
parallel* hybrid
performance
portion
propulsion power
recharging (batteries)
rpm (revolutions per minute)
scenario*
series hybrid
service-based
speeds
tech-savvy
telecenters (also spelled telecentres)
transmission*
upload
vehicle*
via*
well-educated
widespread*

Chapter 6

absentmindedly
affordable
amicable
anticipated*
boom
chain (as in a group of similar
   businesses)
convenience
drama*
effusive
enormous*
executive
flattered
found* (find)
franchises
globalization*
growth markets
imposing*
inadequate*
inclined*
management

marketing
maturing*
mentality*
modernizing
mortifying
multinational
outlets (as in individual
   businesses in a chain)
pizzeria
projected sales
prospered
specialties
startled
succulent
transform*
untapped market
vindictive

Chapter 7

assistance*
atone
atrocities
background
benevolent
childhood
civil*
commitment*
commoners
compelling
conduct*
Confucian
cornerstones
decisions
defender
demilitarization
depressed*
diligent
dynasty
easily
eloquence
enduring
energy*
eradicate
etiquette
expression
founded*
(the) Golden Rule
governmental
holocaust
influential
innovator*
investment*
lament
medical*
modernize

*These words are from the Academic Word List. For more information on this list, see www.victoria.ac.nz/lals/resources/academicwordlist/

250

monitors*
negotiations
notions*
obstacles
outlook
overwhelming
perception*
permeated
philosophical*
political
preparation
prestige
primarily*
principality
promotion*
reared
repression
resigned
responsibility
role*
sacrifice
seized
servitude
strive
suppress
take up the torch
tyranny
valor
violations*

Chapter 8

architect/architecture
articulate
as springboards
assumptions*
authorities*
cavernous
commissions*
compress
conceptual*
conduct*
construction*
contemporary*
contraption
contrary* to popular belief
create*
dedication
deficiencies
design*
diluting
divert
draftsman
dud
exclusives*
experiment

for sure
generate*
genius
in retrospect
insecurity
inspiration
intelligent*
invention
isolated*
major*
marshes
mentor
imaginative
in the light of
on the lookout
patents
persist*
preserved
priority*
publish*
quantity
quotas
research*
rethink
teams*
transmitted*
turbulent
typewriter

Chapter 9

aspect*
aware*
barbarian
bias*
colleague*
constantly*
culture*
despair
distasteful
ethnocentrism
hue
inconceivable*
inhuman
insomnia
irrational*
liberal*
non-Western
objectively*
omission of syntax
open-minded
outcome*
outlook
repugnant
repulsive
self-evaluation

sexual*
subarctic
subgroup
unnatural
world view

Chapter 10

abruptly
accessory
addled
assault
back when things were flush
backslide
burly
carefully
chapter* (of an organization)
clean (in the sense
  of "free from drugs")
clean-cut
cons
contentious
created*
credits*
deliberated
dependency
draft*
extortion
fear
hard-luck
heroin
homelessness
I did my time
imposed*
jailhouse hard
making amends
meaty
modest
nervously
the Old Man
personally
principles*
quickly
responds*
robberies
suspiciously
taxpayer
tic
tradition*
trafficking
underlings
warily
wearily
wrenching

*These words are from the Academic Word List. For more information on this list, see www.victoria.ac.nz/lals/resources/academicwordlist/

Skills Index

Literary Credits